Racial Change and Community Crisis

A Florida Sand Dollar Book

Racial Change
and Community Crisis
St. Augustine, Florida,
1877–1980

David R. Colburn

University of Florida Press
Gainesville

First paperback edition published by University of Florida Press
Copyright 1991 by the Board of Regents, State of Florida
Copyright 1985 by Columbia University Press

Printed in the U.S.A. on acid-free paper ∞

The University of Florida Press is a member of the University Presses of
Florida, the scholarly publishing agency of the State University System of
Florida. Books are selected for publication by faculty editorial committees
at each of Florida's nine public universities: Florida A & M University
(Tallahassee), Florida Atlantic University (Boca Raton), Florida International
University (Miami), Florida State University (Tallahassee), University of
Central Florida (Orlando), University of Florida (Gainesville), University
of North Florida (Jacksonville), University of South Florida (Tampa), and
University of West Florida (Pensacola).

Orders for books published by all member presses should be addressed to
University Presses of Florida, 15 Northwest 15th Street, Gainesville, FL
32611.

Library of Congress Cataloging-in-Publication Data

Colburn, David R.
    Racial change and community crisis : St. Augustine, Florida,
1877-1980 / David R. Colburn. — 1st paperback ed.
      p.   cm. — (A Florida sand dollar book)
    Reprint. Originally published: New York : Columbia University
Press, 1985.
    Includes bibliographical references and index.
    ISBN 0-8130-1066-7
    1. Afro-Americans—Florida—Saint Augustine—History. 2. Saint
Augustine (Fla.)—Race relations. I. Title. II. Series.
[F319.S2C65   1991]
305.896′073075918—dc20   91-2790
                                          CIP

Cover photos by Bill Kuenzel. By permission of *The Miami Herald*.

Dedicated
to my wife, Marion,
and our children,
Margaret, David, and Katherine

Contents

Photographs follow page 108.

Preface to First Paperback Edition

When I completed the research on this book in 1980 and subsequently wrote the conclusion, I argued that, although a decade and a half had passed since the civil rights demonstrations in St. Augustine and the adoption of the Civil Rights Act of 1964, black residents in the nation's oldest city still encountered discrimination, especially in the economic sector where most doors were closed to them. The structure of St. Augustine's economy, based as it was on tourism, did not offer many opportunities for black residents, except in subservient roles as maids, servants, waiters, and cooks. Moreover, black businesses operated only within the black community. Census figures disclosed that the income of black residents stood at less than 63 percent of that for whites, and the educational attainment of black children was three years fewer than that for white children.

The nature of these educational and economic patterns kept black residents in a distinctly subservient and second-class status despite the passage of the Civil Rights Act of 1964 and the Voting Rights Act of 1965 and the integration of local schools in 1970. I observed that in some ways these racial reforms had so angered white leaders that they had deliberately opposed any economic changes that would diversify the economy and improve job opportunities for local blacks. A number of civil rights activists found themselves under such intense scrutiny and economic pressure that they moved from the city in the late 1960s. Economic conditions in general offered so few prospects for black residents that most young blacks who had the opportunity left the community after high school.

The events of the post-1965 period suggested to me that white St. Augustine had yet to accept the full implications of an integrated, biracial society. Despite the civil rights protests of 1964 and 1965 and the adoption of new civil rights laws, the city had to be mandated by the federal courts to comply with the Civil Rights Act of 1964 and to eliminate its dual school system in 1970. Although moderates gradually reassumed positions of leadership in the community in the early 1970s, many whites still resented the protests of 1964 and continued to identify with the philosophy of the John Birch Society. The community's race relations were clearly in transition, but it was not apparent that the reforms of this decade would truly integrate the community and provide black residents with equal opportunity.

Unlike sociologist William Julius Wilson and urban historians like Roger Lane, I did not find the development of a permanent underclass or a ghetto in St. Augustine during this era or at any time before. The spatial distribution of blacks in the city was similar to that in many geographically small southern communities, with blacks and whites residing in close proximity and often across the street from one another. Only the area called Lincolnville on the outskirts of St. Augustine had developed features similar to those found in ghettos in northern urban communities or in some large southern cities. The small size of the community and the migration of young blacks out of the area in the post-1960 era, however, combined to keep Lincolnville from becoming a large ghetto and to prevent the development of many of the social pathologies seen in other ghettos.

In preparing this paperback edition for publication, I wondered if racial and economic patterns had changed significantly in the past decade. As I suspected, the record proved to be a mixed one. A number of developments suggest that racial traditions are moving in a new direction and that, should these changes continue, equal opportunity and an end to racism might become realities for black residents in the next decade. But there remain problem areas that make such developments uncertain.

In looking back over the period from 1960 to 1990, I would be hard pressed to suggest that St. Augustine has not transcended the racial bigotry and segregation traditions of the past. Moreover, many of the recent developments indicate that the community has moved beyond legal equality and is moving increasingly toward full equality for all its citizens. Such changes have occurred in the educational, political, and cultural arenas, but they have not permeated the city's economic life.

The two most visible developments of the 1980s have been the election of Otis Mason to the position of superintendent of schools for St. Johns County and the election of Henry Twine, president of the local NAACP, to the city commission.

As the head of the largest employer in St. Johns County and supervisor of educational policy for the area, Otis Mason has been in a strategic position to improve the quality of life for black residents. He has worked diligently to enhance educational opportunities for all students and quietly to ensure that minority children have access to programs that will remedy any cultural disadvantages. Because he is in such a visible position and thus subject to the wrath of white residents who constitute over 85 percent of the local population, he has also had to work behind the scenes to increase the number of black teachers and black employees. Of the school system's 1,380 employees, 19.5 percent are black, and eight of the thirty-three principals and assistant principals are black (24.2 percent). Until recently, Mason's hiring efforts have been assisted by the federal courts, which have required St. Johns County to submit regular reports on its hiring procedures and on the integration of its schools and staff.

Elected to the city commission in 1984, Henry Twine served two terms during which he actively represented the interests of black residents. Unlike Arnett Chase, the first black elected commissioner who served from 1974 to 1976, Twine pressured the city manager to hire blacks for positions in the police and fire departments and for other positions as well. He also insisted that city resources be used to upgrade streets and electrical, sewage, and water facilities for residents of Lincolnville and other black neighborhoods. Twine became one of the community's principal spokesmen for the celebration of Martin Luther King Day in St. Augustine in 1986. Like King, Twine believed it critically important for young people to understand the past so that the events of an earlier period would not be repeated.

The achievements of Twine and Mason reflected the commitment to racial change that existed in the black community and also the emergence of a group of white leaders who were willing to build on the racial developments of the 1960s and 1970s rather than continue to construct barriers to them. This new group includes representatives from education, business, the city commission, the city manager's office, and the religious community. Responding to initiatives from the black community, these representatives have cosponsored social and cultural events that have highlighted St. Augustine's multicultural heritage, including the statewide celebration of the birthday of Martin Luther King, Jr., in St. Augustine. Although many whites in the community opposed the event, black leaders together with white allies on the city commission agreed to host the first statewide event at which Governor Bob Graham and members of the state cabinet came to pay recognition to King and to the contributions of black St. Augustine in bringing racial change to Florida and the nation. For the first time, the community acknowledged its racial heritage. The King celebration became a time for black residents to assemble to celebrate the role they played in the desegregation of the community and in the passage of the Civil Rights Act of 1964. This celebration has continued yearly, with an annual march around the slave market area in memory of the events of 1964.

More recently, the community held a pictorial exhibit of the work of black photographer Richard Twine in the late spring of 1990, which portrayed life in the black community of St. Augustine. The well-attended exhibit gave many whites their first substantive view of black life in St. Augustine in the first half of the twentieth century and helped to break down their stereotypical views. The black and white communities also continue to cooperate closely in the annual Lincolnville festival in which black culture, folk art, and music are represented.

Few of these changes would have been possible without the intervention of the federal government and the federal courts in the 1960s and their continued involvement in the post-1970 period. Through federal programs such as affirmative action and through federal oversight of voting, educational programs, and hiring practices by government contractors, racial barriers have been removed and black residents have gradually entered many areas of city life for the first time. The Grummen Corporation, the largest private employer in St. Johns County, for example, has six blacks in supervisory positions and blacks in all federally mandated posts. Its predecessor, the Fairchild-Hiller Corporation, had no blacks in supervisory or administrative positions.

Despite these developments, the record of employment and economic opportunity for black residents remains mixed. Of the 244 people employed by the St. Johns County Sheriff's Office, only 15 are black; only 23 of the city's 207 full-time employees are black, and only two of them are in supervisory positions. Moreover, even though the city's black population stands at 14.7 percent, the county and city no longer have a black doctor, dentist, or attorney. And while the Chamber of Commerce talks about soliciting and supporting minority businesses and minority businessmen, it has yet to take any formal steps. Only one black businessman has been able to establish an enterprise that crosses racial lines, and he has yet to be invited to join the Chamber of Commerce. Moreover, median income for the black family actually declined in the 1980s relative to white family income—it is now approximately half that of whites—and most young blacks have continued to leave the community for opportunities elsewhere.

In reflecting on the last twenty years, Otis Mason commented that he has "seen a lot of improvements and a lot of changes in attitudes." Most black residents acknowledge that the challenge for the future lies in the areas of business development and employment. The structure of St. Augustine's economy, however, with over 80 percent of the businesses involved in tourism, remains a major obstacle to black advancement. The white business community and white residents generally show little interest in diversifying the economy to facilitate black employment. The commitments to the community's historic past and to tourism as an acceptable form of economic activity that capitalizes on its historical traditions continue to dominate local thinking and undermine other forms of economic activity.

Although the civil rights leadership of the 1960s fell out of favor in the black and white communities of St. Augustine in the 1970s, it did establish an important tradition of independent black leadership in the community. That leadership reemerged in the 1980s in a different form and with a renewed commitment to the goals of the civil rights movement and to the social and economic needs of black residents in the 1990s. The obstacles that confront this new leadership are still daunting, and the ability of black residents to re-solve these persistent economic problems may depend on more than the leadership and resourcefulness that residents have demonstrated in the past thirty years. Despite the passage of time, economic data reveal that black residents remain in a subservient position.

David R. Colburn
Gainesville, Florida
Summer 1990

Preface

With the collapse of Reconstruction in 1877, the South gradually began to construct a new system of race relations which would insure the dominance of whites and the subservience of blacks. St. Augustine, Florida, the nation's oldest city, was no exception in this regard. Employing a variety of mechanisms including the law, social custom, and violence, by 1900 it restricted black residents to a second-class status, where they remained until the 1960s.

This book examines the evolution of race relations in St. Augustine from the post-Reconstruction period to the present. It shows how racial patterns developed during the Jim Crow period and how these patterns were gradually realigned by the *Brown* decision in 1954 and especially by St. Augustine's civil rights crisis in 1963 and 1964.

St. Augustine became a landmark in the civil rights era when the Reverend Martin Luther King, Jr., and the Southern Christian Leadership Conference selected it as a target city in 1964. Though a civil rights movement had been underway in this historic city for nearly a year before King's arrival, it had gone largely unnoticed in the national press, and no progress had been made toward desegregating the community. King's mere presence changed all that, insuring that St. Augustine would become a major area of civil rights activity and media attention. The civil rights campaign in St. Augustine thus had significance not only for Florida, but for the South and the nation as well.

Very few studies have examined the civil rights movement at the local level and of these even fewer have looked at the effects of the civil rights revolution on race relations after 1965. Yet it was at the community level where black Americans attempted to exercise their new freedoms, and where southern attitudes and traditions confronted these new values. Sufficient time appears to have elapsed enabling historians to make more than a preliminary assessment of the civil rights decade and its impact on the lives of black Americans.

This book then explores the struggle over the color line in St. Augustine and Florida generally throughout the late nineteenth and twentieth centuries. It details the efforts of a racial minority to find an equal place for itself in a society which embraced democracy but refused to compromise with its racial prejudices and social traditions. This dilemma made for a very difficult transition, and one that left many black residents less than satisfied.

This project would not have been completed without the assistance of many people. I would like to take this opportunity to thank them formally.

The staffs at the Federal Records Center in East Point, Georgia, the Manuscript Collections Department at Boston University, the Special Collections Department at Florida State University, the Florida State Archives in Tallahassee, and the Lyndon B. Johnson and the John F. Kennedy presidential libraries all proved most helpful in directing me to source material. I also want to express my appreciation to the staffs at the Federal Bureau of Investigation—Freedom of Information Section and the Community Relations Service for assisting me in obtaining government documents. I am especially indebted to Elizabeth Alexander of the P. K. Yonge Library of Florida History at the University of Florida for her support throughout the project. She used her department's financial resources without hesitation to assist me in obtaining important documents, photocopied materials, and microfilm.

I thank, too, the numerous people I interviewed who patiently answered my never-ending questions. A special thanks to Judge Bryan Simpson, Dr. Joseph Shelley, Hamilton Upchurch, Dr. Hardgrove Norris, Henry Twine, Rosalie Gordon-Mills, Dr. Michael V. Gannon, the Reverend Stanley Bullock, and the Reverend Charles

Seymour, who willingly shared information with me of a private and occasionally personal nature. Without their cooperation this manuscript would lack important information on racial developments and cultural traditions in St. Augustine.

In writing this book, I had the assistance of several busy but generous colleagues. William Chafe, Jim Cobb, David Garrow, Samuel Hill, Elliott Rudwick, and Arvah Strickland read various sections of this book and shared with me their own research and perceptions of the civil rights movement.

As with all studies of this kind, certain people go beyond the bounds of friendship to offer suggestions, criticize, encourage, and just be there at times when you want to discuss a particular concern. James Button, Keith Heim, Elizabeth Jacoway, Steven Lawson, and George Pozzetta each read most, if not all, of the manuscript. Betsy Jacoway took time away from coping with two children to read various sections, while the others were always there to offer help. I also want to extend a very special thanks to series editor, William E. Leuchtenburg, for his encouragement and assistance throughout. They are no doubt as happy as I am that this project has been completed.

To Mrs. Adrienne Turner, who typed and retyped the manuscript with only an occasional protest, I owe a particular debt of gratitude.

This project has been amply supported by grants-in-aid from the American Philosophical Society, the Division of Sponsored Research at the University of Florida, and the Institute for the Study of American Culture. For their financial assistance and encouragement, I am grateful.

Finally, to my wife, Marion, and my children, Margaret, David, and Katherine, I dedicate this book, thanking them in this small way for their patience and loving support.

Despite the generous cooperation of so many people, I must accept sole responsibility for the final outcome. This I do willingly, but not without extending to all these fine people a special thank you.

Racial Change and Community Crisis

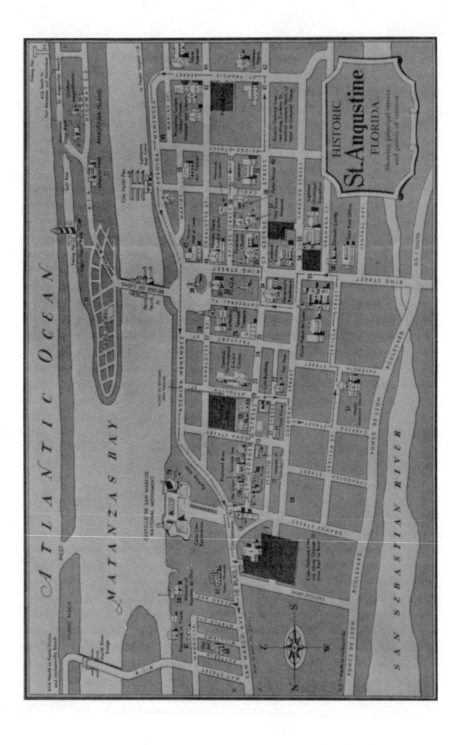

Chapter 1

Shell-Shocked in St. Augustine: The Celebration

After months of demonstrations, arrests, and violence, a large crowd gathered at St. Paul's African Methodist Episcopal Church on June 25, 1964, to discuss ways to end the racial turmoil that had engulfed St. Augustine since 1963. They also met to celebrate the recent passage of the 1964 civil rights bill by the United States Senate and the announcement by President Lyndon Johnson that he would sign the bill into law. Black and white civil rights workers in St. Augustine rejoiced knowing they had helped remove a major obstacle to equal citizenship for all black Americans.[1]

Located in the center of the black community, St. Paul's was a typical Negro structure of the early 1960s made of cheap red brick interrupted by stained glass windows of purple, burgundy, and yellow. A bell tower on the north side of the church gave it a fortresslike appearance. Inside, worn pews fanned out in three directions from the pulpit which dominated the sanctuary. Red and heavily shellacked, the pulpit seemed to capture the strong emotional and spiritual commitment of local blacks. Behind the pulpit stood a cross with the words, spelled in neon light, "This do in remembrance of me." The floor was a yellowish linoleum, cracked in places, and the walls were a faded pink. Paint had peeled away from the walls and ceiling. The windows were opened to provide some relief from the hot, humid summer days that predominated in this southern seacoast community. Two overhead fans turned slowly, barely moving the stagnant air. Providing even less relief were two cardboard band fans with a picture of two well-scrubbed black children on one side and an undertaker's advertisement on another. This particular night the weather was especially oppressive as the usual afternoon thunderstorms had failed to occur to break the heat and humidity. When Wyatt Tee Walker, a chief adviser to Martin Luther King, Jr., was asked why civil rights meetings were held in churches throughout the South, he responded, a Negro "doesn't have a Masonic Lodge, and he's not going to get the public schools. And the church is the primary means of communication, far ahead of the second best, which is the Negro barbershop and beauty parlor."[2]

The meeting began with the singing of an old slave song: "Nobody knows the trouble I've seen. Nobody knows but Jesus." Perspiring heavily from the television camera lights and crowded conditions but enjoying themselves thoroughly, the audience then sang another favorite: "I'm going to sit at the welcome table one of these days, hallelujah!" The song never seemed more appropriate. Near the end of the last verse somebody whispered that Dr. King had arrived and the crowd broke into "When the Saints Go Marching In." People leaped to their feet as he strode in accompanied by his aides. Chanting "Who's our leader—Martin Luther King" and clapping, the crowd began singing the spiritual "Which Side Are You On, Lord?" An Associated Press reporter turned to Marshall Frady of *Newsweek* while listening to the music. "My God, Marshall," he asked, "have you ever heard anything like this?" "Look," Frady responded, extending his arm which bristled with goose bumps.[3]

As he stood there singing the final stanza, preparing to address this large, enthusiastic audience, Martin Luther King, Jr., was at the height of his influence. Only thirty-five years of age, he had become the major spokesman for the civil rights movement in America. He had just recently received the American Baptist's Convention first annual Edwin T. Dahlburg Peace Award and been named *Time* magazine's "Man of the Year."[4] In the fall of the year he would be awarded the Nobel Peace Prize for his role in the movement.

King's style of leadership had proven very effective in rallying blacks behind the civil rights effort and in drawing whites to the movement. Although often aloof and somewhat retiring in his personal relations, King had a warm smile and a dynamic speaking delivery which encouraged people to feel at ease around him. His old-fashioned Negro Baptist rhetoric portrayed the dreams of blacks in ways with which they could readily identify. SCLC veterans maintained that it was not the words but the emotional tone Dr. King expressed that was important, that the Negro South commonly communicated on this level. Often in mass meetings, people who could not understand all the words responded to the tones. Moreover, his influence with presidents and political and economic leaders drew the admiration of black folk, who welcomed such a prominent role for someone of their race. King's religious position and his use of religious terminology also created a bridge to the white community. As August Meier has observed: "To talk in terms of Christianity, love, nonviolence is reassuring to the mentality of white America." In addition, his reference to Gandhi, Hegel, and Marx suggested to middle-class whites that he was a man of intellectual substance, someone to be listened to.[5]

As King addressed his audience in St. Paul's church on the evening of the twenty-fifth, he talked enthusiastically about civil rights developments in St. Augustine and the nation, but he also cautioned his listeners about the difficult work that lay ahead. After his talk, he led the crowd outside St. Paul's in anticipation of their nightly march through the town. Quietly and orderly, approximately 350 people, including nearly 50 whites, queued up. King cautioned the marchers: "We are at the most difficult moment. We must remain calm and not let them provoke us into violence"[6] Led by the Reverend Fred Shuttlesworth, the Reverend Andrew Young, King's young assistant, and Hosea Williams from Savannah—the march was considered too dangerous for King to participate in—the crowd moved quietly through the night toward the center of this historic community.

Hosea Williams had initiated the marches in mid-April to dramatize racial barriers in the town. As one local black leader commented, the marches were designed to provoke the white militants, draw the attention of the media, and bring outside pressure on St. Augustine to desegregate. Another called the marchers "the critical development" in SCLC's campaign to focus national attention on St. Augustine.[7] Because the city had many narrow sidestreets and alleyways and an unsympathetic sheriff and police chief, there was little chance that violence could be avoided during such marches even after Governor Farris Bryant sent an additional 200 state police officers to St. Augustine. One marcher commented that we feared "for our lives every time we went."[8]

The marshaling of white militants and Klansmen in St. Augustine and the confrontations between demonstrators, police, and militants during the afternoon added to the concerns of demonstrators that evening. Earlier that day civil rights leaders had attempted to integrate St. Augustine Beach on two separate occasions. A morning demonstration had ended with only a few minor scuffles and the arrest of one militant who had assaulted the Reverend C. T. Vivian of the SCLC. The second confrontation occurred at 2:30 P.M. when eighty demonstrators, carefully guarded by twenty state and local police officers, marched onto the beach. Nearly eighty white militants waited for them in the water, shouting, "Come on in, niggers. You've got the right to swim." The Reverend Fred Shuttlesworth, who accompanied Vivian on the afternoon demonstration, commented later that he feared more for his life and those with him on that occasion than at any other time during the civil rights movement. "We had no intention of swimming, going out into that deep water and being drowned," he said. That afternoon Shuttlesworth told Vivian, "We're going in just slightly."[9]

Despite the decision by civil rights leaders to force a confrontation with militants, the group was not anxious to face the wrath of the mob and started to walk north on the beach before entering the water. But the extremists quickly moved to intercept them and a melee began. Under orders from Governor Bryant and the Federal District Court to protect the demonstrators, the state patrol attempted to restrain the militants but the ocean current and the waves made their jobs virtually impossible. Nearly exhausted from a month's duty in this violence-torn community, state patrol officers took their frustrations out on those militants they could reach, and several whites received severe head lacerations. A scuffle also broke out between state and local law enforcement officers when a sheriff's deputy objected to the aggressiveness of state police. The beach demonstration marked the first occasion in which police had used such force against the militants. Several white leaders who witnessed the clashes warned state officers that they would get even that night.[10]

During the evening, the civil rights marchers walked through the still night, turning north on Cordova past the old Alcazar Hotel, now housing a museum and city offices. They came to a halt across from the splendid Ponce de Leon Hotel, but few paid attention to it this evening. After once again cautioning marchers against resorting to violence, and saying a brief prayer, the SCLC leaders turned east toward the bay and the town plaza. A local resident who lived very near the center of town commented: "Things would be quiet. Then I'd hear the shuffle of feet. Hair would rise on the back of my bassett. Then I'd hear singing, then police sirens, dogs barking, and people running."[11]

At the center of town, opposite the Catholic cathedral on the town square, a large crowd of perhaps five hundred had gathered at the slave market, a pavilion on the east side of the plaza with benches and tables which were often used by tourists as a place to rest and by residents to play checkers or dominoes. Confederate flags hung from the slave market's roof that evening and signs urging whites to "Kill the Niggers" were carried by the people assembled there to listen to three speakers, J. B. Stoner, Atlanta Ku Klux Klansman and vice-presidential candidate of the right-wing National States Rights Party, the Reverend Connie Lynch, a religious spokesman for segregation, and the local white supremacist leader Holstead "Hoss" Manucy. Each of the three condemned the marches and called on the throng to stop the "niggers" before they destroyed St. Augustine, the South, and the nation.[12]

Increasingly concerned about losing the civil rights struggle after the Birmingham campaign, militant leaders and their followers were determined to make a vigorous defense of segregation in St. Augustine. They saw their world slowly slipping from their grasp and they were more determined than ever to hold on. St. Augustine thus became a major staging area for white extremists.

Stoner and Lynch had made a career of showing up in communities wracked by racial turmoil. According to a report by the House Committee on Un-American Activities, Jesse Benjamin Stoner had been a Klan organizer during the 1940s. He had also founded the Stoner Anti-Jewish Party. Stoner's extremism led to his removal from the Klans of America in January 1950, after he advocated the physical annihilation of "non-Christian Jews." During the summer of 1959 Stoner assumed the role of Imperial Wizard of the new, more militant Christian Knights of the Ku Klux Klan. Within months he denounced the United States Klans for being a "Jew-dominated organization." In 1960 Stoner moved his organization to Atlanta from Louisville, but by 1961, due chiefly to its extremism, it had been reduced to a mere paper organization.[13] Of medium height with a pudgy build and black, curly hair, Stoner told his audiences that "the nigger is not a human being. He is somewhere between the white man and ape. . . . We don't believe in getting along with our enemy, and the nigger is our enemy."[14]

As effective as Stoner was in agitating his white listeners, he played second fiddle in St. Augustine to Connie Lynch, whom one policeman called "one of the best I've ever heard." A committed racist, he saw the white man as the custodian of the Old and the New Testament. He strongly supported an effort to send the country's twenty million Negroes back to Africa. For those who refused to leave, Lynch declared: "I wouldn't blink an eye if it meant every nigger getting killed."[15] Short at 5′4″, curly-haired, with piercing eyes and a jutting jaw, and always wearing a string tie, Lynch had been a crusader for racial separation for many years. As one of ten children of an indigent cotton farmer from Clarksville, Texas, Lynch sympathized with the plight of the poor. But only poor whites. Concerned about alleviating their suffering, he developed "a driving inspiration to do something about it." In 1936 he entered the ministry of the General Assembly of Jesus Christ, a fundamentalist Protestant group. "I never attended no seminaries," he explained. "I just got my credentials."[16]

Lynch, however, did not evince the intense evangelical racism that would characterize his later career until immediately after World War II. Influenced apparently by Adolf Hitler's views on racial superiority and the anti-Communist rhetoric of the postwar era, Lynch entered the Church of Jesus Christ, Christian, a sect founded in 1946 by a former Ku Klux Klan rifle team instructor, Dr. Wesley Swift. Denouncing godless Communism and recognizing a "difference in Biblical history between the races," Dr. Swift emphasized the superiority of the white race. Put in more earthy terms by Dr. Swift's secretary, the organization opposed the white race being "taken over by coons, horses, or anybody."[17]

For nearly ten years, Lynch worked for the Church of Jesus Christ, Christian, in California, performing such traditional tasks as marriages, funerals, and preaching. Continuing the peripatetic lifestyle that had characterized his youth, he moved from congregation to congregation seldom remaining in one place for long. In early 1962, while seeking new ways to combat the "evil conspiracy of race mixing," Lynch organized the National States Rights Party [NSRP] in California. During this period he became a friend of J. B. Stoner's and the two committed themselves to the cause of racial segregation. The extremism of Lynch proved too much even for the NSRP and he was asked to resign. Lynch had required his aides to imitate Hitler's storm troopers by equiping them with black belts, boots, and helmets, and having them march in goose-step fashion. Though Lynch raised considerable sums of money for the organization, his militancy often frightened away potential contributors to the NSRP. By 1961 Lynch had become so involved in the movement to save the white race that he no longer had a home or family of his own. He had been married and divorced twice. All his possessions were kept in the backseat and trunk of his car as he journeyed from one end of the country to the other with Maria Calabria, a large Mexican-American woman, who served as his companion and secretary.[18]

Lynch continued to appear throughout the South during the post-*Brown* years, visiting Little Rock, Oxford, Albany, and Birmingham. A fireball as a speaker, Lynch seldom failed to stir his white audiences to action. He played upon the worst fears of his white listeners by contending that blacks were Satan's children, "devil worshipers," supporters of Communism (King in particular), and sexual fiends lusting after wives and daughters of whites. The sexual innuendos proved most effective in arousing southern audiences. Traditionally concerned about the sexual desires of black men for white women, white southern males believed they had a particular responsibility for preserving the sexual purity of their women. More generally, these people were alarmed at the pace of racial change in the South. Semiliterate, uninformed or misinformed, and removed from decision-making channels, poor whites feared the demise of their society in which, through the color of their skin, they enjoyed a measure of social and economic standing. Given to emotional rather than rational responses, they envisioned the very worst for themselves and their society if blacks should no longer be confined to a second-class status. Lynch and Stoner helped to feed this neurosis, encouraging white fears and urging their listeners to resort to violence to preserve segregation.[19]

Lynch first came to St. Augustine in 1963 to lead the campaign against the civil rights efforts to desegregate St. Augustine's public facilities. Speaking before a Ku Klux Klan meeting in St. Johns County during the fall, he told Klansmen: "We need a strong group in St. Augustine. You come and sign up. But don't come if you are weak or a coward. This ain't no peaceful organization. We aim to do whatever is necessary to put the Nigger back in his place, preferably in his grave."[20] During the winter Lynch drove back to California to work "to repeal the determined effort of the nonwhites to extinguish our race," but the threat of further demonstrations in St. Augustine in 1964 drew him back to the east coast in the spring.[21]

As Lynch spoke to a large audience of whites from St. Augustine and surrounding counties that warm summer evening in June, a crayon poster hanging from the slave market portrayed Martin Luther King's head mounted on the body of a raccoon and captioned: "Martin Luther Coon, And All His Little Coons, Are Going to Go Down, Like Good Tar Went Up." At his frenetic worst, Lynch hollered at his listeners: "Martin Lucifer Coon. That nigger says it's gonna be a hot summer. If he thinks the niggers can make it a hot summer, I will tell him that 140 million white people know how to make it a hotter summer." Misquoting the Bible as was his fashion, he implored his white audience, "Remember the words of Jesus Christ, who said, 'You can't love two masters.' You love the one . . . and you HATE the other. . . ." "Now it may be some niggers are gonna get killed in the process," he ranted, "but when war's on, that's what happens." A voice in the crowd interrupted Lynch, yelling, "Here come the niggers." Lynch picked up the cue: "Here they come, here come the niggers."[22]

Having turned eastward across from the Ponce de Leon, the civil rights group marched toward the plaza, approaching the Spanish Government House on the north and Trinity Episcopal Church on the south. The marchers slowed their pace as 150 state, county, and city police gathered around to protect them from the whites who stood listening to Lynch at the slave market. With the blessing of Lynch, the whites broke away from the rally and sprinted across the plaza toward the marchers helter-skelter. Moments earlier, Fred Shuttlesworth had started singing a Negro spiritual, and others quickly joined in trying to bolster their courage as bricks, firecrackers, and other debris descended upon them.

For one brief moment the singing stopped, and there was silence, much as in the eye of a hurricane. A reporter characterized it as an "eerie silence," adding "You could hear the clicking of stop lights." Then the storm hit.[23]

The marchers tried vainly to hold their ranks and continue on but whites jerked individuals from their lines at will and pummeled them fiercely. In the midst of the violence, one white woman marcher recalled saying to herself, "All whites are not like this! All whites are not like this!" "At that moment if I could have resigned from the white race, I would have done so," she declared. "I forgot every decent white person I knew and at that moment I could not remember any whites who were not like the people in the mob." The organized march quickly deteriorated into an individual search for protection from the onslaught. A young black student, his head bleeding, suddenly burst through the crowd like a halfback, heading toward the Alcazar Hotel and the safety of the black community.[24]

In contrast to their behavior at several previous marches, police, encouraged by a court order, attempted to stop the violence by firing tear gas pellets into the militants, but their efforts were useless. They were overwhelmed by the size and fervor of the mob. Spurred on by the U.S. Senate's passage of the 1964 civil rights bill and the beach violence that occurred during the afternoon, the whites seemed especially determined to make the marchers feel their wrath. The numerous side streets and alleys in St. Augustine added to the difficulty of the police in containing the mob, and some of the local police wearied of trying to stop their friends and neighbors who were committing the violence. State police did manage, though, to rescue all the marchers before any was beaten to death.[25]

While watching the melee and attempting to take notes from the relative safety of the Episcopal church grounds, a reporter felt an arm grasp his leg. Looking down he found a black teenage girl whose dress had been ripped away and who had blood running from a bruise on her shoulder. As he bent down to her, three whites descended upon him demanding: "Let the gorilla go!" The reporter pushed the girl forcefully, urging her to run. She darted away to safety but the reporter who tried to block the path of her pursuers was kicked in the stomach and trampled.[26]

This incident reflected the increasing violence against reporters. From the start of the demonstrations over Easter week through June, over twenty-five reporters and cameramen were assaulted. On May 30 alone ten newsmen were treated for injuries. Carrying heavy equipment, cameramen were especially vulnerable to attack since they could not readily escape. Their filming of the violence infuriated white militants, who began seeking out cameramen even before turning on the marchers. One reporter complained, "I've never seen rednecks as mean as these."[27] Several newsmen became "shell-shocked" by the violence in St. Augustine, and one, it was said, grew to hate St. Augustine because of his experiences. The television networks and newspaper chains began hiring bodyguards to protect their reporters.[28] Ironically, the bodyguards often proved to be whites who had originally been involved in the violence. Not surprisingly, they proved to be less than intrepid defenders of cameramen and reporters. Members of the news media also carried tear gas pistols to keep militants away and an eyewash, provided by a local motel operator, to protect them from acid attacks. For added protection, one reporter revealed, "We learned to recognize the sound of a brick coming through the air."[29] None of this, however, proved very effective on the night of June 25.

The violence lasted only twenty minutes, but it took its toll. Though most of the demonstrators were able to escape to the relative safety of their homes on Central Avenue, not all were so fortunate. Reporter Larry Goodwyn heard the crowd emitting "an eerie cry as it crossed and recrossed the plaza, attacking the dwindling remnants of Negro marchers." Approximately fifty, including marchers and reporters, were assisted by police with their cuts and bruises, while another eighteen suffered injuries serious enough for them to be taken to nearby Flagler Hospital for treatment.[30]

King quickly seized upon the bloody confrontation to

emplore the federal government to come to the assistance of the civil rights movement. "This is a reign of terror that can't be stopped short of intervention by the Federal Government," he argued, adding that "even in Birmingham we had hundreds of children in marches, but they were never attacked." He called St. Augustine the most lawless city SCLC had ever worked in, and asked the Justice Department to "do something about the brutality and violence."[31]

Responding to the violence of June 25 and King's plea, President Lyndon Johnson asked Florida's U.S. Senator George Smathers if he could arrange a settlement. Smathers informed his close friend Herbert Wolfe, a local business leader in St. Augustine, and Governor Bryant of the President's wishes. Smathers asked Wolfe to see if he and other civic leaders could establish a biracial committee to ease tensions and satisfy one of King's demands. When Wolfe called together twenty-five civic and business leaders and informed them of the President's wishes, however, Mayor Joseph Shelley immediately expressed his opposition, telling Wolfe that "You're going to sell the community out and give Martin Luther King a victory." The others supported Shelley completely and called Governor Bryant to inform him of their decision.[32]

To the chagrin of these men, Bryant announced to the press on the following day, June 30, the formation of a biracial commission in St. Augustine to end the crisis. When Shelley called Bryant and asked him what had happened Bryant replied that the "truth of it is, I haven't formed a committee in St. Augustine." Bryant, who was under considerable pressure from President Johnson, decided to make his announcement as a concession to the President even though no committee had been appointed and none would ever meet.[33]

King, sensing an opportunity to leave St. Augustine gracefully, called off further demonstrations, praising Bryant and white leaders for taking "a first important step" toward peace. Having expended considerable time and money during the demonstrations and already committed to the Mississippi Freedom Summer Campaign in 1964, King and SCLC were anxious to leave St. Augustine. The passage of the civil rights bill assured SCLC of its primary objective, but the city's black residents could not be abandoned, given the dramatic deterioration in race relations. The establishment of a biracial committee seemed to offer an opportunity for a constructive peace.[34]

But the crisis was not over. The violence and demonstrations would linger for another two months as city officials attempted to reassert control and remove outside dissidents. Moreover,
local blacks continued to be subjected to physical and verbal threats
for several more months. In fact, the community would be wracked
by racial problems for several years as it tried to adjust to the new
order.

The nature of the crisis and the extent of the violence
baffled onlookers familiar with St. Augustine. How had such a situation developed in a community, they asked, which prided itself on
its historic past, on its peaceful, well-ordered society, and on its harmonious, if somewhat paternalistic, race relations? Why were local
black citizens so upset with the community's racial traditions that they
would invite King and SCLC into St. Augustine? Why had events
deteriorated into a clash between white extremists and civil rights
activists? Where were the community leaders, where were the moderates?

Chapter 2.

Bluebirds and Redbirds
Don't Feed Together

O n Easter Sunday, March 27, 1513, the legendary
Spanish explorer and conquistador Don Juan Ponce
de Leon sighted the eastern coast of Florida while on an expedition
in search of gold and silver. He claimed the land for his country and
named it Pascua Florida (Flowery Easter). After several abortive efforts to establish settlements in the new territory and the threat of
French incursions into northern Florida, the Spanish sent Don Pedro
Menendez de Aviles to explore and colonize the area. On September
8, 1565, Menendez stepped ashore and named the land St. Augustine after the Bishop of Hippo whose feast day the fleet had been
celebrating when land was first sighted. The fleet chaplain, Father
Francisco Lopez de Mendoza Grajales, then celebrated the first mass.
Thus began the earliest continuous settlement within the present
boundaries of the United States.[1]

For over 250 years St. Augustine served as a colony and
military outpost for three separate nations. During nearly 200 of these
years the community enjoyed the stability of Spanish rule, acting as
a buffer against the expansionist efforts of the British southern colo-
nies. The fifty-eight years from 1763 to 1821, however, proved tumultuous for this small garrison community as it moved first from
British rule to Spanish rule and finally to United States control by
the terms of the Adams-Onis Treaty in 1819 (formally proclaimed in
1821). The town suffered economically throughout this period as its

trade declined sharply during the wars. Its territorial status within the United States proved no panacea: the town's economy moved sluggishly through the Seminole War in 1836 and the Civil War and Reconstruction.[2]

Economic and social conditions underwent a dramatic metamorphosis following the visit of Henry M. Flagler, former partner of John D. Rockefeller in the Standard Oil Company, during February 1885. Flagler became sufficiently impressed with the location, climate, and attractiveness of the community to invest several million dollars in its development as a tourist mecca. Besides building the stately Ponce de Leon Hotel to attract wealthy visitors from the North, he added the Alcazar and Cordova hotels for people of more moderate means. Flagler spared no cost in equipping and furnishing these buildings. He also purchased the railroads in the area to improve access to St. Augustine. The town's population and economic life surged forward during the late nineteenth and early twentieth centuries.[3] In the decade of the 1880s the town more than doubled from 2,293 to 4,742, and several hundred tourists added to the total each winter. Following World War I, St. Augustine and Florida basked in the prosperity of the roaring twenties with 6,000 people moving permanently into the city to increase its population to 12,111 by 1930.[4] Although Miami and West Palm Beach had superceded St. Augustine as the major tourist centers in the 1920s, many visitors were still attracted to the nation's oldest city and to Flagler's hotels. Yet despite the growth of the town after 1880, it remained relatively small even during the post–World War I period. Residents described it as the sort of community in which "everybody knew everybody."[5]

The constant in-migration of extremely wealthy and socially prominent people from the North during the winter season seemed, nevertheless, to have left its mark on St. Augustine. A hierarchically ordered society gradually developed during the twentieth century based upon wealth, family heritage, and religion. Hamilton Upchurch, a prominent political leader in the community, described it as "a stilted society" during his youth in the 1930s. He observed that his mother and father always referred to their neighbors as "Mr. and Mrs." and that on Sundays one would get formally dressed to call on neighbors and to wait "for others to call."[6]

During the period from 1930 to 1960 when the popula-

tion remained fairly static and the social order remarkably unchanged, the "old English" residents, as they were referred to by local citizens, comprised the most important group in this society. Many
of these natives lived along Matanzas Bay on Water Street, directly
north of the Castillo de San Marcos. They included approximately
fifty families who were generally well educated and had been political
and economic leaders during the nineteenth and early twentieth centuries. These residents placed great emphasis on one's heritage and
took pride in tracing their roots in St. Augustine back to territorial
and early statehood days. This enabled them to separate themselves
socially from those who had recently acquired wealth and status. The
influence of this old English group and the "blue bloods" from the
north permeated the rest of society. Local residents often copied their
customs, style of dress, and interests. They exercised little political
influence after the Great Depression, however, tending to confine their
activities to the arts, cultural events, historic restoration, and their
business activities. They took an active role in the religious affairs of
Trinity Episcopal Church, the oldest such church in Florida.[7]

Political and economic leadership in St. Augustine was
provided principally by the business and professional class. They
comprised a very large, rather amorphous group of five hundred people, including a number of old English residents, who had resided in
the community for one or more generations. Two studies of St. Augustine's leadership in the early 1970s revealed that the most respected business and professional leaders all knew one another well
in this small town. Their relationships were further intertwined by
their mutual involvement in such groups as the Chamber of Commerce, the St. Augustine Historical Society, the Country Club, and
Kiwanis. These men frequently sat on the city commission from 1930
to 1960. During the years they did not sit on the commission, they
were consulted by commission members whenever important issues
arose. They deliberately avoided controversial issues and did not "want
to excite passions," which might jeopardize community development
and their business interests. One leading businessman commented,
"We don't always agree on everything, but when we do disagree we
don't do it publicly."[8]

A third important voice in the community came from the
Minorcans, a large white ethnic group of nearly one hundred families

who tended to intermarry and thus retain their ethnic identity. Their ancestors had originally migrated to St. Augustine from New Smyrna, a coastal community 64 miles south of St. Augustine, in 1777, but despite their long residency in the community, the Minorcans in the 1960s still formed a very distinct, identifiable social group.[9] Catholic in a community that was predominantly Catholic, they took an active part in the life of the cathedral which served as the headquarters of the north Florida diocese. A number of Minorcan families had achieved considerable economic and social progress during their residence in St. Augustine. Most Minorcans, however, were below the median income level for the city during the twentieth century, engaging in such activities as construction, fishing, and shrimping.[10]

A fourth group in St. Augustine included fishermen, railroad, construction, and other blue collar workers. This very disparate group of approximately four thousand people (including Minorcans below the median income level) shared very little in common other than a fundamental Christian faith (whether Catholic or Protestant) and their racial heritage. They participated in little of the prosperity of St. Augustine's tourist trade. No unions existed in the community during much of the twentieth century because of the opposition of Flagler and other business leaders and the antiunion sentiment that permeated the South during most of this century. They were also excluded from political influence because they exercised little social or economic power and voted irregularly.[11]

The final group in St. Augustine comprised the city's 2,480 black residents (23.2 percent of the population) whose subordinate status had been defined by custom and law. Segregation denied blacks full and equal access to the railroad station, bus depot, restrooms, drinking fountains, public schools, city hospital, and library, and blacks attended separate churches. Blacks made a living in St. Augustine by waiting upon white needs as servants, maids, migrant workers, tenant farmers, and menial laborers, and the city's reliance on the tourist industry emphasized dramatically that subordinate role. Black residents lived in the southwest section of the city and in an area just west of the city limits. Whites commonly referred to the section in the city as "colored town," although several white families also resided in this rather well maintained area. The area west of town housed a slightly larger number of black families and exhibited the poverty more frequently associated with black ghettos in the South.[12]

Blacks had resided in the historic community of St. Augustine almost as long as whites. Spain had, in fact, established a free black colony in the St. Augustine area in 1739, but this experiment had ceased by 1763. During the post–1821 era, as tensions increased between the North and South, St. Augustine retained a relatively large black population. The 1830 census revealed that the overwhelming majority of blacks were enslaved and that they constituted almost one-half of the city's population. According to the historian Thomas Graham, the sheer size of the slave population and the urban locale led to a more relaxed system of slavery than commonly found on cotton plantations during the antebellum period. Owners allowed slaves to hire themselves out to railroad contractors, lumbermen, and fishermen. While the money earned through these agreements went to the owners, slaves occasionally received a small income from part-time work. This provided them with a small measure of financial independence which they used to support their own grog shops, clubs, and churches. Many slaves also resided outside the master's home in a separate area of the city where they felt free to express themselves.[13]

The 1830 census also disclosed 240 free blacks in a population of 4,000 blacks, or 6 percent, about three times the statewide average. Most of St. Augustine's free blacks were descendants of the earlier colonists and of Georgia's runaway slaves. During this period they held a very precarious place in St. Augustine, occupying a position only slightly removed from slavery. They could not hold meetings without receiving permission from white authorities, were restricted in the types of jobs they could obtain, and were forced to live in one section of the community where their activities could be observed.[14]

The place of blacks, especially slaves in St. Augustine, greatly concerned local residents in the antebellum period. George R. Fairbanks, a leading citizen and slaveowner, warned his neighbors that they would be faced with serious problems if they continued to allow their slaves to live independent lives. Local residents took his warnings seriously. Following the example of other southern cities between 1840 and 1860, local slaveholders reasserted their control by tightening slave codes and selling nonessential slaves to rural areas of the South.[15]

Throughout this period, white residents in St. Augustine insisted that blacks were very content as slaves, but many aspects of slavery suggested otherwise. Whites, for example, found it necessary to lock their doors, guard their fields with watchdogs, and maintain night patrols to prevent slaves from stealing, running away, or committing acts of violence.[16]

Less than a year after the Civil War broke out, the town fell to Union troops, causing a significant disruption in traditional racial customs. Slaves from surrounding areas began arriving in large numbers, seeking freedom and protection. The army hired slave men and also employed free blacks to prepare defenses for the city and to begin filling the ranks of all-black regiments being formed in the South. With the end of slavery in sight, masters complained that their slaves had become increasingly lazy and disobedient. They observed with disgust the cheers blacks accorded the news of Union victories on the battlefield and the announcement of the Emancipation Proclamation.[17]

During the post–Civil War period, race relations continued on an unsteady course as blacks and whites adjusted to the end of slavery. Several black families attempted to separate themselves from their former owners by establishing an independent settlement south of town called "Africa." This effort failed, however, and most blacks asserted their independence by maintaining their own churches (principally Baptist and Methodist) and by seeking jobs which were distinct from past slave work. They also eagerly embraced the educational and welfare services offered by the Freedmen's Bureau during and after the war. Moreover, blacks joined with white unionists to form the Union Conservative Party, and several blacks were elected to local office. William Van Dyke was selected as town marshall in 1873 and 1877 and John Papino succeeded him in 1885; Edward J. Houston also served as tax collector in 1882 and 1885.[18]

With the end of Reconstruction in 1877 and the removal of the Union Army, southern whites gradually reasserted their control of community affairs. A few blacks managed to maintain a degree of independence as ministers, bankers, shoemakers, tailors, and barbers. But as the century wore on, most blacks could only find employment as domestics and common laborers. During the 1880s the town was divided into wards, and most blacks were confined to one ward for local elections. This effectively killed the Union Conservative Party. Blacks also felt the pressure of the emerging paternalistic system in social matters. Beginning in the 1890s whites invited blacks to take part in an annual cake walk. The leading black people dressed in their finest clothes for the occasion and paraded before a white audience. Other blacks sang Negro spirituals, and the waiters performed a variety of dances. Whites apparently used the event to render approval for certain patterns of black behavior and dress. Race relations reached their nadir in 1902 with the shooting of John Papino, who had just recently been elected to the city council (the last black to hold public office until 1973). His killer, who apparently was not charged, contended that Papino would not keep quiet when he was trying to address the council.[19]

The establishment of the tourist industry by Henry Flagler during the same period seemed to prevent racial antagonisms from worsening. Indeed, in order to insure the continuation of a profitable tourist economy, whites and blacks became dependent on one another. Whites needed black labor to assist in the advancement of the new tourist trade. Blacks in turn appear to have been more than happy to escape from tenant farming and domestic work to enjoy the greater economic benefits and freedom that evolved from tourism. There thus developed a more civil relationship between black and white residents.

The integrated housing patterns in the area of the city known as colored town and in other sections scattered throughout the city helped to maintain civil relations between the races. Blacks often resided next door or across the street from whites. This neighborhood arrangement remained from the days when slaves commonly lived in quarters behind the master's house or in the immediate vicinity. These patterns also reflected the small size of the town, little more than twenty square miles, which forced blacks and whites to reside in close proximity.

Despite these economic and residential conditions which ameliorated race relations, white St. Augustinians were no less committed to implementing segregation than their southern neighbors. Thus by 1900, white waitresses had replaced black waiters in hotels and restaurants, and the white minstrel show had superceded the cake walk. In addition, very few blacks could vote because of the state's poll tax and multiple ballot law. Whites in St. Augustine also joined with residents in other sections of the state in fully supporting segregation of public facilities and a ban on interracial marriages.[20]

The progressive period in Florida and St. Augustine conformed to C. Vann Woodward's portrayal of the South during this era as a region "for whites only." Segregation laws and customs effectively excluded blacks from any role in local political and economic affairs. Blacks in St. Augustine, however, were not subjected to acts of intimidation and physical abuse that blacks encountered in other parts of Florida and the South. Though not blessed by racial progressiveness, St. Augustine did manage to escape the racial violence so characteristic of the region at the turn of the century. Thus when the opportunity occurred for blacks to leave St. Augustine, as it did during and immediately after World War I, most chose to stay, believing race relations were as good there as everywhere else.

Even when whites made overtures to blacks in St. Augustine, however, they did so within the context of the paternalistic values that shaped race relations. In 1921, motivated by a desire to strengthen the local economy, a delegation from the Chamber of Commerce visited the president of Florida Baptist Academy, a black school in Jacksonville, and persuaded him to move the school to St. Augustine in exchange for land and financial considerations. Renamed the Florida Normal and Industrial Institute, the college followed the precepts of Booker T. Washington, emphasizing accommodation, hard work, service, and technical education. These aims squared nicely with the place white St. Augustinians had constructed for blacks. The presence of the college in the community during the next four decades helped develop a stronger sense of racial identity and social vitality through a variety of social, cultural, and political events, yet always within a separatist matrix. The latter usually took the form of distinguished blacks or white political leaders addressing students and faculty on the wisdom of Washington's philosophy of self-help. Black residents were invited to the events sponsored by the college and frequently asked to participate in the planning and preparation. Thus, while the leadership of the college tended to be quite conservative in outlook, it provided an important institutional mechanism for black awareness. It should be emphasized, however, that the college did so almost exclusively within the confines of the Jim Crow system.[21]

A small but influential black professional class also moved to St. Augustine in the 1920s, enhancing black leadership and helping to maintain peaceful relations. The relocation of Florida Normal College, relatively stable racial traditions when contrasted with the rest of the South, and a pleasant environment apparently attracted such men to the community. They not only helped provide leadership, but their professions also served as a bridge to the white community. The majority of the black dentist's patients were, in fact, white St. Augustinians. By and large black professionals accepted the status quo, but there were occasions in which they protested their exclusion from professional gatherings. Because of their economic success and their educational background, these professionals served as role models for young blacks. The chances of local blacks achieving similar professional and economic success were very small, however, since none of the black professionals was a native of St. Augustine. Indeed, they had all moved to the community from elsewhere, and they alone in the black community commanded sufficient wealth to send their children to college.[22]

Although the onset of the Great Depression caused major economic and social problems in Florida, race relations did not noticeably worsen in St. Augustine as it did in the Florida Panhandle, where racial violence and lynchings, increased significantly. The tourist industry in St. Augustine had been eclipsed earlier by the development of Miami and West Palm Beach in 1915, so the general collapse at the end of the 1920s did not cause a major readjustment. Few blacks lost their jobs in this sector of the economy during the twenties, although there was a decline in wages. Most of the black unemployed (approximately 15 percent) managed to survive these years through handouts from family, friends, the church, and, on some occasions, from white residents.[23]

Although race relations remained calm during this period, blacks were careful not to challenge the segregation barriers. Those who contemplated such action could expect an immediate response from local police as well as discouragement from leaders in the black community. No one appears to have given even passing thought to contacting NAACP officials about racial conditions. Life thus continued at a rather leisurely pace for blacks and whites during the 1930s, but it was carefully circumscribed by racial customs.[24]

Throughout this period the church provided moral and spiritual comfort for residents of the black community that enabled them to cope with discrimination and persecution. Ministerial leaders told their parishioners that God would ultimately vindicate the righteous and long suffering. "Seeing little or no hope in this world," wrote sociologists Benjamin Mays and Joseph Nicholson, "the Negro has done what other people have done, he has projected his hopes in a heaven above." The church also helped develop a strong sense of family and community by sponsoring numerous social activities and an occasional recreational function. It thus forged a sense of community and provided a sense of purpose to the lives of black residents during these often difficult times.[25]

Despite the peaceful race relations in the community and the reemergence of prosperity at the end of the 1930s, black St. Augustinians enjoyed few economic or educational benefits from residing in this seacoast community. Census data for the 1940s disclosed that 75 percent of all black male workers were employed in service, operative, and manual labor activities. Forty-eight percent of Negro women workers were employed in private homes with another thirty percent engaged in service occupations. Only 3.8 percent of the black population were professionals, a surprisingly small figure in view of the black faculty who worked at Florida Normal College. By contrast 8.7 percent of the whites were professionals. Ninety percent of all black workers earned under $3,000 per year with 41 percent earning less than $1,000. Only 63 percent of white workers received less than $3,000 with 26 percent of this group earning under $1,000. A mere .8 percent of the black population earned over $5,000 compared to 8.2 percent for the white race. The median education for black St. Augustinians stood at 7.3 years as opposed to over ten years for whites. Very few blacks graduated from high school and even fewer went to college. One hundred and twenty-five blacks in the community had attended college, but this figure was inflated by the black professors at Florida Normal College.[26]

Little progress occurred for black residents during the 1950s: 60 percent of all black female employees were engaged in domestic or service work. Significantly, black women held nearly eighty more types of jobs than black men. Slightly more than 20 percent of all black males were involved in service positions. The overwhelming majority of black employees worked in service trades, farming, railroad, and construction jobs. The black family median income stood at approximately $3,500 (white family median income averaged $5,000) but over four hundred black families earned less than $3,000 per year. No black worker received over $7,000 while six hundred white families did. More than two-thirds of the individual black workers garnered less than $2,500, while less than one-half the white population earned below this figure. Blacks attended school for only 7.4 years compared with 11.2 for whites. The educational gap between whites and blacks had increased in the past decade by one full grade level. Only 178 blacks had attended college in 1960, an increase of fifty-three from the 1950 figure.[27]

These census figures demonstrated that blacks encountered very limited economic opportunity in St. Augustine during their lifetime and that their children found similar restrictions. Most black children, probably encouraged to do so by their parents, dropped out before high school to help support the family and acquire a skill. These limitations also meant that both husbands and wives had to work if their family was to enjoy more than a poverty-stricken existence. Employment for blacks outside the service area, railroad and construction work, and tenant farming was virtually nonexistent. Teaching and preaching offered the only areas of advancement for blacks. Reflecting on the lack of opportunity for local residents, black Assistant Superintendent of Schools Otis Mason declared that "education for me was the only salvation."[28]

Despite the pervasiveness of segregation and economic discrimination, race relations continued to be characterized by what the historian William Chafe calls civility—"a way of dealing with people and problems that made good manners more important than substantial action." While whites expected blacks to defer to them, relations between the races appeared cordial, indeed often friendly. Blacks and whites frequently exchanged pleasantries on the street and often sat in discussion on the park benches in the plaza. Catholics and Episcopalians even attended services together, though only on special religious occasions. Whites considered the relations between black and white to be "excellent." "Less segregation, less anomosity" existed there, according to the reporter and native southerner Hank Drane, "than in many communities in Florida."[29] The historian David Chalmers noted in a similar vein that St. Augustine permitted a greater degree of racial intermingling than "hundreds of other Southern towns." Even local blacks observed, "You really weren't too conscious at that time of the difference that existed." Otis Mason portrayed it as "an harmonious thing." The paternalistic system in St. Augustine thus functioned more flexibly than it did in many other southern and Florida communities.[30]

Because of such interracial involvement, local black leaders felt St. Augustine would be relatively easy to integrate. "We never anticipated it being so much trouble," a civil rights leader reflected. But all was not racial bliss in this southern town, and some leaders envisioned difficulty for those seeking to improve the lot of black residents. "Racially, there was no concern on the part of most of the white people there as to the black," a ministerial leader commented. "They were servants. They were kept in this position and there was no attempt much to help them except to help them to the extent that you would keep them in their place." Moreover, local whites never exhibited a genuinely progressive attitude toward race relations that might lead to a breakdown of segregation barriers. In private and public conversations white residents repeatedly indicated that they had no intention of surrendering their control of the political and social process.[31]

During the post–World War II period St. Augustine remained a relatively stable society in a state that was experiencing rapid socioeconomic changes. Prosperity accelerated due to a resurgent tourist trade but otherwise the community seemed little changed from the prewar era. The leadership still came from the legal, banking, and business community. The majority of newcomers who arrived seemed to come chiefly to retire. According to local observers, they generally shared the prevailing values of the community. It was a society "not terribly interested in change," a local clergyman noted and "not terribly interested in being disturbed."[32]

Living in the nation's oldest city. St. Augustinians were especially conscious of their past. According to one historian who spent several years studying the city's early history, the postwar white leadership exhibited a craze "for genealogy." Several residents took pride in tracing their ancestry back to the period of British and even Spanish occupation. Here then was a very stable, personally close, and structured community on the verge of being confronted by a civil rights crisis of considerable magnitude.[33]

The decision of the Supreme Court in *Brown* vs. *Board of Education of Topeka* had virtually no immediate impact on race relations in St. Augustine. Whites in the community did not like the decision, but few expected St. Augustine to be affected seriously by it. The editor of the *St. Augustine Record* urged that the issue of desegregation be kept out of politics and that "a solution based on reason and the public's welfare" be sought in order to avoid "hatred, heartaches, and misunderstandings." Blacks were pleased by the pronouncement but most, no doubt, thought that the Court's decision would somehow be evaded in St. Augustine.[34]

As in the rest of the South, Florida initially responded calmly to the Court's pronouncement. Senior senator Spessard Holland said he hoped the decision would be met with "patience and moderation," and that he believed there would be no "violent repercussions" in the state. The editor of the *Tampa Tribune* urged restraint, calling the *Brown* decision inevitable.[35]

But this is not to suggest that the *Brown* decision had little significance for Florida. In the spring of 1954 Florida was one of only four states with no school integration whatsoever, and thus the Court's action had grave implications for the state's traditional pattern of public education. The state gave an indication of its subsequent response to the *Brown* decision when the Cabinet decided not to modify its $120 million school construction program in light of this verdict. State School Superintendent Thomas Bailey commented that "the Negro schools should be constructed as planned." Reflecting the views of other cabinet members and most white Floridians, Bailey added, "My presumption is that Negroes attending a good school are going to prefer to remain there." St. Augustine's school leaders followed the state's leadership, going ahead with construction plans which included a new Negro high school for West St. Augustine.[36]

By 1956 Florida and the South generally had abandoned their moderate position on the *Brown* decision. The White Citizens' Council movement, which began in Indianola, Mississippi, in July 1954, spread into Louisiana, Alabama, Texas, Arkansas, Georgia, and Florida. The shift in southern temper reflected hostility to the Supreme Court's second *Brown* decision in May 1955, which directed the lower courts to begin the process of desegregating public schools in the South "with all deliberate speed." While implementation of the decision started slowly in the fall of 1956, it took on a degree of inevitability that it had lacked before. In addition, numerous state and local elections occurred during the spring and fall of 1956 throughout the South at which time southerners and their representatives denounced the Court's edict and promised if elected to block enforcement of the *Brown* decision.[37]

Florida avoided the "massive resistance" approach of states like Virginia and the racial turmoil that engulfed much of the South during this era due to the moderate leadership of Governor LeRoy Collins, but Collins was unable to erode public and legislative support for segregation and a dual school system during his six years in office. He tried to convince several school boards to comply voluntarily with the Supreme Court decision by offering them financial inducements, and he appointed a biracial committee to assist communities in this process. But when he left office in 1960 only Dade County had desegregated (and the desegregation involved only four black children attending one elementary school). St. Augustine joined with other Florida communities in ignoring the Governor's request and maintaining two separate school systems as it entered the new decade. Florida and other Southern states were under no pressure to desegregate until 1968 when the Supreme Court in *Green v. County School Board* (New Kent County, Virginia) dismissed the "freedom of choice" plan in favor of a desegregation plan that "promises realistically to work now."[38]

Collins' successor, Farris Bryant, had been an avowed opponent of desegregation since the announcement of the *Brown* decision and had championed an interposition resolution as a member of the state legislature in 1956. He also campaigned for governor as a segregationist in 1960. In one of the first acts of his administration, Bryant indicated he would reappoint Collins' statewide biracial advisory committee. The chairman soon resigned, however, alleging that Bryant wanted a committee composed of people "whose opinions would be congenial with his own." Bryant later announced he had chosen a new chairman, but he refused to name him and the committee subsequently dissolved.[39] Thus in 1961, Florida had begun to take a more dogmatic stance against desegregation under the leadership of Governor Bryant. School segregation and other Jim Crow features continued almost completely intact as the state entered a decade of racial change.

Like the state, St. Augustine, too, was slow to respond to the changes portended by the *Brown* decision. County school board officials, as noted earlier, went ahead with plans to build a new black high school. The community was thus remarkably unaffected by the Court's edict or by racial developments in the latter part of the decade. Local residents watched with alarm as events unfolded during the Little Rock school crisis of 1957, but most apparently attributed developments there to an irrational governor, to school officials who should not have desegregated Central High School, and to the federal courts for interfering in a state matter. The bus boycott by blacks in Montgomery in 1956 went largely unnoticed by residents of St. Augustine.

Local blacks clearly wanted greater freedom and opportunity for themselves and their families, but they were fearful that protests would only worsen relations. While they applauded the actions of Martin Luther King, Jr., no one proposed similar steps in St. Augustine. Until they had ample evidence that protest could lead to improved conditions and until a leader emerged to coordinate such activities, local blacks hesitated to act. An NAACP chapter did exist in the community and had been reactivated in the 1950s by the Reverend Thomas Wright of St. Mary's Baptist Church, but the organization proposed no radical change in racial practices during this decade. Under Wright's leadership, the organization sought financial support for additional recreation facilities and a community library in the black section of the city. Since neither request threatened traditional racial customs, city commissioners approved both requests. The NAACP also conducted an active voter registration campaign in the aftermath of the Supreme Court's rejection of a white primary law in Texas (*Smith v. Allwright*, 1944), and, although nearly 500 blacks were added to the voting lists, they only constituted 20 percent of the electorate. Since there were no significant political divisions in St. Augustine, black political influence would remain unchanged.[40]

The commitment of white St. Augustinians to segregation, however, was apparent to anyone who wished to challenge it. In the summer of 1961 Henry Thomas, a young black student who had just returned home from a workshop on sit-ins at Howard University, decided to seek service at Woolworth's lunch counter. Although it was customary for blacks to purchase food at such places, they were not permitted to eat there. Thomas was quickly carried off to jail once the waitress realized what he was attempting to do. The police transferred Thomas to the hospital during the night, seeking to have him ruled insane and committed to a mental institution. Only Thomas's reputation in the community, as well as the apparent reluctance of the doctors, prevented police from having him locked away.[41] Encouraged by Thomas' example and that of the North Carolina A. & T. students in Greensboro, the Reverend Wright planned additional sit-ins during the summer of 1962 using students from Florida Memorial College, but they never took place because of opposition from college officials.

What Thomas' personal demonstration and Wright's abortive plans revealed was an increasing interest by black residents in some form of protest against the Jim Crow system. In this regard, the Greensboro sit-ins which began in February 1960 played a critical role. The success of this protest effort and the rapid spread of the sit-in to many other communities in the South persuaded several black leaders in St. Augustine that such demonstrations could facilitate racial change.

The efforts of Thomas and Wright, however, had little or no effect on white attitudes or segregation practices. "At first whites helped us," Wright reflected, "but as we applied more pressure and asked for more assistance, we received more opposition." White leaders seemed generally unaware of emerging racial problems during the first

two years of the 1960s and, as one leader noted, if there were demonstrations, they were conducted by one or two people "who were
put away." Whites remained convinced that blacks in St. Augustine
were quite content with the racial traditions of the past and saw no
need to change them.[42]

Organized demonstrations did not occur in St. Augustine until 1963 after Dr. Robert B. Hayling assumed the leadership
of the Youth Council of the National Association for the Advancement of Colored People. He had arrived in St. Augustine in 1960 to
take over the dental practice of Dr. Rudolph Gordon. Hayling's
background, education, and temperament, made him ill-prepared for
living in a small, segregated community. Born in Tallahassee on November 20, 1929, he was the second oldest of four children of a professor in industrial education at Florida Agricultural and Mechanical
College for Negroes. Although black, the Haylings suffered few dep-
rivations in Tallahassee. The father's occupation insured the family
a comfortable living and a position of social leadership in the black
community. The family also benefitted from the absence of overt racial hostility in Tallahassee in the 1930s. Hayling attended the segregated public schools in the city and then matriculated at his father's school, the state's only publicly supported black college. He
achieved superior grades in school, especially in the sciences, and received a B. S. in zoology in 1951. Perhaps, because of his academic
interests, friends found him to be "a withdrawn type" who "didn't
exert positive leadership." He did not engage in civil rights activities
during these years although neither did most black students. He seemed
more interested in pursuing a professional career in dentistry and in
achieving the social and economic security such a career could offer.[43]

In 1951, during the height of the Korean War, Hayling
volunteered for Air Force duty to avoid being drafted into the Army.
He entered Officer's Candidate School, and after his commission,
served four years at the Aero Medical Research Center at Wright-
Patterson Air Force Base in Dayton, Ohio. It was during his Air Force
career that he first encountered overt racial hostility. Living in the
black community in Tallahassee and attending black schools and a
black university had insulated him from displays of racial animosity.
During his Air Force career, however, he left the confines of that

community to enter a branch of the service that was overwhelmingly white. He apparently heard a number of racial epthets during his Officer's Candidate training. In the face of this hostility, Hayling later remarked about his Air Force experience, "I've never been a person you could push around. If you pushed me to the corner, I would always fight."[44]

Upon completing his military obligation in 1955, Hayling pursued his dental education at Meharry Medical College, a leading black medical and dental school in Nashville, Tennessee, where he became actively involved in racial issues. The state of Florida provided him with a $1,000 scholarship to attend the all-black medical school since none existed in the state. During these years he took part in his first civil rights demonstration after the home of a black city commissioner was bombed. Hayling accompanied several other Meharry students as they paraded in front of city hall, demanding the arrest of the bomber and denouncing the Ku Klux Klan.[45]

After moving to St. Augustine in 1960, Hayling concentrated on maintaining and expanding Dr. Rudolph Gordon's dental practice. As Gordon had done, Hayling continued to treat a large number of white residents, including several who were members of the Klan. During this period he joined the State Dental Association, the first black admitted to this professional organization. However, Hayling's professional experiences were not uniformly pleasant. The white medical figures in St. Augustine were a very conservative lot who refused to associate with him on a personal or professional level. As with his racial encounters in the Air Force, Hayling seemed unprepared for this development. Being an outsider, Hayling also saw problem areas in this historic community which natives frequently overlooked.[46]

Dissatisfied with his own experiences in St. Augustine and inspired by civil rights developments elsewhere, especially in his home town of Tallahassee, Hayling soon joined the local NAACP. The NAACP was essentially a low-keyed operation in the early 1960s which, with the exception of the Reverend Wright's activities, had done relatively little to break down racial barriers. Most members, including its two leaders in 1963, Mrs. Fannie Fullerwood and Mrs. Elizabeth Hawthorne, were rather conservative in their efforts to desegregate St. Augustine. They tried to persuade rather than coerce whites to abandon segregation. Moreover, they were anxious to avoid alienating white leaders, fearing economic reprisals and physical threats. Significantly, the NAACP was very small, with perhaps no more than twenty to thirty active members. The majority of the Negro community showed little more than passing interest in the organization and its activities. In this respect the local NAACP had much in common with numerous other branches in small communities throughout the South in 1962.[47] Hayling's presence would soon change the direction of NAACP activities, however.

Aiding Hayling in mounting a civil rights movement in St. Augustine were the numerous racial developments elsewhere, especially the Albany and Birmingham campaigns and the Freedom Rides, and the growing support for civil rights throughout the country. From 1961 to 1965, in fact, several public opinion polls identified civil rights as the most important issue confronting the nation. Sociologist Doug McAdam has suggested in a book on black insurgency that during such times a cognitive liberation often occurs in which people "collectively define their situations as unjust and subject to change through group action." In St. Augustine, Hayling's leadership and the developments of the era helped mobilize a civil rights movement.[48]

Throughout this period Hayling was something of an enigma to St. Augustinians. Mrs. Rosalie Gordon, wife of Dr. Gordon, thought him to be "quiet, unassuming, very pleasant, [and] quite intelligent." Several local blacks described him as a "friendly, intelligent, and hardworking man," while others who worked with him in the St. Augustine movement, contended he was "a committed egotistical man," "a bull head." One black leader would later accuse Hayling of making hysterical telephone calls to black and white leaders throughout the country, exaggerating conditions in St. Augustine. Hosea Williams, who helped organize demonstrations in 1964 for the Southern Christian Leadership Conference, claimed that Hayling "didn't understand the weakness of violence." Mrs. Gordon added that as she got to know him better she realized "he had a deep down anger with conditions facing blacks in America," and, no doubt, in St. Augustine. Certainly Hayling's actions and personal relations hardened as race relations worsened, and as he and his family became the objects of militant threats, but he never resorted to violence nor did his supporters.[49]

Acting as personal adviser to the Youth Council of the NAACP, Hayling recruited members from the college and community and laid plans to desegregate public facilities. The council was a natural vehicle for Hayling to turn to. While originally founded at the national level in 1936, it had come into its own during the 1960s as an effective direct action arm of the NAACP. Comprised of youthful idealists, it was a potent force for change in the early 1960s throughout Florida and the South. When Hayling assumed leadership, the St. Augustine Youth Council had approximately fifteen members, most of whom were high school students, although a few attended Florida Memorial College.[50]

Throughout 1963 and 1964, Hayling's support came principally from young people in the community. Older residents saw him as a newcomer and something of a troublemaker, who did not understand how things were done in St. Augustine. Even among older blacks who supported the efforts of the NAACP there was a general belief that Hayling lacked patience and often spoke without thinking. Young people, however, who were tired of waiting for racial change, found in Hayling a leader who shared their desire for a quick end to segregation and who was willing to pursue aggressive tactics to achieve this goal.[51]

At the beginning of 1963 NAACP officials developed plans for desegregating the community by exerting pressure at the local and national level. Black leaders requested a parade permit from city officials to protest the continuation of segregation in the city, but the city manager rejected the petition without comment. In March NAACP leaders, with Hayling's encouragement, wrote Vice-President Lyndon Johnson asking him to cancel his visit to St. Augustine to dedicate a historical Spanish landmark. In their letter Mrs. Fullerwood and Mrs. Hawthorne complained of widespread segregation in the city, and the refusal of city leaders to meet with them, establish a biracial commission, or grant them a parade permit. Hayling told reporters that he would try to disrupt the Vice-President's visit if blacks were not allowed to take part in the proceedings. Johnson responded on March 7, indicating he would not take part in any segregated event. Dr. Royal Puryear and eleven others, but not Hayling, were selected to represent the black community by white leaders who specifically excluded NAACP officials and Hayling. Apparently Roy Wilkins, national president of the NAACP, called Hayling, supporting the compromise and urging Hayling not to disrupt the proceedings.[52]

Johnson promised during his one day visit to have his press secretary George Reedy meet with local black leaders and the city commission on the following day. But on March 12 black leaders arrived at city commission chambers only to find City Manager Charles Barrier, his secretary, and a tape recorder present. No observers from Washington and no commission members were in attendance. The group protested the absence of city commissioners and representatives from Johnson's staff, but Barrier replied that commissioners had not been asked to attend, and he had not heard from George Reedy, who had departed with the Vice-President. Barrier indicated that he would provide transcripts of the tape to commissioners. The black leaders expressed concern about the continuation of segregation in public facilities, the lack of black employment in city government, and the absence of suitable housing for middle class blacks. Barrier encouraged the group to meet with commissioners in private or at a public meeting in the near future to discuss these matters.[53]

Two weeks later, black leaders met with three members of the commission to discuss the issues raised at the meeting with Barrier. At that time black leaders requested the desegration of the public park, the city-owned pier, and the courthouse, more skilled job opportunities for blacks in city and county government, employment of one more black policeman, and hiring of Negro workers for city and county polling work. The three commissioners said they had not had time to study the requests, and because the full commission was not present they would meet with the group at a later date. It appeared, however, that commissioners were stalling until new commissioners had been elected in May, thereby forcing them to handle this brewing controversy.[54]

Dissatisfied with the city's delays, Mrs. Fullerwood and Mrs. Hawthorne wrote President John Kennedy on May 4, again at Hayling's urging, asking that he oppose a federal grant of $350,000 for the city's quadricentennial observance to avoid publicizing "this truly undemocratic city." They alluded to widespread segregation in city schools, public facilities, and city employment and pointed out that city commissioners had failed to keep their promise to meet with a delegation of Negro citizens following Vice-President Johnson's visit. Using a popular Cold War appeal of the NAACP, the two local leaders called on the President to "prove to the Communists and the entire world that America's oldest city can truly be a showcase of democracy." They also asked that the President appoint at least one Negro member to the Quadricentennial Commission. President Kennedy had designated Herbert Wolfe chairman of this commission and had also appointed several prominent Americans, none of whom was black. While the White House monitored the situation in St. Augustine during 1963, Kennedy's staff did not respond to the requests made by the NAACP. J. Edgar Hoover did approve FBI surveillance of civil rights developments in the city, however, and on June 5 Jacksonville agents sent the first of numerous daily reports to FBI headquarters in Washington.[55]

City Commissioner James Lindsley asked City Manager Barrier to reply to the accusations made by the NAACP in its letter to President Kennedy. Barrier responded that the public schools were operated under the County School Board and that private businesses set their own policies. Furthermore, Barrier stated that "Negroes are given every opportunity to fill vacant positions" in city government and that 27 out of 150 city employees were black. What he failed to mention was that nearly all those employed were secretaries or garbage men. He concluded by noting that the city commission had never refused to meet with anyone and that no promise had been made for commissioners to meet with representatives of Vice-President Johnson.[56]

Frustrated by the response from city commissioners and the federal government, Hayling called recently elected city commissioner and acting mayor Harry Gutterman (Mayor Joseph Shelley was on vacation), informing him that he could no longer control local Negroes unless the commission took some action to end segregation. Promising to get back in touch with him, Gutterman hastily met with Commissioners John Bailey, James Lindsley, and H. L. McDaniel, City Manager Barrier, and City Attorney Robert Andreu at his home on the following evening. They agreed to meet with black leaders on June 16 to hear their grievances.

At the beginning of the meeting, black leaders requested that civil service examinations for all city positions be open to citizens regardless of race, creed, or color, city-owned facilities be fully desegregated, picketing within city ordinances be permitted, and commissioners express their views openly on desegregation. After a remarkably frank three-hour discussion between the four commissioners and nine black leaders, the commissioners announced that no city ordinance prohibited "the use of municipal facilities to any citizen of the community," and that all signs "which in any way restrict the use of such facilities would be removed." The commission agreed to meet with black leaders again on June 20.[57]

Between the first and second meeting with commissioners, three matters became public which angered commissioners and stymied further negotiations. The first was a letter from the NAACP to Barrier and city commissioners on June 18. The NAACP acknowledged that the city did not control several areas of racial discrimination, but contended that it did have responsibility for segregation signs that existed on city property. In addition, NAACP leaders mentioned the salary discrimination in the city, noting that not one black employee received a raise among the several recently granted by the city. City leaders were urged to "correct the community atmosphere" and appoint the necessary committees "until the desired results are attained." The consequences, black leaders warned, would "bring an ugly Birmingham situation to St. Augustine and will mean *TOTAL COLLAPSE* for our economy and tourist business." City leaders were angered by this threat, calling it blackmail. Second, the *St. Augustine Record* made public the efforts of other NAACP branches to assist the St. Augustine NAACP in blocking the appropriation of federal funds for the quadricentennial celebration. Lastly, Hayling, responding to telephone threats he had received, angrily told reporters on the nineteenth that "Passive resistance is no good in the face of violence." He declared that he and other NAACP members "have armed ourselves and we will shoot first and ask questions later." "We are not going to die like Medgar Evers," Hayling asserted (Evers had been murdered in Mississippi only seven days earlier). Hayling later commented that Police Chief Virgil Stuart was a segregationist and that he would not provide the movement with adequate protection, and that "all hell would break loose" if city commissioners did not meet with black leaders. NAACP officials tried to lessen the impact of Hayling's comments by stating that racial feelings in the black community were well under control. But white leaders were infuriated by Hayling's threats.[58]

At the scheduled meeting between Negro leaders and commissioners on June 20 only two commissioners attended. Gutterman announced that each citizen would be given three minutes to speak but only Clyde Jenkins, local NAACP vice-president, spoke and, after requesting the establishment of a biracial committee, he asked to hear the commissioners' views. Gutterman and McDaniel both replied that the city had desegregated its public facilities and that the rest was up to the private business community. (This was not entirely accurate since the library and a city golf course were still segregated.) City Attorney Robert Andreu also informed black leaders that no city law prohibited picketing as long as there was law and order. Gutterman then adjourned the meeting, inviting black leaders to attend the regularly scheduled commission meeting on June 28.[59]

Calling the meeting unsatisfactory because commissioners failed to support a biracial committee and end the segregation of public facilities, Hayling announced that demonstrations would not be put off any longer. On June 21, blacks canvassed lunch counters and drug stores to determine if they employed or served blacks. Despite the contention of city officials that all community-owned facilities were desegregated, a group of black teenagers were turned away from the municipal putting course during the afternoon. Demonstrations formally began on June 25 when five black teenagers carried signs in front of Woolworth's which read, "If We Spend Money Here Why Can't We Eat Here?" Four members of the Youth Council also picketed the St. Augustine Civic Center. The following day twenty-five teenagers conducted sit-ins at McCrory's, Woolworth's, and Service Drugs. The store managers immediately closed the lunch counters and took up all unoccupied seats.[60]

The events of June 18–25 represented a turning point in black-white relations in St. Augustine. The statements of NAACP leaders and Hayling awakened whites to the presence of an active civil rights movement. Moreover, the angry remarks made by Hayling led several conservative white leaders to believe they were dealing with a black extremist. Reluctant to change racial traditions in any case, they now became dogmatically opposed to what they perceived as a militant-led movement. Hayling's comments also made it exceedingly difficult for a moderate group to emerge and act as a counterforce to conservative attitudes. Moderates, who had yet to express themselves on the civil rights efforts, found it virtually impossible to propose a compromise after the developments of June 18–25. When they did indicate their support for a biracial committee, they were denounced by their white friends and neighbors who contended that compromise was not possible with extremists like Hayling. Mayor Joseph Shelley became the leading spokesman for this position and persuaded his fellow commissioners to side with him.[61]

From 1963 to 1965 Mayor Shelley consistently resisted efforts to establish a biracial committee or reach a compromise with the civil rights forces. Shelley came by his conservatism naturally. Born and reared in rural Florida by a father who was a self-made man, Shelley was very much an individualist who prided himself on being his own man. A veteran of World War II, army reservist, and product of the Cold War, he was especially concerned about Communism, which he regarded, in some ways, as a much graver and more insidious threat to America than that posed by Hitler. His medical associates shared and helped reinforce these views about the Communist menace. In particular, his close friend and colleague Dr. Hardgrove Norris, organizer and leading spokesman for the conservative John Birch Society, believed "that there was a tremendous number . . . of Communists in this country."

Shelley refused to recognize the legitimacy of the civil rights movement and was convinced that the movement was Communist inspired. Sounding much like former Senator Joseph McCarthy of Wisconsin, Shelley announced after the civil rights crisis had become full-blown that he had fifteen documents "which irrefutably show how deeply the civil rights movement had become involved with Communism." He also could not accept the position that because a person believed a law was improper, he could violate it. For Shelley the United States had very few, if any, such laws in the first place.[62]

Shelley claimed to be "very sympathetic to blacks," and there seems to be nothing in his past to suggest that he was not. He treated more blacks in his practice than whites, and he was apparently one of few physicians in the community who treated them willingly. Blacks in return supported Shelley in his 1963 city commission race. Nevertheless, Shelley did not regard blacks and whites as racial equals. Indeed, his views on race relations were very much shaped by his background. He had known blacks only as second-class citizens— as economically and educationally backward people. He genuinely believed blacks were genetically inferior to whites. "I consider myself a segregationist," he once declared. "God segregated the races, as far as I'm concerned when he made skins a different color. You don't find bluebirds and redbirds feeding together at the same trough, and you certainly don't see them breeding together." Shelley's views were paternalistic and clearly racist. He thought whites ought to help blacks, and that they needed better jobs, a better education, and better living conditions, but he never thought blacks could become equal to whites. Therefore, they should remain segregated.[63]

The reactionary position of Shelley, Norris, and nearly all members of the medical community in St. Augustine was probably typical of most southern physicians. Nearly all the doctors in this community were born and reared in the South and their experience inclined them to support segregation. In addition, their professional education and experience left them ill-prepared to cope with the racial changes occurring in society. Their education emphasized a practical rather than a philosophical consideration of society's needs. Few, if any, had contemplated developments that might lead to major societal changes. Their professional experience, especially that of doctors like Shelley who treated a large number of black patients, added to their prejudices against racial change. Their encounters with poor blacks, particularly in emergency room situations where family and neighbor conflicts had resulted in injuries, led Shelley and his colleagues to stereotype blacks as racially inferior to whites and to resist vehemently efforts to equalize their position in St. Augustine.[64]

While Shelley was on vacation with his family in Kentucky, Mrs. Fullerwood and Mrs. Hawthorne had written City Manager Barrier asking to meet with city commissioners on June 28. Shelley returned in time to preside over the meeting. Through their attorney

L. J. Shaw of Jacksonville, NAACP leaders again requested that city civil service examinations be open to all citizens regardless of race, creed, or color; all city-owned facilities be desegregated; picketing of segregated facilities be permitted; the mayor and commission issue a statement on desegregation; the city establish a biracial commission; and commissioners encourage religious leaders to promote racial harmony in St. Augustine.[65]

Sitting behind a long, curved table with his fellow commissioners on either side, Shelley responded by noting that the city had desegregated all public facilities: "There is no city ordinance providing for segregation." In fact, St. Augustine had never adopted a formal segregation law, although racial customs established in the antebellum and postbellum periods provided for separation of the races. Shaw replied correctly that the public library and municipal golf course refused to serve blacks. City Attorney Andreu immediately called the two agencies and reported that they had agreed to serve blacks. Speaking for the commission, Shelley acceded to the third request, provided that the pickets carry small signs due to the narrowness of St. Augustine's streets. He also noted that he had already expressed his views on segregation. To the demands for a biracial committee made by the NAACP, Shelley declared that he and his fellow commissioners believed they had no right to interfere in the affairs of private business. Gutterman suggested that black leaders contact private business leaders and set up such a committee with them, and Shelley observed that blacks in Orlando had done this. But business leaders in St. Augustine had no interest in creating such a committee or serving on it, as commission members were well aware because four of them were businessmen. The Reverend Goldie Eubanks of the First Church of God commented that some commissioners had told him during the campaign they would support a biracial committee.

Although civil rights workers remained concerned about a variety of racial issues, they decided to concentrate their efforts on establishing a biracial committee, believing that through this mechanism they could eliminate other racial barriers. Eubanks told commissioners that support for such a committee would encourage merchants to desegregate. But the commission refused to budge. They also passed an ordinance limiting the size of signs used by picketers and prohibiting loitering or barring entrances to business establishments. This ended formal contact between black leaders and city officials for the remainder of the year.[66]

Dissatisfied with the commission's unwillingness to support their key demands, NAACP leaders increased the number of demonstrations and began to encounter physical violence for the first time. On July 2 five Negro youths under Hayling's direction demonstrated in front of the Tourist Information Center in St. Augustine with signs proclaiming "America's oldest city unfair to Negro citizens." On the same day Hayling led a small group that integrated St. Augustine beach. No violence occurred at either demonstration although later that evening three white teenagers fired birdshot into a group of blacks gathered outside Hayling's home. Four blacks received minor wounds. Police arrested the three teenagers as well as three blacks who were charged with firing a weapon into an occupied automobile even though police found no weapons on the Negro teenagers and no bullet holes in the car. Hayling received two telephone calls early the following morning in which the callers said "they were sorry they had missed him and there will be another night."[67]

During nearly three weeks of demonstrations conducted principally by the Youth Council, protesters avoided arrest by leaving local businesses before police arrived, but that changed with dramatic consequences for the youthful participants on July 18. A sit-in at a local pharmacy resulted in the arrest of sixteen young blacks, including seven juveniles when they refused to end their demonstration. County Judge Charles Mathis, Jr., ordered the seven "delinquent children" to spend the night in jail when their parents would not promise to keep them from participating in future demonstrations. Mathis later ordered all juveniles removed by police from picket lines because of the danger of violence and turned them over to the juvenile officer. The juvenile officer was instructed by Mathis to warn the parents against allowing their children to participate in future demonstrations before releasing them into the parents' custody.[68]

On July 23 Mathis informed the parents of the seven juveniles that he would release their children only if they promised to keep them away from future demonstrations. Mathis opposed the civil rights movement, contending that it was Communist inspired, and his decision to detain the seven children and remove others from demonstrations can only be viewed as an attempt to undermine the

movement. The parents of three children agreed to the judge's stip-
ulation but the parents of Audrey Nell Edwards, Jo Ann Anderson,
Samuel White, and Willie Carl Singleton refused to do so.[69]

The following evening approximately 100 angry black
residents gathered at the county jail to protest the continued detention of the children and became involved in a violent clash with police. Mrs. Louise Cook, wife of the jailer, happened to be alone in
the jail when they arrived. In the confusion that followed, Mrs. Cook
claimed she was knocked down, kicked, scratched, and dragged along
the ground by the demonstrators. Sheriff L. O. Davis and his deputies, who were in the adjoining stockade, arrived shortly after the
crowd gathered. Davis called the demonstration "worse than anything I've seen since Birmingham." In dispersing the crowd, Davis,
his deputies, and demonstrators became involved in a shoving match.
The confrontation ended with police assaulting the protestors with
nightsticks. A photographer who tried to film the incident had his
camera seized by deputies.[70]

In the aftermath of the jail disturbance, Mathis transferred the two juvenile boys from the county jail to the Florida Industrial School for Boys because Davis contended he lacked the facilities to care for them, and the two girls were sent to Ocala
Correctional School for Girls four weeks later. Prison officials at both
reform schools expressed concern about housing juveniles who had
only committed a misdemeanor with those who had committed more
violent crimes. Attorney General James Kynes asked Mathis to reconsider his decision, but the judge refused, saying "I'm not gonna
release them." He later told friends, you cannot do business with those
darkies. County officials promised Mathis that he would receive the
full cooperation of the Board and the County Attorney's office, and
congratulated him "on the manner in which he has handled these
matters to date."[71]

When the parents tried to reclaim their children, they
encountered a legal maze which left them frustrated and angry. Earl
Johnson, NAACP attorney in Jacksonville, who represented the
teenagers, told Mathis in mid-November that their parents were now
prepared to accept his probation terms. But Mathis alleged that he
had lost custody of the cases by their transfer to state reform schools.
The Assistant State Attorney General, however, claimed that, since

the four youths were not accused of any crime, but merely of being delinquents, they could not be freed. The District Court upheld the Attorney General's opinion.[72] With no one claiming custody of the case, the four youths languished in state institutions through Christmas.

By this time the case had become a cause célèbre for the NAACP, and pressure began to be exerted locally and nationally for the release of the children. A staff member of the United States Commission on Civil Rights wrote Tobias Simon, secretary of Florida's Advisory Committee on Civil Rights, in disbelief about what was happening. "Can such a thing be true in this country?" he asked. Under pressure from state and federal organizations and private groups, Governor Bryant convened the Correctional Institutions Board (comprising members of the State Cabinet) and signed a release. Nevertheless, the order let stand Judge Mathis' finding that the four were delinquents and also required them to refrain from further demonstrations.[73]

During the course of the imprisonment of the four youths, the St. Augustine NAACP, refusing to be intimidated, had accelerated its demonstrations. Throughout July, August, and September the Youth Council conducted almost daily demonstrations against various restaurants and public facilities. The students achieved a few breakthroughs during this period, persuading Woolworth's and McCrory's stores, both national concerns, and Del Monico's restaurant, a local operation, to join Howard Johnson's in serving blacks.[74] But these gains did not represent a trend. Indeed, they would be the only victories by the civil rights forces in St. Augustine until the passage of the Civil Rights Act in 1964. Moreover, three of the businesses had desegregated principally because they were chain stores and feared economic reprisals against their stores elsewhere.

The more typical response by the community came during July 1963, when white leaders began employing a variety of economic and legal measures to keep blacks from continuing the demonstrations. Three black men lost their jobs for participating in demonstrations: Arthur Funderberk had been employed at the Bozard Ford dealership for three and one-half years, Ted Conway at Meadow Brooks Dairy for nine months, and James Hauser as a schoolbus driver for over one year. Shortly after these firings, the white shop steward at the Fairchild Stratos Corporation, an aircraft manufacturing plant and second largest employer in the area, called a union meeting of all black workers and, with the apparent support of company officials, threatened them with the loss of their jobs if they took part in any further sit-ins or picketing. Women workers and wives of men who were involved in the civil rights protests, and who worked in motels or as domestics, were also intimidated by employers. Additionally, local judges began levying fines of $100 or jail sentences of forty-five days for each violation by demonstrators. Sheriff Davis notified employers when their workers were arrested for participating in a demonstration. Hayling recounted that "since most of . . . [these jobs] involved no contracts, no tenure, no seniority . . . then these people could be summarily dismissed . . . from their jobs." NAACP leader Henry Twine asserted you were branded as a "crazy or bad nigger" if you took part in the sit-ins. Moreover, despite the promise of city officials, blacks were still denied access to the municipal library, golf course, and the city stadium.[75]

Business and civic leaders found support for maintaining the status quo in race relations from Governor Bryant. Bryant had expressed his opposition to the proposed civil rights bill while appearing before the Commerce Committee of the United States Senate. He argued that a motel owner, for example, should have the right to refuse service: "That's simple justice. The wonder is really that it can be questioned."[76]

The local John Birch Society which had been established in 1963 also encouraged community leaders to resist the pressures to desegregate. St. Augustine housed a very active, conservative chapter called the St. Johns Chapter of the Florida Coalition of Patriotic Societies. Maintaining an office and reading room on St. George Street in the heart of the old Spanish quarter, the chapter, headed by Dr. Hardgrove Norris, sponsored weekly lectures by conservative speakers. The organization had approximately fifty active members, but numerous citizens were known to be sympathetic with its views, and Norris was perceived by many people as being very influential in community affairs. One man remarked that whenever Norris became involved in a new project numerous other residents soon followed suit.[77]

A significant minority of the white leadership was convinced by Norris and his Birch allies that the civil rights movement was Communist inspired. They perceived the movement as a radical departure from the traditional pattern of race relations and, having imbibed thoroughly from the well of the Cold War, put Communism and civil rights together in their minds and saw red behind the community's racial crisis. In this view they were quite sincere; they did not seek merely to tarnish the reputations of people like Hayling and other NAACP leaders. Because the movement threatened the stability of community life in St. Augustine and because the country had just emerged from the Cold War decade of the 1950s, it should not be surprising that they identified Communism with civil rights activism. Moreover, because they lived in such a historic community, white leaders had an unusual commitment to the past and a desire to preserve their society in its present form.[78]

That the influence of the Birch Society extended well beyond Norris and the organization's fifty members was attested to by assistant States Attorney Hamilton Upchurch, who noted that if "you proposed anything even . . . at a cocktail party that was in any way conciliatory . . . you were ostracized by this extreme right wing." Very few people spoke in favor of a biracial committee. Dr. Ron Jackson, a veterinarian, who advocated establishing an informal biracial committee, suddenly found himself without friends. Jackson observed that as race relations deteriorated, "You got pushed to one side or another. If you tried to stay in the middle your friends became your enemies."[79] The militant position occupied by Shelley on one side and Hayling on the other, especially in the eyes of white leaders, made it very difficult for white residents like Jackson to pursue a moderate course of action.

Significantly, Shelley and other white leaders who opposed integration believed that they had gone more than halfway in meeting the NAACP's demands. The mayor repeatedly referred to the absence of segregation in city facilities and the decision by the county school system to desegregate its facilities in the fall of 1963. But what he failed to note was that the county chose to desegregate under Florida's Pupil Placement law which has been designed to allow counties to avoid the real intent of the *Brown* decision. The plan called for the integration of six black children at Fullerwood elementary school with no plan for further desegregation. The county's desegregation plan also took place under the shadow of a suit by the NAACP which called for the complete integration of the county schools.[80]

Equally important, the vast majority of whites in St. Augustine were unaffected by the civil rights developments of 1963 and largely ignored the demonstrations. Most white residents, as a *New York Times* reporter learned, still believed race relations were excellent. Those who gave more than passing thought to what was occurring laid the blame for St. Augustine's racial disturbances on the Klan and uppity black militants. One resident commented that "not until agitators moved in from Jacksonville and other towns did we have any trouble, and if violence breaks out it will be the work of outside agitators." Hamilton Upchurch declared that businessmen "attributed their problem to a pushy nigger [Hayling]."[81]

Few white citizens in St. Augustine understood the concerns of blacks and very few tried to determine what they were. "Colored folks wanted to ride on the bus and wanted to vote," one man declared, "but they could do both here." Most whites assumed that they knew what was best for black residents, an attitude that carried over from the days of slavery, and the civil rights demonstrations in 1963 had failed to make them question this assumption. Despite the daily sit-ins conducted by the Youth Council, tourism dropped only slightly in St. Augustine, and few businessmen thought the decline had anything to do with the protests.[82]

With relationships between the races rapidly disintegrating, the Florida Advisory Committee to the United States Commission on Civil Rights announced that it would visit St. Augustine on August 16th. Established by the 1957 Civil Rights Act, the commission organized state committees to assist it in investigating violations of voting rights and equal protection of the laws. The Florida Advisory Committee had conducted hearings in several cities in the state before coming to St. Augustine. During the single day the committee heard testimony, not one member of the city commission, and only one of the "invited business leaders," appeared as witnesses. The committee noted that "in none of the other cities [in Florida] . . . has there been such a boycott."[83]

Testimony from blacks and whites revealed that widespread discrimination and racial unrest existed in the community. Dr.

Puryear, president of Florida Memorial College, described his four-teen years in St. Augustine as especially frustrating: "In Mississippi, my birthplace, things were pretty bad, but you could get people to sit down and talk." He told the committee of being required to sub-mit to fingerprinting after he brought a Chinese scholar to the col-lege, because the sheriff's office claimed that this had been requested by the House Un-American Activities Committee. He also reported that during the past year the college had had the opportunity to re-ceive a $20,000 grant from a national foundation if the school could get matching funds. But after writing over 550 letters, the college had received only three gifts from the community. Puryear stated that the trustees had voted to move the college from St. Augustine in 1966 due to the lack of support from white residents. Louis Mitchell of Daytona Beach, a white Episcopal minister and executive director of the Florida Council on Human Relations, compared conditions in St. Augustine with those in Birmingham, Alabama, in 1963 before the violence erupted. Several other black witnesses appeared and re-counted the difficulties they had experienced in dealing with city of-ficials. They also told of threats on their lives, police harassment, and job discrimination.[84]

Two company officials from the Fairchild Stratos Cor-poration, W. A. Baker, manager of industrial relations, and E. A. Bowe, personnel manager, were the only businessmen to appear be-fore the committee, apparently because the company feared cancel-lation of its federal contracts. Both men denied discrimination at the plant. Further testimony revealed, however, that of the company's thirty-eight black employees, all but five worked as "strippers," which was considered to be the most dangerous job at the factory. No white workers at Fairchild performed this job.[85]

After completing the day-long hearing, the committee recommended that the federal government intervene to protect black residents. It proposed that the United States Civil Rights Commis-sion seek to halt the use of federal funds for St. Augustine's quadri-centennial celebration in 1965. The committee also urged that fed-eral contracts be withheld from the Fairchild Stratos Corporation for its discriminatory practices and that steps be taken against the Ma-chinists Union at Fairchild for its intimidation of black employees. Lastly, the committee asked that the federal government withhold funds from the State of Florida until the two teenage boys at Marianna Correctional Institute were released (the two teenage girls were still in the county jail and not subject to state control at this time).[86]

The committee's recommendations served to alienate even further St. Augustine's white leaders, who were incensed by the suggestion that the federal government cut off funds for the quadricentennial observance and federal contracts to the Fairchild Stratos Corporation. Most whites boycotted the committee's one-day inquiry because they thought the city had no racial problems except those created by a black militant and because they assumed they would not receive a fair hearing. Shelley, had, in fact, drafted a letter to the Advisory Committee contending that no racial problems existed but did not send it, believing that the committee's members had already made up their minds. Shelley and several supporters were also convinced that little would be gained by testifying before the group and that it would be easier to ignore the committee's recommendations if they did not participate.[87]

Shelley immediately denounced the committee's report, stating once again his opposition to a biracial committee: "We have no biracial committee here because it could do nothing we have not already done." The mayor also expressed his dissatisfaction with the committee's suggestion that the black teenagers be freed from jail and not be required to abide by Mathis' demands. "This is something required of all juvenile offenders and their parents," he declared, "whether they are black, white, or green." Steve Payton, Fairchild's public relations director, called the charges against his company unjust, and alleged that morale among all employees at the St. Augustine plant was the highest of any of the company's five divisions. Thus, rather than opening channels of communication between the races and ending the stalemate over a biracial committee, the report by Florida's Advisory Committee only increased animosities. Whites regarded the report as one-sided, although the committee's assessment had certainly been influenced by the failure of white leaders to appear.[88]

Confronted by increasing hostility from white residents, but with the support of the Florida Advisory Committee, NAACP leaders and particularly Hayling's Youth Council moved to maintain pressure on the community. Sit-ins, lie-ins, and picketing continued

daily throughout the final ten days of August. A massive voter registration drive was also conducted in September after it was revealed
that nearly 300 blacks had been removed from the voting rolls since
1952. The NAACP campaign led to the registration of 500 black
voters, bringing their total to 2100 of 2500 eligible voters.[89]

As the protests continued and momentum for the civil
rights movement began to build, more and more people, especially
teenagers and college students, joined the demonstrations. Anxious
to see racial improvements in their lifetime, the young people proved
to be enthusiastic, if somewhat impatient, participants. The protests
not only grew larger in size, but the young activists began to employ
different tactics. The lie-ins, for example, were utilized to frustrate
police and to show white residents that civil rights demonstrators were
determined to achieve desegregation by using all forms of nonviolent
protest. By the first of September these demonstrations also included
more older blacks who were inspired by the actions of the young.
Hence action generated a sense of achievement which laid the foundation for mobilizing more black participation.[90]

On Labor Day 1963, 125 NAACP leaders and supporters
conducted their first mass demonstration on the plaza to protest continued discrimination and the commission's unwillingness to appoint
a biracial committee. Civil rights leaders also sought to show white
residents that the demonstrations had gained considerable support in
the black community. Participation in this demonstration represented a departure from traditional practices for the NAACP. Having pursued legalistic methods to challenge discrimination in the past,
the NAACP had been gradually placing greater emphasis on direct
action. The growing influence of SCLC and the Congress of Racial
Equality in black communities through their direct action techniques
no doubt encouraged the NAACP to involve itself in such activities
to avoid losing its dominance.[91]

Police quickly moved into the plaza to disperse the demonstrators who, they charged, lacked a permit. Using their newly acquired dogs and cattle prods, they halted the proceedings and arrested twenty-seven people. Several people including the Reverend
Goldie Eubanks were struck with cattle prods or clubbed by police
even though no one resisted arrest. Eubanks was subsequently charged
with and found guilty of resisting arrest by a six-man white jury and

sentenced to six months in jail. The others arrested were fined $100 and court costs. Angered at their treatment by police, black leaders conducted a massive march through the center of town that evening.[92]

Police violence, which had been minimal initially, had increased steadily as demonstrations mounted. Police officers in St. Augustine as elsewhere were poorly trained in crowd control. Additionally, most officers opposed the integration of schools and public facilities. Police Chief Virgil Stuart failed to restrain his deputies because, like so many others, he thought the movement was allied with Communism. A very conservative man, he openly sided with local John Birch Society members in their opposition to the NAACP's efforts. One resident characterized Stuart as an "extreme right winger. He saw a Communist behind every bush, he didn't *think* there was one, he *saw* one."[93] Sheriff L. O. Davis had been seen initially as a friend to local blacks. His brother had a grocery store on Washington Street near the heart of the black residential area and Davis had gained a reputation for being fair in dealings with blacks. However, Davis did not envisage a society in which whites and blacks were equal and shared power. As the demonstrations accelerated in frequency, Davis, like Stuart, became increasingly hostile. With city commissioners and other white leaders expressly opposed to the sit-ins, Stuart and Davis felt no restraint in dealing forcefully with civil rights activists.[94]

Police violence now became a major issue for black leaders. In mid-September NAACP President Fannie Fullerwood asked City Manager Barrier for a parade permit to conduct a rally on the plaza on September 21 protesting the police brutality at the Labor Day rally. Barrier refused, and, at the urging of city commissioners announced that all parades, demonstrations, and large public gatherings were being suspended indefinitely.[95]

Heightening the tension in the city was the Florida East Coast Railroad strike which had entered its eighth month marked by bombings and shootings. Over 1,300 employees had walked off their jobs on January 13, 1963, or refused to cross picket lines. While most of the workers came from Jacksonville and other Florida cities, approximately 100 workers lived in the St. Augustine area. The evidence suggests that some of the strikers used their free time to threaten civil rights demonstrators, especially after the Negro firemen refused to walk off their jobs in support of the strike. William Rosencrans, who had dynamited Florida East Coast Railroad facilities as well as a black home in Jacksonville, was subsequently arrested in St. Augustine by the FBI where he apparently had assisted militant whites in terrorizing black St. Augustinians.[96]

Civil rights developments in St. Augustine were influenced considerably by events in Jacksonville. The large black community in this New South city had developed its own institutions and leadership early in the twentieth century. An active, aggressive civil rights movement emerged in 1960 with the sit-ins, and thereafter black leaders campaigned for an expansion of black rights through school desegregation, integration of public accommodations, and increased voter registration. In addition to an activist black community, Jacksonville also had a militant Klan population. Five separate Klan organizations with nearly 1,000 members operated in the city. In August 1960, Klansmen used ax handles to discourage further sit-ins. Over the next three years, Klansmen engaged in numerous beatings and several bombings of black homes and businesses in an effort to intimidate black activists. Much of this violence carried over into the St. Augustine civil rights movement with Klan forces and civil rights leaders from Jacksonville participating in the demonstrations there.[97]

The integration of St. Augustine's public schools which bagan in the fall failed to stem the tide of racial unrest. The two separate teacher organizations were merged into one with no overt opposition, but with little enthusiasm or public note. No racial problems occurred within Fullerwood Elementary School where five black children attended or Ketterlinus Junior High School where one black teenager was enrolled, although both schools were emptied by bomb threats in October. However, Bungum Roberson, whose child went to Fullerwood, had four Molotov cocktails thrown at his home, and Charles Brunson and his wife, who also had a child in Fullerwood, had their car firebombed while attending a PTA meeting at the school. A pink Ford belonging to a local Klan leader was seen in the area, but sheriff's officers were unable to connect him with the explosion.[98]

During the midst of the racial conflict, city officials stood on the sidelines, refusing to recognize the growing crisis and the desire by black residents for change. Mayor Shelley commented in a letter to a supporter that the NAACP did not represent the interests of black St. Augustinians. "I think one of the best indications of the way the Negro and the white citizen feel towards each other," he observed, "has been the fact that in spite of every effort by the leaders of the NAACP to stir up large demonstrations and incidents, they have failed miserably."[99] White residents generally shared Shelley's view even after the large demonstration on Labor Day.

Despite the opposition of the white community to racial change, civil rights activists continued to make gains and remained generally optimistic about the future. Apparently bowing to pressure from the federal government, the Fairchild Stratos Company had upgraded the positions of eight black employees. Willie Ludden, an NAACP field director from Atlanta, expressed pleasure at this development and declared that many "white persons have come out openly in support of NAACP efforts."[100] But Ludden's observation about white support had little basis in fact and events of the late fall of 1963 would prove that wishing did not make it so.

Pressure began to be exerted increasingly from the militant right in September 1963 to block any further desegregation. The Reverend Connie Lynch had arrived in a pink Cadillac from California and, after meeting with Klan leaders from Jacksonville and vicinity, urged whites to demonstrate their displeasure with the civil rights activities. Klansmen from Jacksonville and surrounding areas eagerly volunteered to assist local militants in St. Augustine in suppressing civil rights demonstrations.[101]

The most dramatic racial episode occurred on September 18, 1963, at a Ku Klux Klan rally north of St. Augustine's city limits and one half mile west of U.S. Highway 1. Handbills had been distributed by Lynch and his allies during the several days before the meeting urging all white people to attend. A huge cross, nearly twenty feet in height, wrapped in burlap and soaked with gasoline stood at the center of a crowd of 300. "Robed klansmen and klanswomen, two dozen strong, walked in a circle around the burning cross," an observer wrote, "giving a sort of sloppy, left-handed sign of obeisance." The meeting was called to order shortly after dark and a prayer said. Lynch was then introduced and at his vitriolic best harangued his audience for nearly one hour and a half. Referring to the recent bombing of the Sixteenth Street Baptist Church in Birmingham and the resulting death of four black girls, Lynch asserted, "It wasn't no shame they was killed. If there's four less niggers tonight, then good for whoever planted the bomb. We're all better off." The crowd screamed approval.[102]

Calling Hayling a "burr-headed bastard of a dentist," Lynch told his audience, "If you were half the men you claim to be you'd kill him before sunup." He denounced racial developments in St. Augustine and urged on his audience to join the Klan fight against the demonstrators. "This ain't no peaceful organization," he insisted. "We aim to do whatever is necessary to put the Nigger back in his grave." The crowd shouted for more as Lynch left the speaker's platform. He was followed by another speaker from MacClenny, Florida who tried his best to retain the crowd's enthusiasm but without much success. Bored and restless, the crowd was beginning to break up when someone shouted: "Niggers! Niggers! Niggers!"[103]

Accompanied by James Hauser, James Jackson, and Clyde Jenkins, Robert Hayling had decided to drive out to the Klan meeting after seeing one of the pamphlets. They had been watching it from the federal highway when Jenkins alleged they "decided to turn around on a dirt road," and get closer to hear what was being said. FBI evidence suggests, however, that Hayling may have planned to confront the Klansmen at the meeting. Earlier that day, Hayling had called WFGA-TV, Channel 12 in Jacksonville and informed a newsman about the Klan rally near St. Augustine. He gave the reporter directions to the rally and advised him to bring a camera crew. The reporter told Hayling that Klan rallies were commonplace and were not normally given special coverage. Hayling reiterated that there might be news value for Channel 12 at this meeting.[104]

As they pulled onto the dirt road, a carload of whites, trying to get to the rally, pulled in behind them and shouted: "How about pulling in so we can get past." When they did, the other car came beside them and suddenly rifles protruded from the windows. Hayling and his friends were told to get out and, after being searched, were escorted to the Klan meeting.[105]

Lynch jumped from the platform, grabbed a gun from his

car, and raced to where the blacks had emerged. Others quickly followed. Hayling was recognized by a Klansman as "the nigger who wants to be king." Two white men stripped away their shirts and began to beat them with their fists. The blacks fell in a heap with legs and fists hitting them from all directions. The women stood watching, encouraging their men to "Castrate the bastards!" "Kick their balls out!" and "Knock their heads off!" A woman in a Klan robe told her husband to "Go get the head chopper . . . and get the rope, and for God's sake, take your robe and leave it in the car. You don't want to mess it up." Before he lost consciousness, Hayling heard someone say "work on his right hand—he's a right-handed dentist!" When he revived he found himself piled on his three friends "like firewood." A Klansman told his comrades "Did you ever smell a nigger burn! Just wait until [our] Klan brother . . . gets back with five gallons of gasoline and then you can. It's a mighty sweet smell."[106]

But before the men could be killed, Sheriff Davis arrived, summoned by the Reverend Irwin Cheney, associate director of the Florida Human Relations Council and an eyewitness to the violence, and a news correspondent and photographer for WJXT, a television station in Jacksonville. Although a bonded deputy for Sheriff Davis, the photographer made no effort to stop the beating beyond calling Davis. Cheney had called the FBI, the Governor's office, and the sheriff to insure that someone would arrive to rescue the men. Davis arrested four Klansmen who were huddled over the pile of black bodies and took the blacks to Flagler Hospital with deep scalp wounds, abrasions, and broken bones.[107]

In the jury trial that followed, the Klansmen's cases were dismissed when Hayling and his colleagues failed to identify their attackers. Deputy Sheriff Guy Rexrood, the first officer on the scene, claimed he did not see the actual beating although he found the four Negroes lying on the ground badly beaten and the four Klansmen in robes standing over them. An all-white jury of six, however, subsequently found Hayling guilty of assault but not battery after the testimony of two Klansmen. Judge Marvin Grier, apparently unconvinced of Hayling's guilt, did not sentence him to jail although he did fine him $100.[108]

City officials refused to comment on this violence and they refrained from discouraging militant whites who were becoming increasingly more violent and threatening to local blacks. Because of their silence, the control of events in the city began rapidly slipping out of their hands. Carloads of whites armed with shotguns could be seen most evenings in October riding through the black sections of the city.[109]

The heightened violence between the races culminated on the evening of October 24 when a carload of young white men rode through the Lincolnshire section of St. Augustine—a section already hit by gunfire and Molotov cocktails. Holstead D. Manucy, son of local militant leader Holstead R. "Hoss" Manucy, drove the car, and William Kincaid, his friend, sat next to him with a loaded shotgun. As they roared through the black section of town looking for trouble, eight to ten shots were fired from the shadows of a home on Palm Street. Kincaid was hit in the head and died immediately. His finger had been on the trigger of his gun when he was hit; it jerked back causing the gun to fire, blowing a hole in the floor of the car. Manucy told officers on the scene that he, Kincaid, and their two other companions had been out dove hunting and were returning home when the incident occurred, but evidence showed only Kincaid's gun had been fired recently. Several black residents were questioned about the shooting and the Reverend Goldie Eubanks and his son Richard were arrested. The case was never brought to trial, however, and the murderer of Kincaid was never discovered although he apparently was murdered by a black resident in the area.[110]

The death of Kincaid angered militants and led to additional violence. On October 28, two hundred Klansmen from St. Augustine and surrounding counties attended Kincaid's funeral, and afterward heard Connie Lynch address a closed meeting. That evening, shotgun blasts and rifle fire tore through the Harlem Gardens, a local Negro nightspot with a juke box and bar. No one was injured but only because a live hand grenade, which had hit the roof of the building, failed to explode. Two Negro homes were also fired into on the same evening and one man was slightly injured. Sheriff Davis arrested Hayling at Harlem Gardens that evening for allegedly "hindering the investigation." Hayling in turn criticized Davis and his deputies for failing to protect local residents from the continued violence.[111]

Some local blacks, angered by these developments, added

to the racial tension in the community by arming themselves. In early October six blacks threw rocks indiscriminately at passing white motorists. A gun was taken from a young black man, Rob McClain, in the county courthouse while he was being tried for assault and battery against two white women on October 29. The gun had been removed from Hayling's home, which seemed to connect the civil rights movement with the violence and suggested to local whites that the movement was becoming increasingly militant. After being convicted of assault and battery, McClain turned to the two women as he was being escorted from the court room and announced: "I'll see you later." Two nights after the Harlem Gardens shooting, six rifle shots were fired into a white home in a predominantly Negro section. The white community had been further aroused by an armed robbery and rape case involving a local Negro.[112]

After a public silence on racial matters for over two months, Shelley appealed to black and white citizens to stop the accelerating violence. "Do not be coerced or provoked into retaliation or acts of violence which can only result in bringing grief to yourselves and families," he urged. A. H. Tebeault, Jr., editor of the *St. Augustine Record,* blamed Kincaid's death on militant forces of both races, especially the refusal of juvenile pickets to obey court orders, mass civil rights and Klan meetings, gun battles between whites and blacks, and confrontations between radicals in the NAACP and Klan. Most whites including Shelley agreed with Tebeault's assessment.[113]

Nevertheless, the shooting death had shocked Shelley and the city commission from their lethargy. The mayor asked and received from Governor Bryant the assistance of thirteen state highway patrol officers. He also apparently gave Davis orders to stop the marauding by whites in black neighborhoods. To aid police, city leaders asked parents to curtail Halloween activities for their children and to keep teenagers at home.[114] These steps brought a halt to the violence, but the continued refusal of city commissioners, led by Shelley, to negotiate with black leaders about a biracial commission suggested that it would only be temporary.

In the midst of the racial violence, the NAACP had petitioned the federal court to enjoin the city from arresting civil rights demonstrators. On November 14 United States District Court Judge William McRae dismissed the suit arguing that the NAACP "did not come into court with clean hands." Singling out Dr. Hayling, McRae characterized his leadership as showing "a lack of restraint, common sense, and good judgment, and an irresponsibility which have done a disservice" to the civil rights movement. McRae specifically referred to Hayling's threat in early June to arm himself and his subsequent exhortations to shoot first and ask questions later. The judge apparently had access to FBI records in which Hayling had told a Jacksonville FBI agent that he had given guns to several of his Youth Council members to protect themselves. While acknowledging the opposition of the NAACP to armed violence, Hayling said this was not his policy and he would not abide by it.[115]

Hayling and the civil rights movement suffered another sharp rebuke in early December. The grand jury of the circuit court of the Seventh Judicial Circuit, operating with the assistance of Judge Howell Melton and States Attorney Dan Warren, had decided to examine the racial unrest in St. Augustine. They subpoenaed Dr. Puryear, Douglas Hartley, superintendent of schools, local clergy, businessmen, school teachers, and bank officials. They did not invite those "directly involved in the racial disturbances," contending they wanted "the true feeling of this cross-section of the citizens of the county." This excluded NAACP officials and city leaders.[116]

After a two-day inquiry the grand jury blamed the racial crisis on Dr. Hayling and the Reverend Goldie Eubanks for using "extremely bad judgment in attempting to present their problems and grievances to the duly elected officials." Jury members contended that city leaders were expected "to accede to the demands of this group" from which "there was no compromise." The jury did add that the "impasse was exploited by the Ku Klux Klan," although they suggested that the Klan represented "many *outside* voices."[117]

City officials received nothing but praise from the sixteen white and two black members of the jury. The report declared that St. Augustine "has made certain definite steps toward racial harmony," including the presence of blacks on grand juries, on the police force, and in the public schools. The grand jury added that "duly elected officials and law enforcement officers have shown remarkable restraint" in handling the crisis. While falling short of recommending the establishment of a biracial committee, the grand jury declared that if both races were "given the chance to sit down and discuss these difference [sic] that they will be able to resolve the same, in so far as is humanly possible."[118]

The immediate impact of the grand jury report was to force the resignation of Hayling and Eubanks from their leadership roles in the NAACP. One student of the crisis observed that Roy Wilkins, president of the NAACP, had told Hayling to resign or "he would withdraw the local chapter." In announcing their resignation, the two men expressed their hope that "others less militant than ourselves will be more acceptable to the white powers and can make progress in eliminating the remaining divisions" in the community.[119]

The resignation by these two men, however, did not produce a change in strategy by NAACP leaders. Over the preceding six months, Hayling and Eubanks, especially the former, had emerged as spokesmen for the civil rights movement in St. Augustine. Despite their resignations and the grand jury report, they were still looked to for leadership by NAACP members and the Youth Council. Indeed, the two had such a large following that no further steps could be taken apparently without consulting them. Civil rights workers generally believed that the resignations were unwarranted and that the grand jury report was inaccurate and biased. One local leader criticized the NAACP, observing that "we couldn't even get an NAACP official to spend the night here."[120]

More importantly, the inflexibility of city commissioners against creation of a biracial commission stymied any reconciliation between the races. After the resignations of Hayling and Eubanks and a pause in demonstrations, Mrs. Fullerwood approached the city commission at its January meeting and asked for a closed door session to discuss the possibility of establishing a biracial committee. Commissioner John Bailey, an insurance man, asked her if Hayling and Eubanks were still spokesman for the NAACP. Mrs. Fullerwood reported that they no longer served as leaders, but were still members of the organization. Commissioner Lindsley also wanted to know if the NAACP still sought Congressional support to block the appropriation of federal funds for the quadricentennial celebration. Mrs. Fullerwood stated that no further action had been taken on this matter since the summer, although the NAACP continued to oppose the appropriation of federal funds until the city ended all vestiges of segregation. Her answer did not satisfy city leaders, and Shelley informed her that the commission would take her request under advisement. Certain that they had been vindicated in their past actions by the grand jury and dissatisfied with Mrs. Fullerwood's comments, the city commissioners refused to hold a private meeting with NAACP officials or reconsider their position on the appointment of a biracial committee. Municipal officials felt confident that with Federal Judge McRae's decision and the grand jury report the entire racial crisis would soon disappear.[121]

With the city commission unwilling to assert leadership on the desegregation issue or allow for the appointment of an independent advisory body, Klan members and local militants allied with the Klan on the desegregation issue moved in to fill the void in leadership. Having been mobilized into action in late 1963 by the death of William Kincaid and the arrival of Connie Lynch, and having been relatively unrestrained in their activities by local law enforcement officials, these groups became more assertive in early 1964. Despite the grand jury contention that white militants came from outside the community, police arrest records disclosed that the vast majority were local citizens. Operating out of "Hoss" Manucy's Ancient City Hunting Club and utilizing two-way radio communications in connection with their activities, militants accelerated their program of intimidation against blacks. States Attorney Dan Warren found pressure being "applied by young white hoodlums against prominent colored residents." Near the end of January, a Negro worker at the Fairchild plant was badly beaten while returning home from a night class on blueprint reading, and another employee had seen white workers carrying hand grenades. On a Saturday morning in early February four loads of buckshot were fired into the home of Hayling, killing his boxer dog which sat in the living room but missing his wife and two children who were asleep in the bedroom. Hayling was at his dental office at the time of the shooting.[122]

Mayor Shelley, who had said little about the escalating violence, deplored the shooting. "No matter how individuals feel about integration or segregation," Shelley declared, "acts of this kind should not and will not be tolerated." The *St. Augustine Record*, which had opposed the civil rights activities in the city, also condemned the violence. And in its first criticism of city leaders, the editor declared, it was "high time that elected public officials demanded and enforced

the municipal and state laws to the maximum of their abilities."[123]
Despite the statements by Shelley and editor A. H. Tebeault, Jr.,
civil rights leaders wondered whether white leaders could control events
in the city any longer.

Three days after the shooting Hayling went to Tallahassee and asked Governor Bryant's secretary, Mal Ogden, for state assistance in protecting the lives of blacks. Hayling argued that the Klan
was concentrated in the area and yet Police Chief Stuart showed little concern over this development. Hayling did say that Sheriff Davis
had become much more aware of the seriousness of the situation but
lacked the manpower to deal with it. Ogden promised to keep in touch
with him and inform the governor. After receiving Ogden's report
and talking with him, Bryant dispatched another state highway police contingent to assist Sheriff Davis, and he sent state investigators
to look into the shooting.[124]

Despite the intervention of state authorities and a growing awareness by white leaders of the explosive conditions in the
community, whites remained opposed to further desegregation in the
community and reluctant to suppress the activities of white militants. The decision by Judge McRae and the grand jury report had
completely undermined the legitimacy of the NAACP and the civil
rights demonstrations in the eyes of white leaders and citizens. Although no one, including Shelley, liked the violence that had occurred, most white residents viewed it as a pitched battle between
militant groups, neither of which was representative of St. Augustine. They would attempt to repress the activities of these groups and
the confrontations between them for the sake of peace in St. Augustine, but they would certainly not negotiate with either of the militant factions. Of the two, the civil rights group, no doubt, was more
feared by whites. The Klan and Klanlike elements had always existed
but had posed no serious threat to their society. The civil rights
movement, especially in light of developments elsewhere, however,
did endanger the continuation of St. Augustine's segregated society.
But the threat in the eyes of many white St. Augustinians went beyond this. What they saw was a militant, Communist-inspired civil
rights movement attempting to undermine the very social, economic, and political traditions of the United States, the South, and
St. Augustine.[125]

Hayling's pledge to arm himself and his young assistants

lent credibility to the Birch position and increased support for the organization's position on civil rights in the community. Little evidence exists to suggest that white leaders would have been more responsive to the NAACP demands if Hayling had been more circumspect in his public comments. It does appear, however, that his rhetoric and leadership assisted the cause of the John Birch Society while at the same time helping to silence the voices of moderation in St. Augustine. In particular, Hayling's comments made it virtually impossible for white moderates to organize and to effect a compromise which would lead to the desegregation of public facilities. More importantly, it made their position untenable as they encountered increasing criticism from an aggressive Birch Society and unsympathetic neighbors.

Although none belonged to the Birch Society, the prominence of Birch supporters in city government further undermined the cause of peace and racial progress. Nearly every city leader, including the mayor, city attorney, police chief, sheriff, county judge, and school superintendent, agreed with the Birch position and opposed a change in St. Augustine's race relations. Their opposition went beyond a simple belief that the old ways were best. Rather, they viewed these demands for change from a doctrinaire set of values that made moderation and compromise unthinkable.

Thus, the opportunity for a peaceful discussion of racial conditions in the community and the gradual removal of the most obvious racial barriers which had seemed possible in the summer of 1963 had been lost by the beginning of 1964. A firm commitment to the racial traditions of the past, a widespread perception by white residents, whether accurate or not, that Hayling was an extremist, and an inflexibility by city commissioners, especially Mayor Shelley, had ruptured lines of communication and allowed white militants to seize the initiative. Most local black leaders now concluded that because of these changes they could not continue as they had in 1963 without outside assistance. Otherwise, the racial caste system would remain intact, and this prospect was unacceptable to the civil rights workers. Since the national NAACP had expressed displeasure with the civil rights leadership in St. Augustine, black leaders led by Hayling and Eubanks felt they had to turn elsewhere for help.[126]

Chapter 3

The Invasion

On March 6, 1964, Dr. Robert Hayling, the Reverend Goldie Eubanks, Henry Twine, and several other black leaders from St. Augustine drove in two cars to Orlando, Florida, to meet with aides of the Reverend Martin Luther King, Jr., who were attending the annual state meeting of the Southern Christian Leadership Conference. They went with the blessing of civil rights workers in the Ancient City who were dissatisfied with the NAACP, especially its ambivalence on direct action techniques, and "because we needed help." Black leaders and their white opponents in St. Augustine both thought the integration drive was losing momentum in the first months of the new year, and blacks feared the movement would cease to exist without the assistance of a major civil rights organization.[1]

In Orlando the St. Augustine group met privately with the Reverend C. T. Vivian, a member of SCLC's Board of Directors and personal advisor to King. Recounting the difficulties of 1963 and the unwillingness of the NAACP to support a stepped-up desegregation campaign, they asked Vivian if SCLC would assist them. Vivian refused to commit the organization but agreed to visit St. Augustine on his return to Atlanta.[2]

SCLC had been watching events unfold in St. Augustine since July 1963, when King had inquired about the use of federal funds for St. Augustine's quadricentennial celebration and been informed by Vice-President Johnson that no such funds were being used.

The Reverend Wyatt Tee Walker, executive assistant to King, had also written Hobart Taylor, Jr., executive vice-chairman of the President's Committee on Equal Employment Opportunity, in August seeking the committee's cooperation in improving the racial situation in St. Augustine. In responding to Walker, Taylor indicated that the city was "not amenable to Federal action" and that city officials thought they had gone far enough in desegregating local facilities. Taylor also reported that there were no openings on the quadricentennial commission to which a Negro could be appointed. Despite this unsatisfactory response, SCLC chose not to involve itself further in St. Augustine developments at this time.[3]

SCLC's position changed dramatically, however, after Vivian's report on his visit to St. Augustine. Convinced by conversations with local leaders that blacks needed outside assistance, Vivian urged King and the SCLC to intervene in St. Augustine. He made particular reference to the presence of so many white extremists in the community and the absence of strong black ministerial leaders. "I recommended that the SCLC go into St. Augustine because of the desperate needs of local blacks and because we had not been in Florida before." He thus saw the SCLC's involvement as a way to facilitate desegregation in St. Augustine and strengthen the organization throughout the state.

King and SCLC's Board of Directors approved Vivian's recommendation and by the second week in March 1964 the organization had begun mobilizing its forces for a major drive against segregation in St. Augustine. SCLC based its decision on the plight of black leaders in the community, especially in light of Klan violence and a hostile police department. SCLC leaders also thought that because St. Augustine was a heavily Catholic community, the church could be used as a force for social change. As will be noted later, however, this did not prove to be the case. John Herbers of the *New York Times* has argued that King and SCLC leaders were additionally concerned about the growing violence among black Americans in response to white racism. Herbers believed that SCLC was anxious to renew the desegregation drive in 1964 to demonstrate to blacks throughout the country that nonviolence was a much more effective instrument for change. SCLC leaders called the St. Augustine campaign an attempt to give "new dignity to the movement," emphasizing the need to have the St. Augustine movement "pull the nonviolent thrust of the Negro back on center."[4]

Perhaps most important from SCLC's perspective in 1964 was its concern with the passage of the civil rights bill. In the March issue of the SCLC newsletter, King wrote that enactment of the bill was "so critical for the domestic health of our national community that we must mobilize every force and pressure available to see to it that the civil rights bill before the Senate gets through—*as is.*" When the Reverend Fred Shuttlesworth was asked if the St. Augustine campaign was seen as a way to pressure Congress into adopting the civil rights bill, he replied, "Yes, yes definitely." Vivian also acknowledged that "passage of the civil rights bill was a primary goal of the SCLC in St. Augustine." SCLC thus went into St. Augustine to prevent southern senators from tying the civil rights bill up in committee or successfully filibustering it on the floor of the Senate.[5]

Having made its decision to intervene in St. Augustine, SCLC chose to begin its campaign over Easter week, March 28–April 2, in order to capture national attention and to enable the organization to bring in white college recruits from the North who were on vacation. The organization moved quickly to mobilize its forces for the two-week deadline. By 1964 SCLC had developed a sophisticated machinery for its campaigns. Hosea Williams, special projects director for the organization, served as coordinator for the St. Augustine campaign with assistance provided by SCLC's national board and staff. In addition to the support SCLC received from the black community, it received substantial aid from whites in the Northeast. White participation had symbolic meaning for SCLC, since, as Vivian noted, "it belies the segregationists' argument that white and Negro cannot and will not live together." Furthermore, it permitted "Southerners with a conscience" to contrast whites in the demonstrations with Ku Klux Klan types.[6]

A letter was quickly prepared and sent out over Dr. Hayling's signature to college students in New England, asking them to spend their Easter vacation assisting the struggle to desegregate the nation's oldest city. "This call is issued because of the particularly intolerable conditions within the city of St. Augustine," Hayling wrote. "It may well be that the oldest historic city in the United States is one in which the patterns of discrimination, hatred, and violence are most deeply entrenched." SCLC chapters in the New England states distriubted the letter to college campuses. The Massachusetts chapter described St. Augustine as "one of the most segregated cities in the country" and asked all volunteers to plan to spend at least four days in the city. Both the Massachusetts and New Haven chapters warned students that arrests were not planned, "but students must be willing to accept it" and be prepared to post bail. In addition to sending the recruitment letters, King and his aides personally contacted ministerial and faculty supporters in the Boston area. Assistance was also sought from the federal government. King wrote Attorney General Robert Kennedy noting that "400 years of local control and states rights have not led to the betterment of relations but a denial of basic human rights."[7]

St. Augustine's white leaders quickly got wind of these developments. In the middle of March, Mayor Shelley received a letter from a student at a New England college, who was a native of St. Augustine, warning him of SCLC efforts to recruit students for an Easter invasion of the community and sending him a copy of a recruitment flyer. Shelley immediately drafted a statement of his own which denounced Hayling's letter and SCLC allegations. In an attempt to persuade northern students to stay home, Shelley's letter claimed no segregation existed in the city's public facilities and that blacks encountered no discrimination in seeking public positions. He also pointed out that Federal Judge William McCrae had reprimanded the NAACP and Hayling in 1963 for provoking the racial crisis while generally praising civic leaders for their efforts to end the turmoil. The mayor received a long distance call shortly thereafter from a reporter for the *Boston Globe* who asked Shelley if he had ever heard of Mrs. Malcolm Peabody. Shelley replied that he had not. The reporter informed him that she was the wife of an Episcopal Bishop in Massachusetts and also the mother of the Governor of Massachusetts, Endicott Peabody, and was planning to participate in the St. Augustine demonstrations during Easter. He asked Shelley what he would do if she violated segregation laws. Shelley responded, "If she comes down and breaks the law, we are going to arrest her."[8] His threat to arrest Mrs. Peabody demonstrated that Shelley, and it could be said of the white community as well, was ill prepared for SCLC's intervention.[9] No one in St. Augustine foresaw the potential consequences, and city leaders took no steps to prepare the community for the Easter demonstrations.

SCLC aides began arriving on March 20 with the initial delegation responsible for setting up food kitchens and arranging accommodations for those coming from outside the state. The first contingent of college students entered the community two days later. On Thursday, March 26, Hosea Williams, accompanied by SCLC staff members from Atlanta, reached the city and began preparing local civil rights workers and northern supporters for the demonstrations. By Friday, over sixty students had joined the civil rights effort along with several ministerial leaders, Mrs. Peabody, and her close friends.[10]

When Williams entered St. Augustine, he found conditions explosive. He and his assistants ordered blacks to put away their weapons, and they established classes in nonviolence for young and old. As part of the preparation for demonstrations, SCLC aides encouraged trainees to be prepared to offer their bodies as living sacrifices. The training program was a rigorous experience with participants being taunted and threatened by leaders to see if they could retain their composure. Those who could not were turned away and asked not to take part in future demonstrations.

The first demonstrations began quietly on March 25 when a white minister, accompanied by four northern college students, picketed the Tourist Information Center and passed out leaflets urging visitors to "bypass St. Augustine, America's oldest segregated city." The pamphlet made special reference to Hayling's beating by Klansmen and the violence against black parents whose children attended desegregated schools. Three days later, following the arrival of Williams, the demonstrations escalated as twenty-six protesters conducted sit-ins at segregated restaurants; all were arrested by police. On Easter Sunday several mixed groups attempted to attend religious services at white churches, but they were turned away. Church leaders told reporters that the groups sought to demonstrate rather than worship. That afternoon the Reverend David Robinson, a Yale University chaplain, led a large group to the Monson Motor Lodge where another thirty-nine people were arrested for trespassing. Refusing to admit the protests were a result of local racial problems, Mayor Shelley instead attributed the demonstrations to northern "scalawags" and contended that racial difficulties in St. Augustine had been nearly resolved when they "came down here with the idea of getting in jail."[11]

The first mass demonstration took place on March 31 with 150 people, mostly black students from St. Augustine's Murray High School, parading through town singing "We Shall Overcome." They walked around the plaza to the Ponce de Leon Hotel and then entered the hotel restaurant. The police asked the students to leave without success before using police dogs and cattle prods to round them up and put them in jail.

As events unfolded, SCLC's strategy became increasingly clear. Specifically, the organization sought to fill the jails and then exploit the conditions created by overcrowding. This approach had worked very effectively in obtaining national support for the civil rights movement in Birmingham. More generally, SCLC sought to disrupt the community's tourist economy over the holidays through picketing and numerous demonstrations.

The most highly publicized event during the Easter demonstrations occurred on the afternoon of the thirty-first, when Mrs. Peabody accompanied by an integrated group which included the Reverend England, Dr. Hayling, and Mrs. John Burgess, wife of a Negro Episcopal bishop, attempted to integrate the restaurant at the Ponce de Leon Motor Lodge. While on her way to the restaurant, Mrs. Peabody encountered an old friend from Philadelphia. "How wonderful to see you," the friend declared. "What are you doing here?" "I'm in the process of being arrested," she replied proudly.[12] Shortly after her group had taken their seats in the restaurant, Sheriff L. O. Davis arrived and asked them to leave, warning that they would be arrested for violating the state's undesirable guest law. Mrs. Peabody refused to move, asking the sheriff to read the statute to her. Caught off guard, Davis mumbled something, then retreated to his car to find a copy of the law. After several minutes he returned, read the law, and announced they were under arrest. Mrs. Peabody recalled in court that it was "a very long law with a great many words in it." "I realized that I couldn't fit some of those parts of it that described why I should leave," she said. "I think I was neither drunken or disorderly and there was something about hurting the good name of the establishment, [and] I decided that must be it. . . ." "Did the sheriff ever tell you?" her lawyer asked. "No," she answered, "I think he took it for granted I was all those things." Mayor Shelley immediately sought to belittle her, asserting that "people like the Peabodys live in exclusive suburbs. They don't practice what they preach. They are the true hypocrite."[13]

The arrest and the subsequent imprisonment of this seventy-two-year-old grandmother, however, drew the nation's attention to racial conditions in St. Augustine as no other incident had. It was a watershed development in the community's race relations. Prior to Mrs. Peabody's involvement, events in the city had received attention in local and area newspapers but only sporadically had the national newspapers covered events in the city. The involvement of Mrs. Peabody changed all that. Over fifty reporters gathered at the jail to interview her and her jailers. Not only did she and the Easter demonstrations attract a national audience, but they also raised the interest of the federal government and Congress in this historic community. In a telegram to Mrs. Peabody, Martin Luther King, Jr., praised her "creative nonviolent demonstration" and noted her contribution to the achievement of "the American Dream" in which racial segregation was abolished. From March through the remainder of the year, events in St. Augustine would unfold before the eyes of an attentive nation.[14]

Mrs. Peabody was not unaware of the impact she and her friends had on race relations in St. Augustine. She told reporters, "We got involved in this because we think it'll go faster if we do it together. It puts the spotlight on the city, and gives them unwelcome publicity." If her arrest had dramatic implications for St. Augustine, it did not come as any great surprise to her family. "That's the kind of thing she always does," commented her husband of forty-seven years, Bishop Malcolm Peabody.[15]

Mrs. Peabody had known Martin Luther King for several years through her husband and had assisted SCLC in its fund-raising drives. She had probably been informed of the St. Augustine Easter campaign by the Reverend William England, a family friend. She decided to participate, declaring she was after a "better deal" for Negroes. Before getting arrested, Mrs. Peabody had telephoned her son. "Endicott, we feel that we should be arrested. I'm not worried about myself, of course, but I am worried about you." Governor Peabody told her not to worry—"Mother, do what you think is right." Mrs. Peabody refused to accept bail after her arrest believing that "it wouldn't be right to just come in and go out again."[16]

While Mrs. Peabody's imprisonment overshadowed other

developments, the demonstrations continued through Easter Sunday. Hosea Williams directed daytime marches to the slave market and sit-ins were conducted throughout the community. So many people had been arrested that there was no space left at the county jail but standing room. SCLC decried these conditions and the racism in the community, but chose to end the demonstrations on April 2 as prearranged, having yet to decide whether it was prepared to invest the necessary resources for a full-scale campaign in St. Augustine.[17]

In reflecting on the Easter-week protests and the general dissatisfaction with the outcome, a King aide, who had participated in the demonstrations, declared that "it may be necessary to bring in part of our nonviolent army that we have recurited from all over the country." He told reporters that King would decide shortly whether to do so. Little had been achieved in the community as a result of the Easter demonstrations other than widespread media visibility. White officials had not changed their attitudes and most expected the city to return to normal with SCLC and Mrs. Peabody's departure. Adding to the interest of SCLC in renewing the campaign in St. Augustine was the fate of the civil rights bill. It was still tied up in the Senate and passage seemed uncertain. King wired Dr. Hayling on April 1 declaring that St. Augustine had aroused the attention of the nation and indicated that SCLC would be sending additional help on May 1.[18]

SCLC's concern about race relations in this historic city were clearly warranted as evidenced by the white response. Speaking for the more militant segment of the community, Dr. Hardgrove Norris described the Easter protests as "an invasion." He opposed any negotiations between the two sides: "If you are invaded, you don't talk with your invaders and . . . try to arrive at a reasonable understanding." Even the more moderate people in the community were reluctant to support a compromise solution, believing "St. Augustine was used for publicity reasons."[19]

White leaders, who had predicted that the racial problems of 1963 "would blow over" in 1964, now realized that they may have been mistaken. This realization was shocking in itself. Added to this, however, was the widespread criticism being leveled at their city by the national media at the same time local leaders were preparing a media blitz of their own publicizing the four hundredth anniversary. The clash between their plans for the anniversary celebration and the portrayal of St. Augustine as a racist community shocked and angered white citizens. "We're a target city," one man commented, "not primarily because of segregation or racial discrimination, but because we are the nation's oldest city. This gives dramatic impact to the civil rights movement."[20]

In their anger about these developments, white leaders took forceful steps to punish local blacks for joining in the Easter demonstrations and to dissuade others from participating in future demonstrations. Bungum Roberson, local SCLC treasurer, and Lucille Plummer, SCLC secretary, were both fired from their jobs as were five other civil rights activists. Flagler Hospital released Plummer after warning her on several occasions about her civil rights activities. At the same time several white doctors told blacks they were increasing the cost of office visits for them. Even Florida Memorial College succumbed to white pressure when Dr. Puryear warned students that they would be suspended if they participated in further demonstrations. White leaders apparently told Puryear that community financial assistance would be withheld from the college if he did not make such a statement.[21]

The consensus achieved by the white community in the aftermath of the Easter protests was reflected in the policies of Sheriff Davis and Judge Mathis. Mathis refused to accept the bonds written by a professional Negro bondsman from Daytona. He made this decision after a local bondsman had declined to write bonds for the nearly two hundred demonstrators. He also ruled against the demonstrators in every instance, fining them $100 to $300 per count. Sheriff Davis added a further obstacle to the efforts of the demonstrators to free themselves by not accepting any checks in the payment of bonds.[22]

Civil rights attorneys appealed the rulings of Mathis and the policies of Davis to the Federal District Court, contending that their clients could not receive a fair trial in St. Augustine. In particular, lawyers William Kunstler and Tobias Simon complained that there had been no acquittals in the St. Augustine cases in the state courts. Judge Bryan Simpson, however, ruled against SCLC's appeal in early April. He responded to Kunstler and Simon's complaint by suggesting that "there have not been many who should be acquitted. Somebody who sticks his head in a noose and complains that the rope burns his neck—well, I don't think he has any complaint." More pointedly, Simpson declared that "whether they can be acquitted is not the test anyway. It's whether they can get a fair trial."[23]

Round one had ended for SCLC, and St. Augustine appeared more resistant to desegregation than it had at any point earlier. Civic leaders felt confident, especially after Judge Simpson's ruling, that they had withstood SCLC's challenge. But many were clearly concerned about the possibility of SCLC returning to St. Augustine, and the actions taken against local activists sought to discourage further appeals to SCLC.

Despite the efforts of local officials, events quickly demonstrated that St. Augustine had not heard or seen the last of its protagonists. In a series of well-coordinated steps, SCLC supporters publicized racial problems in St. Augustine. On April 8 the Reverend William Sloane Coffin, chaplain at Yale University and close ally of SCLC, wrote a letter to the *New York Times* in which he outlined the tactics SCLC would pursue in its subsequent efforts to desegregate this historic community. Coffin urged the federal government not to contribute to the city's 400th anniversary. He also called upon northerners to avoid the city on vacations into the South and encouraged young people in St. Augustine to continue the demonstrations.[24] Six days later Mrs. Peabody appeared on the NBC "Today Show" and described her reasons for going to St. Augustine and her subsequent arrest. She portrayed the community as one of hatred and violence. The national spotlight remained focused on St. Augustine when demonstrators picketed the Florida pavilion at the New York World's Fair.[25]

Despite the continued pressure on the city, white leaders refused to bend, and on April 14 the County Commission approved a motion initiated by Dr. Shelley asking the "Today Show" to give equal time to Shelley and other public officials to rebut the "derogatory, incorrect, and misleading statements" made by Mrs. Peabody. The City Commission passed a similar resolution three days later, although Commissioner McDaniel expressed concern about continuing to publicize the civil rights activities in the community. Shelley responded that remaining quiet in the face of Mrs. Peabody's comments would only prove more injurious to the city. The commission voted five to nothing in favor of the county's resolution.[26] On May 19 Shelley and Earle W. Newton, director of the quadricentennial observance, gave an interview to NBC newsman Ray Schearer in Washington during which they refused to concede that there were racial problems in the community. In response to a question concerning Mrs. Peabody, Shelley claimed she did "a disservice not only to St. Augustine but the nation as a whole" by participating in the Easter demonstrations. Reiterating a viewpoint he had expressed on several occasions, he contended that steady progress had been made in the community toward removing racial barriers and that her actions and those of other radicals, such as Hayling, had done "irreparable harm" to these advances. Overstating city initiatives in eliminating segregation, integrating its public schools, and hiring Negro policemen, Shelley sought to portray the ancient city as a racially progressive community. He also reemphasized the belief held by nearly all white residents that St. Augustine had been selected as a target city by SCLC only because it was the oldest city in the United States and not because of a breakdown in race relations.[27]

White St. Augustine further indicated its determination not to yield on the civil rights crisis by reelecting L. O. Davis as sheriff in May with over 70 percent of the vote. Davis had emerged during late 1963 and 1964 as one of the major opponents of the civil rights movement. A rather easygoing person not unlike Sheriff Laurie Pritchett of Albany, Georgia, Davis had treated demonstrators evenhandedly in his initial encounters with them, but by the fall of 1963 he and his deputies had begun physically threatening civil rights activists. Davis' reaction was particularly important because, not only was he the county's chief law enforcement officer, he was also a major political force in the community, as the recent election returns had demonstrated. In addition, he had close ties with both civic leaders and white militants.[28]

Despite the civility he had shown toward black residents in the past, Davis was not at all sympathetic to a change in the city's racial patterns. Davis was very much a product of his society and the times; he never questioned the separation of the races because he believed blacks were racially inferior. Nothing angered him more during the civil rights protests than to see a black boy and white girl walking hand in hand, for it challenged the very essence of southern race relations. Davis' views were also shaped by his participation in World War II and his friendship with Drs. Shelley and Norris, Police Chief Stuart, and Judge Mathis. Davis saw the civil rights movement as a Communist conspiracy to take over the United States and he had no doubt that Martin Luther King was a communist.[29]

Davis had been concerned about the movement of Ku Klux Klan elements into St. Augustine in late 1963 and 1964, but when King and SCLC entered the community, his interest in KKK activities seemed to wane. He viewed the KKK as a real threat to peace in the community when the local civil rights movement appeared to be declining in late 1963. With the dramatic change in events in 1964, however, he apparently saw the KKK as a way to help rid St. Augustine of the SCLC.[30]

Aiding Davis' change of attitude was the pro-Klan sentiment among his deputies. He claimed he might have had one Klansman as a deputy but he was not positive. Deputy Robert Pittman Gentry, however, told the House Un-American Activities Committee in 1965 that he had belonged to a Jacksonville Klavern since 1961, and that three other deputies were all active in this Klavern. Gentry said that Davis was not a Klansman but he "allowed Klan meetings to be held in the county jail and also loaned sheriff department automobiles to the Klansmen."[31] Although Davis denied Gentry's charges, he did allow "Hoss" Manucy and J. B. Stoner free access to his office during the spring of 1964. Davis also told a close friend that if he hadn't been sheriff, he would have taken a baseball bat and knocked Martin Luther King's teeth out. Moreover, he stated that during his reelection campaign in 1964 he went to the black district and told residents not to vote for him: "I used the word 'nigger' so they would know I meant it."[32]

Davis' hostility toward the aims of SCLC and his personal dislike of King appears to have persuaded him to act as an intermediary between civic leaders and Klan leaders, keeping each apprised of the intentions of the other. Davis met regularly with Shelley, Judge Mathis, and City Attorney Robert Andreu during the crisis, and there seems little doubt that they could have restrained Manucy and Stoner if they chose to. The opposition of civic leaders to the aims of the civil rights leaders was apparently conveyed to Klansmen by Davis and his deputies, encouraging them to pursue their violent tactics. Throughout all of this Davis acted as something of a show-man. He had made a great display of arresting Mrs. Peabody and holding press conferences on Mrs. Peabody's condition during her twenty-four hour imprisonment.[33]

Behind this façade, Davis took the civil rights move-ment very seriously and was determined it would not succeed in St. Augustine. He and Mathis together had raised the bond from $100 per count to $300 and finally to $1,500 per count to discourage peo-ple from participating in the demonstrations. When William Kun-stler came to bail out his clients Davis told him, "These bums will all be back here for holding hands with niggers."[34]

The response of Sheriff Davis and other white leaders to the civil rights movement in St. Augustine received added encour-agement from the leading Democratic gubernatorial candidate Hay-don Burns, mayor of Jacksonville, who based a large part of his cam-paign on racial issues in the spring of 1964. In virtually every speech, Burns denounced the civil rights bill and promised to utilize "every legal means" to prevent its implementation. While campaigning in St. Augustine, he expressed his support for the mayor and city offi-cials and condemned the illegal actions of civil rights demonstrators.

Burns' rival, Scott Kelly, state senator from Lakeland, Florida, added his opposition to the civil rights movement. He des-ignated himself as the "symbol of opposition to civil rights in Flor-ida" and promised to ignore the civil rights measure if he were elected governor. Kelly also opposed further desegregation of the state's pub-lic schools. Such statements from the state's leading political figures only increased the defiance of local leaders.[35]

Since the departure of SCLC in early April, the move-ment seemed to have lost much of its local initiative and only two demonstrations had been conducted during the rest of the month. Both had been led by the Reverend A. H. Taylor, a visiting minis-ter, who had been brought in by SCLC to assist Hayling. The dem-onstration at the Castillo de San Marcos on April 23 had been widely advertised and television crews from local and national networks covered the event, but only seventy-five college and high school stu-dents participated in the hour of songs and speeches. The second protest at the Tourist Information Center involved only a handful of demonstrators. Precisely what had happened to the local movement is not completely clear. It appears that a split had developed between civil rights activists, led by Hayling and SCLC leaders, and more conservative black leaders, led by Puryear, Mrs. Gordon, and some black ministers. Increased social and economic pressure from the white community had clearly discouraged many older black residents from supporting the movement and from allowing their children to participate. In addition, conservative black leaders felt SCLC was trying to move too fast and was, as a consequence, causing serious problems between blacks and whites in the community.[36]

In an effort to recapture the initiative in the community, SCLC sent Assistant Project Director John L. Gibson to St. Augustine. On May 2 he called together fifty black leaders and persuaded them to work cooperatively for "an all-out push" tentatively set for early June to coincide with the reentrance of SCLC forces. Following the meeting, Gibson and Hayling had dinner with Dr. and Mrs. Canwright, who had recently retired to St Augustine from New Jersey and were sympathetic to the civil rights movement. The Canwrights agreed to approach white moderates in the community and see if they could encourage support for a biracial commission.

SCLC's selection of the Canwrights to assist them demonstrated graphically the lack of support SCLC had in the white community. Outsiders, such as the Canwrights, had very little influence in this community where family ties and social connections played such an important role. SCLC obviously hoped that Dr. Canwright, as a retired physician, would be listened to by medical leaders, especially Mayor Shelley. Unfortunately, they ignored his supplications.[37]

In a move to strengthen local black support for further demonstrations and to portray the organization in a moderate light, SCLC established a seven-member negotiations committee, headed by conservative leader Dr. Puryear, to meet with a white committee when and if it were appointed. Gibson reported to King that by this step SCLC would be seen as "working for the good of the community and not to gain 'glory.' " Gibson and SCLC aides also began going door to door on May 3 to revive support for the civil rights effort. In addition, they made plans for mass meetings in black churches three nights a week and open-air rallies at the fort once a week.[38]

In reporting to SCLC headquarters in Atlanta, Gibson sketched a scenario of events SCLC might follow during the first two weeks of its return in St. Augustine—May 24 through June 7. He recommended that "nonviolent workshops . . . be held daily for high school and college students and those adults recruited in mass meetings." Throughout the demonstrations, Gibson suggested that negotiations be sought with white officials, although he was unclear on how this would be done. If SCLC sought to "pull out the stoppers" in May and June, Gibson proposed a massive jail-in and a march, led by Reverend C. K. Steele, from the Georgia-Florida border to St. Augustine. He also called for "some major 'symbols' from the national office . . . [to] join and lead crowds to jail." To undermine the city's plans for the 400th anniversary, Gibson recommended that SCLC's New York office set up a meeting of African delegates with King to urge France, Spain, Great Britain, and Mexico to withdraw their support from St. Augustine's celebration. Gibson commented that "this would be in keeping with the UN's actions against the segregation which now exists in South Africa."[39]

Despite Gibson's report and King's letter to Hayling, SCLC was still undecided about its involvement in St. Augustine. At the executive staff meeting in Atlanta on May 4, King chose to wait another ten days before deciding whether to mobilize SCLC's nonviolent army for demonstrations in Washington, D.C., or St. Augustine. SCLC leaders were apparently unsure which demonstrations would have the greatest impact on the Senate. Ultimately, they decided upon St. Augustine because of concerns that demonstrations in the nation's capital might alienate congressional leaders.[40]

Once the decision had been made, SCLC sent the Reverend Wyatt Tee Walker, King's executive assistant, to St. Augustine to assess the local movement and further refine Gibson's battle plan. Clearly concerned about the need to give direction and purpose to the movement in St. Augustine after the failure of the Albany, Georgia, campaign in 1962 and tactical mistakes in Birmingham in 1963, SCLC spent considerable time in preparation for the forthcoming campaign. The selection of Walker to visit St. Augustine indicated the seriousness with which SCLC approached the forthcoming campaign. Walker was generally recognized as the ablest administrator in the organization and one who "thought things through very carefully." Mindful of the influence of the national media on the public's perception of the movement, Walker wrote, "Somehow, we must recapture the moral offensive so that it can not be suggested that the nonviolent revolution has become surly, irresponsible, and undisciplined. THIS IS AN ABSOLUTE MUST." Walker characterized the local movement as "raggedy" and said that at times it appeared as if SCLC was trying to "out-Snick" SNCC by minstrellike demonstrations with dancing, shouting, and singing. He recommended that participants in the demonstrations appear neat and clean, walk erect, be courteous, and disciplined. He reported that the movement in St. Augustine suffered from a lack of direction and discipline and that these changes were designed to correct that.[41]

Walker believed that St. Augustine was particularly vulnerable in two areas and they ought to be exploited: its dependence on tourism and its desire for federal assistance for the quadricentennial observance. He proposed that SCLC attack these two areas by making the national community aware of racism in St. Augustine and by persuading President Johnson to block any commitment of federal funds to the anniversary celebration.[42]

Walker's battle plan, which was essentially that followed by SCLC, called for the first mass protest on May 26 with a march around the slave market to alert the nation to conditions in St. Augustine. From May 27 until June 8, a series of evening marches and daytime demonstrations would be conducted as recommended by Gibson. Beginning on June 8, Walker suggested that SCLC seek a dialogue with city leaders. Simultaneously, demonstrations would be led by prominent figures from around the nation during the 10–12, followed by a massive drive for a settlement, commencing on the fourteenth. To insure that SCLC controlled events throughout and that the organization was not itself controlled by local developments, Walker's plan called for staff meetings every morning to discuss the demonstrations of the previous day and plans for the day. He also proposed that SCLC designate one person to represent the organization to the press and that a citizen's committee, as in Birmingham, be apointed to coordinate local activities.[43] Walker's proposal received approval from King and SCLC's executive board in mid-May, setting the stage for renewed demonstrations at the end of the month.

Having committed itself to the St. Augustine campaign, SCLC proceeded to mobilize its national and local forces to bring maximum pressure on the community and to implement Walker's plan to insure that the problems experienced in previous campaigns were avoided in St. Augustine. Despite the intense planning and the economic vulnerability of St. Augustine, SCLC's leaders did not anticipate a quick victory. Indeed, SCLC officials were already beginning to portray the forthcoming campaign as a long, hot summer in the nation's oldest and most racially restrictive community—an exaggerated description to be sure, but one which Williams and others felt would help mobilize northern support and media interest.

Chapter 4.

You're Going To
Have To Integrate

On May 18, King formally announced that SCLC would return to St. Augustine and requested federal support. Calling the city "a small Birmingham," he promised a "very strong direct action campaign" with "our nonviolent army." King told reporters that President Johnson had agreed in 1963 to help establish lines of communication between whites and blacks in the city. "We will remind him of his pledge and urge him to use the full weight of his office to help achieve a peaceful solution in St. Augustine," he stated.[1] Shortly after his conference with the press, King wired Attorney General Robert Kennedy pointing out that the situation in St. Augustine "highlights the need for the protection of minorities provided by the Civil Rights Bill," and urged him to employ federal forces to halt the violence and brutality against black residents.[2]

Hosea Williams and Willie Bolden returned to the city five days later to prepare local blacks for the second wave of demonstrations. Circulating a code of discipline, which included eleven "commandments," to supporters in a meeting at St. Paul's Church, Williams and Bolden urged them to abide by the principles of nonviolence and emphasized the importance of not carrying guns or knives. "Nonviolent direct action is a way of overcoming injustice without becoming unjust yourself," the code stated. "It's a way of conquering fear without being overcome by it yourself."[3]

With Dr. Hayling's assistance, Williams quickly galvanized black youth for SCLC's plans, but found the "old people wanted
nothing to do with me or Hayling." Accustomed to racial traditions
and concerned about their jobs, most older black St. Augustinians
worried that the civil rights movement would create further instabil-
ity in the community without any improvement in black rights and
opportunities. They expressed concern not only about their jobs but
also about further violence in the community. Most of the participants in SCLC's demonstrations were teenagers from St. Augustine,
college students from Florida Memorial and northern schools, and
clergy and other sympathizers from throughout the nation. Few residents over thirty, who were not involved in civil rights organizations, became involved in the protests. The absence of strong ministerial leaders in the civil rights effort no doubt influenced the actions
of older citizens.[4]

Despite the lack of support from older residents, nearly
400 people gathered at First Baptist Church on May 26 at 8:00 P.M.
to hear Dr. King, who had arrived earlier that day, and to receive
instructions from Hosea Williams about the evening's march. At nine
o'clock Dr. King entered the building amid shouts of greeting and
praise. People in the church reached out to touch him as he walked
up the center aisle to a seat at the front of the church. In the few
years since the Montgomery campaign he had become a Christlike
figure to many poor blacks who hoped to be somehow spiritually en-
riched by touching him. It was a poignant moment in the civil rights
movement as the cheers, hallelujahs, and amens resounded throughout the church. King told the audience, "You are proving to be the
creative anvils that will wear out many a physical hammer." It was a
favorite phrase of King's and seemed to calm his listeners, who were
anxious to begin their first night march but also nervous about the
white community's response.[5]

Hosea Williams followed King to the podium, and he
spoke slowly about the need to be nonviolent and to pay attention
to his orders during the course of the march. Williams joined SCLC
after spending several years leading the civil rights effort in Savannah for the NAACP. Employing a variety of tactics, some of which
were controversial (the evening marches in particular), Williams and

his aides successfully desegregated the community in 1963. Dissatisfied with the NAACP for its lukewarm support, however, Williams
decided to join SCLC and became director of the Field Staff in 1963,
a position he would hold until 1970. As part of his new duties, Williams visited southern communities which requested SCLC assistance
and reported back to the Board of Directors. If the site was designated as a target community by SCLC, Williams would be sent in to
organize the leadership and coordinate local activities. It was in this
capacity that Williams had arrived in St. Augustine during Easter week
1964.[6]

A dynamic speaker and an aggressive person, Williams
assumed control of local planning shortly after his arrival, a move
that caused considerable tension between him and Dr. Hayling. Although the two were alike in many ways and shared many of the same
goals, both men had large egos and each sought to direct the St. Augustine movement. Hayling perceived Williams as an interloper who
spent his time telling residents what to do instead of listening to their
concerns. Williams considered Hayling to be too outspoken and too
willing to resort to violence to be effective in St. Augustine. Hayling's middle-class background, education, and occupation contrasted
sharply with Williams, who was reared in poverty in rural Georgia by
his mother. Williams appears to have had reservations about the
commitment of professional blacks to the movement and the extent
of their concern with conditions faced by poor blacks.[7]

After reemphasizing the importance of nonviolence,
Williams called for volunteers to join him in a march to the slave
market. "The invitational periods at the mass meetings, when we asked
for volunteers, were much like those invitational periods that occur
every Sunday morning in Negro churches, when the pastor projects
the call to those present to join the church. By twenties and thirties
and forties, people came forward to join our army," King recalled.
Led by Williams and the Reverend C. T. Vivian, four hundred
marchers gathered outside the church on that pleasant spring evening in late May and began their walk to the center of town. As they
paraded through the heart of the black community, participants from
other areas were struck by the relative neatness and attractiveness of
it. Single-family homes lined Central Avenue and Washington Street

with small but rather well-kept front yards. This was not an impov-
erished black community housed in dilapidated tenements, but housing had never been the chief concern of blacks in St. Augustine.[8]

The marchers arrived at the slave market at 10:30 P.M.
clapping and singing "We Shall Overcome." To the surprise of many,
no segregationists had gathered in the downtown area to harass them.
"I think we caught them off guard," one marcher observed. Local
police allowed the marchers to stop to pray and sing several hymns
before they returned to First Baptist Church.[9]

The following evening the same scenario unfolded but as
the marchers approached the intersection of King and Cordova Street,
a block and a half north of the slave market, a police lieutenant intercepted Williams and warned him that a large group of whites had
gathered at the slave market. He advised Williams to turn around
and return to Washington Street. Sheriff Davis and Police Chief Stuart
also approached the marchers, asking that they not go downtown because "there were not enough police to protect them." Davis commented that there were reports "that the town is full of Klan types,
armed with sticks, metal rods, chains, [and] knives." Some of the
older people and small children left at this point, but approximately
350 marched silently around the plaza. Many white teenagers heck-
led the marchers and threw a variety of objects at them. No one
was hurt but several marchers declared that they had seen gun barrels
pointed at them. Events were heating up. The state highway patrol
sent in fifteen patrolmen the following day, anticipating a difficult
Thursday.[10]

On the evening of the twenty-eighth, 400 demonstrators
marched past the slave market, accompanied for the first time by
television cameramen and reporters. The segregationists stood in the
market area shouting epithets at marchers. When the camera lights
were turned on them, they suddenly burst out of the market area and
attacked the cameramen. NBC sound man Irving Gans and James P.
Kerlin, an Associated Press photographer, received severe beatings
and lost their cameras in the process. The segregationists also turned
on the marchers; one of whom was hit on the head with a club while
several others received an assortment of bruises from chains, tire irons,
and fists.[11]

Local police, angered at having to protect the marchers

whom they blamed for the trouble, stood aside as the attack continued. Exclaiming to his partner "there's that nigger lover," a deputy
sheriff allowed his police dog to attack Harry Boyte, white aide to
King, and then, claiming he and Boyte became entangled in the dog's
leash, fell on Boyte and slugged him several times. When Boyte got
to his feet, he asked a deputy what happened to his camera; the deputy told him to "let Khrushchev buy you another one."[12]

Following the daytime demonstrations and the evening
march, SCLC held a mass meeting during which there were reports
of the day's activities. According to one observer, the mass meetings
were "the heart of the freedom movement, for here people have an
opportunity to come together, release some of their pent-up emotions with singing, hear reports on the things that have happened
during the day, volunteer for service the next day, and gather strength
and courage from each other and from their faith." Reports were given
by those who had been hurt or injured during the day and others
who had taken part in the demonstrations. SCLC leaders also showed
demonstrators what to do if someone in the march was assaulted,
pointing out how those nearby should fall on top of the person being
beaten to prevent him from being severely hurt. SCLC spokesmen
repeatedly stressed that nonviolence must be practiced and demonstrators should not fight back.[13]

Unlike the racial confrontations of the previous two evenings, the violence did not cease with the conclusion of the evening
meeting. Boyte and his son were followed back to their motel by another car. Noticing someone driving up behind him as he parked,
Boyte pushed his son down onto the front seat just as a shotgun blast
exploded the rear window. A few hours later, King's rented house at
St. Augustine Beach was hit by gunfire.[14]

Reporters for local and regional newspapers had received
an anonymous telephone tip earlier in the day that King was staying
in a beach cottage. The *St. Augustine Record* published the story with
the address of the cottage in the evening edition. Early the following
morning the cottage was struck. Two reporters felt the tip had come
from someone active in SCLC or in the local movement and was
designed to elicit just such a response from the segregationists. Hank
Drane remains convinced that SCLC sought to use the threat on King's
life to obtain federal assistance. No evidence exists to support the

reporter's contention but such a step was not beyond the fertile imag-
ination of Hosea Williams, who felt that SCLC needed an aggressive
strategy keyed to winning federal support for the desegregation effort.[15]

King did wire President Johnson the following day asking
that he "immediately provide federal protection through the Department of Justice" for civil rights workers. Claiming "all semblance of
law and order has broken down at St. Augustine, Florida," King
maintained that "we have witnessed raw and rampant violence even
beyond much of what we have experienced in Alabama and Mississippi." He refused to suspend the demonstrations because of the
mounting violence and the danger to the lives of his aides, arguing:
"We cannot in good conscience postpone our nonviolent thrust merely
because violence has erupted against us, but we sincerely believe that
as American citizens our right to peaceably assemble must be guaranteed and not abridged because of the unrestrained lawlessness of
the Klan element."[16]

The importance of King to the St. Augustine movement
was readily apparent to Dr. Hayling and other local leaders. Although they had written President Kennedy several times in 1963,
they had never received a reply. King on the other hand had sent off
his telegram on May 29 and received a telephone call from Lee White,
Johnson's Associate Special Council on Racial Matters, the following evening. A letter from White to King and Hayling arrived on
June 12.[17]

In the telephone conversation, King sought federal assistance by arguing that local police authorities were no longer capable
of handling developments in the city. White promised Dr. King that
he would "alert the Justice Department and do whatever he could."
White asked Burke Marshall, Assistant Attorney General in charge
of the Civil Rights Division, to contact the FBI and "make sure that
they stayed on top of the situation in St. Augustine and supplied up-
to-the-minute information."[18] After directions were given to the FBI,
White called Governor Bryant, informing him of King's concerns.
Bryant told White he was watching St. Augustine "on a continual
basis." Captain Prater of the Florida State Police had been stationed
in the city and had been authorized by Bryant "to call sufficient state
patrolmen to handle any situation in St. Augustine."[19]

Black leaders generally perceived the FBI's involvement in the civil rights movement as a mixed blessing. The agency's presence in a community suggested that the federal government was closely monitoring events there. It thus often encouraged white leaders to pursue more actively a solution to the crisis. But the presence of the FBI was not without its cost to the civil rights movement. In St. Augustine the FBI encouraged members of the NAACP to serve as informants, providing details not only about right wing activities in the community but also about developments within the movement itself. Those who were dissatisfied with the local leadership, especially Hayling, and the involvement of SCLC often provided the FBI with information. Indirectly then, the FBI helped to promote discord within the movement, thereby undermining its unity and credibility. The FBI, for example, received letters from R. W. Puryear and NAACP members who criticized Hayling for militant statements he made at meetings. Other anonymous sources within the NAACP also served as sources of information for the FBI on developments and strategies within the movement. The FBI also jeopardized the civil rights movement by repeatedly revealing to local law enforcement officials the movement's plans. Since the sheriff's department and the city police department were opposed to the movement, they used this information to impede the efforts of the SCLC. Moreover, since Holstead "Hoss" Manucy, a militant leader, chatted daily with Sheriff Davis, he often had access to this information and used it to threathen and harass demonstrators. The Reverend Vivian later observed that most members of the FBI were southerners who hoped the SCLC would lose. "They wanted to maintain the status quo," he declared. Although no evidence exists to suggest that the FBI deliberately sought to undermine the civil rights movement in St. Augustine, the conclusion is inescapable that the FBI aided the forces of resistance.[20]

The FBI was not the only federal agency monitoring events in St. Augustine; the White House also had Lee White's office follow the situation in St. Augustine closely, but White and the President were, at this time, unwilling to intervene directly. The White House's position reflected the political environment in 1964. Johnson probably thought forceful intervention by the federal government would jeopardize passage of the 1964 civil rights bill. More importantly, such action by the federal government would alienate

Johnson's southern supporters and, perhaps, create a serious threat to his presidential campaign in 1964. In addition, Johnson believed restraints should be imposed by the federal courts, not the government.

With the federal government reluctant to intervene, King's aides initiated discussions with city leaders in an effort to reach a compromise. Mayor Shelley met with Andrew Young and Harry Boyte, who presented the organization's demands. They included: desegregation of all hotels and restaurants in thirty days; establishment of a biracial committee with two-thirds of the black members to be named by SCLC; dropping all charges against demonstrators; acceptance by the city of Negro job applications; and employment of five black firemen, four policemen, and three office workers within ninety days. Shelley refused to consider the demands, and, according to the Mayor, Young and Boyte "made it obvious that they were going to continue to harass the city."[21]

Although Shelley rejected SCLC's demands, he was anxious to remove the organization from the city and stop the demonstrations. On June 1 the city commission held a special meeting to consider statements by Sheriff Davis and Chief Stuart that they could no longer prevent rioting between marchers and segregationists and destruction of property in the downtown area. Without discussion, Shelley and his fellow commissioners unanimously approved an ordinance making it unlawful for any minor under the age of eighteen to appear on city streets or in a public place between 9:00 P.M. and 5:00 A.M. They also forbade anyone from parking in the downtown area during the same hours. Since the majority of marchers were under eighteen (as were many segregationists), the commission's action effectively stymied the evening demonstrations. SCLC immediately challenged the ordinance in court. Eight days later, on June 9, Federal Judge Bryan Simpson declared the city ordinance in violation of the demonstrators' First Amendment rights of speech, assembly, and petition.[22]

Angered at Simpson's ruling and at the press reporting of events in the community, city leaders moved noticeably into the background, refusing to negotiate with SCLC leaders as they prepared to launch a second wave of demonstrations. Viewing King and his SCLC aides as "Communists" and "professional agitators," commission members led by Dr. Shelley repeatedly denounced the activities of SCLC in Cold War terms. White residents also contended that newsmen and photographers consistently portrayed the city in an unfavorable light despite improvements in black-white relations. In a radio news broadcast, one citizen characterized SCLC workers as a "highly paid group that is followed around the 'trouble spots' they select by a corps of newsmen and photographers . . . experts themselves . . . in civil rights demonstration strategy. Police . . . learn what's happening . . . from this corps of newsmen." When Harry Boyte asked Herbert Wolfe to use his influence to persuade city leaders to remove racial barriers before the violence became worse, Wolfe told Boyte he saw nothing wrong with the status of blacks in St. Augustine and refused to intervene.[23]

With no initiatives or statements emerging from city hall, reporters turned increasingly to police and segregationists for an expression of local attitudes. By their decision not to meet with SCLC leaders and not to discuss developments with the press, city leaders, especially Mayor Shelley, permitted St. Augustine to be presented to the nation as a reactionary, militantly segregationist community when, in fact, it was no different from many other southern cities that resisted racial changes portended by the *Brown* decision and the sit-ins. It was unusual, however, in the dogmatic, often doctrinaire stance taken by civic leaders and in the influential role played by the Birch Society.

As city leaders withdrew from the racial crisis, segregationists stepped forward quickly as the new representatives of the community. During this period Holstead R. "Hoss" Manucy emerged as the leading spokesman for the militant faction. Manucy headed the two-year-old Ancient City Hunting Club, a Klan-like organization, which he claimed had 1,486 members. "We're better organized than the niggers are, and the niggers know it." Manucy told reporters. "That's the only way we can win. Us white people have got to stick together." He insisted, however, that he and his organization had no connection with the Klan. "Now I'm definitely not knocking the Klan," he declared. "It's a wonderful organization." But "who ever heard of a Catholic being a Klansman anyhow?" Nevertheless, the

FBI considered Manucy a Klansman and their reports referred to him as the Exalted Cyclops of the Klan in St. Augustine.[24]

Manucy resided six miles north of St. Augustine in a dilapidated house with his wife, fourteen children, a yard full of dogs, a few farm animals, and little else. Few people in the community knew Manucy prior to 1964. One civic leader called him "a low life" who was not "very responsible." Indeed, he often appeared as a caricature of the southern redneck, wearing a large, black cowboy hat and blue jeans. Short and considerably overweight, Manucy looked especially uncomfortable with stomach hanging over his belt buckle. He carried a loaded pistol which he kept on the front seat of his car.[25] His support of the Klan reflected an attitude that was popular among many lower-class whites in St. Augustine, including a number of Minorcans. While economic competition had not been a source of friction between races, poor whites were anxious to keep blacks in their place, thereby providing themselves and their families with some status in this historic community.[26]

Working closely with Stoner and Lynch and receiving considerable assistance from Klan members in Northeast Florida, Georgia, South Carolina, and Alabama, Manucy and his allies were well organized, utilizing two-way radios to mobilize supporters at short notice. "We've got a better communications system among ourselves than the police," Manucy told reporters.[27] Because St. Augustine had become a target city for SCLC, Klansmen turned out in full force to strangle the movement. Manucy appeared at all KKK rallies in the area where he denounced the efforts of King and his allies. Not a very effective speaker, however, Manucy played second fiddle to Lynch, Stoner, and other Klan leaders.[28]

The white militants also received considerable cooperation from Sheriff Davis' office. Davis and Manucy were close friends, having known each other since Manucy's high school days when he played football under Davis. Moreover, as noted earlier, at least four of Davis' deputies were active in the Klan. Manucy and Stoner had daily access to the sheriff's office and were frequently seen conversing with Davis. During civil rights demonstrations in late May and early June, Manucy had also been observed by the FBI riding with deputies of the sheriff's office. Davis denied appointing Manucy as a special deputy, although he admitted that he had added eighty special deputies to his staff and some may have been Klan members. Deputy Sheriff Guy Rexrood told FBI officials, however, that he had seen Klansmen at the sheriff's office, and he seemed sure that several were serving as special deputies, including Manucy. The FBI in Jacksonville informed J. Edgar Hoover that several regular deputies and special deputies were "known members of [the] St. Augustine Klavern."[29]

Because of the close association between Manucy's men and the sheriff's office, the militants were often unimpeded in their efforts to intimidate civil rights workers. Following the voluntary withdrawal of civic officials from leadership positions on the civil rights issue, Klansmen conducted numerous raids against black activists. Shots were fired frequently at blacks in their homes, and militants followed civil rights workers in their cars and fired shotgun blasts at them. Early in the morning of June 8 King's cottage was ransacked and burned.[30]

Concerned about the breakdown in civil authority and the danger to his son's safety, Martin Luther King, Sr., telephoned the Justice Department seeking federal action. Burke Marshall told the Reverend King that events could best be handled by local and state officials, but he agreed to inform Governor Bryant of his concerns. Lee White reached Bryant at the National Governors' Conference in Cleveland and informed him of the destruction of King's cottage and of Judge Simpson's decision. Bryant "evidenced considerable concern" about Simpson's decision but assured White that he would take steps to prevent any further violence.[31]

Bryant had sent Elmer Emrich, his special assistant on law enforcement, to meet with St. Augustine's law enforcement leaders prior to his trip to Cleveland. Emrich informed the Governor on his return that relations in St. Augustine were highly explosive and that even "the more responsible law enforcement officers" thought that without the city ban there would be "violence and bloodshed." Emrich proposed that Bryant send additional members of the highway patrol and sheriff's deputies from neighboring counties to forestall serious rioting.[32]

Before state reinforcements arrived, however, SCLC leaders and over 300 supporters assembled at St. Mary's Church on June 9 in preparation for another evening march. King told the audience, "We are determined this city will not celebrate its quadricentennial as a segregated city. There will be no turning back." With the crowd cheering, he pledged, "We are going through with massive demonstrations, sit-ins, and marches to protest to the nation the racial injustices in this city." The Reverend Andrew Young, echoing King, told the marchers, "We have to see whatever is suffered in this town have [sic] not been suffered in vain. We have to get out there much stronger than before."[33]

Young and the Reverend England, recently returned from Boston, led the marchers down Washington Street toward the plaza. Alerted by Simpson's decision, segregationists waited at the slave market in anticipation of the march. A young white militant turned to a friend and, in a loud voice so that reporters could hear, said: "Just let them sorry niggers come." Another reponded, "Wouldn't you love to see Martin Luther Coon come down that street?"[34]

As the marchers approached the intersection of St. George and King Street, a group of white men emerged from the darkness of the grounds around Trinity Episcopal Church and began pummeling Young and England. Two local policemen, angered at Simpson's ruling, sat in their car within sight of the beatings but refused to come to their aid. A young black boy ran from the crowd of marchers and fell on England who had been taking a fearful beating from a large white man. One officer finally exited from his car and shoved the white man away. Civil rights aides took England back to the black section of town while the remaining marchers regrouped around Young. As the march proceeded past the symbolic slave market, Young was slugged again as were several others in the group. Slowly the marchers withdrew to Washington Street but not before a third group of whites emerged from a side street to add to a few parting blows.[35]

On the next day, prodded by this new outbreak of violence and his investigator's report, Governor Bryant ordered 100 additional state highway partolmen to St. Augustine and placed all law enforcement officers under the command of Major John Jourdan. An additional twenty conservation officers and twenty beverage officials were assigned to police bars and taverns. Bryant also ordered the establishment of an independent communications network to avoid the need to use the county sheriff's facilities, which were suspected of being monitored by segregationists.[36]

That same day cloture was achieved on the civil rights

bill in the Senate, insuring SCLC of its principal goal. Rather than withdrawing from St. Augustine, however, SCLC leaders chose to adhere to the agenda established by Gibson and Walker and remain in the community until their work had been completed. Thus, while the desire to insure passage of the civil rights bill had been mainly responsible for SCLC's intervention in St. Augustine, it did not determine the organization's timetable once events began to unfold in the city.

The crisis continued to worsen during the middle of June with King, local militants, the Governor's office, and the White House all involved. Representatives of the Florida Highway Patrol, St. Johns County Sheriff's Office, St. Augustine Police Department, and the Governor's office met with Andrew Young, who criticized the handling of demonstrators by police on the ninth. The Highway Patrol and local police promised Young that adequate protection would be provided for marchers in the future if SCLC would notify them of the time and route of the march in advance. Young agreed to provide this information as long as violence was prevented.[37]

King, who had not participated in any of the previous demonstrations, announced that he would personally take part in a sit-in at Monson's Motor Lodge on June 11. King and his aides sought to increase the pressure on the city by forcing his arrest. SCLC was aware that Bryant's office and the White House were closely following events in the city and that his arrest might be sufficient to insure their direct intervention and the establishment of a biracial commission. Sit-ins had been conducted regularly by SCLC and local leaders against the Monson restaurant, which was managed by James Brock. His motel became the target because Brock was prominent in the motel and hotel business, serving as president of the state association and past president of the St. Johns County association, and because a large group of reporters stayed at the Monson. Publicity would thus be easy to arrange.

At 12:22 P.M. King arrived with seven aides at Monson's for lunch. The press had been forewarned by SCLC of what was to occur, and King and his party were "surrounded by a horde of cameramen." Brock, a short, mustachioed man, had also been notified of King's arrival. He stood on the red welcome mat in front of the restaurant waiting for King's party. As the crowd of demonstrators and reporters descended upon him with King in the center, Brock announced that this was private property. He then turned toward King and asked, "What is your name?" "Martin King," came the response. Brock introduced himself and the two tried unsuccessfully to talk privately but microphones were jabbed between them. With cameras flashing and clicking, King told Brock, "You're going to have to integrate." Brock, a rather mild-mannered, religious man who suddenly found himself thrust into the middle of the civil rights controversy, said he would if you have a "federal court order or if a group of St. Augustine businessmen prevail upon me." Then, as if hoping that King would suddenly go away, Brock asked, "Won't you leave?" King, wearing a black button with a white "Equal" on his lapel, had no intention of leaving. "He was there to be arrested," reported Gene Miller of the *Miami Herald*.[38] In this carnivallike atmosphere King began to sermonize, "We are standing here in a nonviolent manner." He was interrupted by a white man who hollered to Brock, "Are you open or not?" "Yes," Brock replied. With that the man shoved the Reverend Ralph Abernathy forward knocking him into King. The white man turned to King and called him a "black bastard."[39]

Reporters and television cameramen meanwhile had created a sideshow of their own as they circled to get the most audible comments or take the best picture. Shouts of "Duck your head," "Out of the way," and "Get that flashgun down, you're blocking the [television camera] lens" were heard as reporters jockeyed for position.[40]

Within a few minutes Police Chief Virgil Stuart arrived and asked Brock if he was "lookin' for us?" Breathing a sigh of relief, Brock told Stuart that he had asked King and his aides to leave three times and that they were trespassing on his property. Stuart told the group: "You're under arrest. Follow me."[41]

With King's arrest, SCLC accelerated pressure on the federal government to intervene in St. Augustine. Aides to Dr. King argued that community leaders were not responding to sit-ins or the marches and that only action by the federal government could force them to sit down and negotiate. SCLC's interest in directly negotiating a solution with local leaders was somewhat suspect, however. Beyond Andrew Young's initial discussion with Mayor Shelley, no SCLC leader including Dr. King had attempted to contact city officials again. Perhaps they had taken the advice of local black leaders who, on the basis of their own experiences, suggested such efforts would be fruitless. More likely, however, SCLC believed its bargaining position would be enhanced considerably if the federal or state government entered on its behalf.

The day after King and Abernathy's arrest, Harry Boyte telephoned federal officials about recent developments and also about King's criticism of the federal government for failing to protect the rights of the demonstrators. Boyte pointed out that despite the presence of 175 police officers during the marches of June 11, whites had still managed to infiltrate police lines and assault marchers. Expressing concern for King's safety while in jail, Boyte claimed that "the Klan element has complete free run of the jail," and he portrayed Chief Stuart as being "sympathetic to the segregationists and . . . [unlikely] to provide protection." Boyte urged that greater efforts be made by Governor Bryant and the federal government to avert further violence. Wyatt Tee Walker also telephoned White House official Douglas Cater, to say that in light of President Johnson's promises to St. Augustine civil rights leaders when he visited the city a year earlier, it seemed appropriate for the President to send a federal mediation team.[42]

At a meeting between Cater, White, and Johnson, it was decided that the federal government would refrain from intervening in St. Augustine until the civil rights bill became law. At Johnson's suggestion White returned Walker's telephone call two days later, indicating that the Administration would continue to monitor events and that he considered the situation "hopeful" in light of the recent empaneling of a grand jury to examine civil rights developments. White also told Walker that "the less the Federal Government [was] involved in the situation, the more likely there was to be fruitful discussions and negotiations."[43]

In an effort to avoid federal intervention, state and local leaders took steps to ease the crisis. After returning early from the National Governors' Conference in Cleveland, Governor Bryant talked to President Johnson's advisers on June 12 and expressed his belief that law and order could be maintained in St. Augustine without federal troops. He informed them that he planned to send an additional fifty state troopers to the community on the thirteenth and promised to do anything necessary to preserve peace. On June 11,

States Attorney Dan Warren, with the support of Governor Bryant, arranged with Judge Howell Melton to empanel a grand jury to seek to resolve the racial turmoil in St. Augustine. The following day the grand jury urged that all citizens avoid demonstrations and asked for "a good faith effort to examine ways and means to open up meaningful lines of communication between the two races."[44]

Following the recommendation of the grand jury, Herbert Wolfe, president of the largest bank in St. Augustine, and four executives with the Fairchild Stratos Corporation met privately with Mayor Shelley at the Monson Motor Lodge on June 12. Wolfe and the others tried to persuade Shelley to support the establishment of a biracial committee which they felt would lead to the withdrawal of SCLC. But Shelley was adamantly opposed to a biracial commission, regarding it as a sign of surrender. Wolfe and the Fairchild executives decided not to appeal to the public because Shelley's position was widely endorsed in the community. Support for Shelley's stance also came from U.S. Senator George Smathers who wired King on June 13 denouncing him and "other outside professional agitators who frequently violate local, county, and state laws, create tensions, divisions, and problems that not only stop the progress that is being made, but turn the clock back with antagonism, divisions, and recriminations." He called on King to leave the state so that elected officials can "solve their own problems."[45]

The county commission quickly followed with its own endorsement of Shelley's position, deciding to examine the law to "see if there are any grounds on which St. Johns County could file a slander suit against Martin Luther King and the Southern Christian Leadership Conference." The county also contacted Senators George Smathers and Spessard Holland and Representative John Mathews, and asked if they would get the FBI to investigate conditions in St. Augustine. Angered by what they characterized as an unjustified civil rights invasion, unfavorable publicity, Simpson's judicial ruling, and a sudden decline in the tourist economy, county commissioners, like their city counterparts, refused to consider negotiating with SCLC leaders. The alienation of the county leadership was reflected in a letter by County Attorney Donald Buck, who suggested that a brass band with someone selling hot dogs and balloons "lead the civil rights parade each night."[46]

Amidst these conditions and in keeping with Walker's

battle plan, King called for more help. Appeals went out to a number of southern communities where SCLC had strong organizations. "We need people as quickly as possible," King told them. Utilizing a tactic developed by Hosea Williams in Savannah, SCLC decided to fill the jails, forcing the police department and the city and county judicial process to a standstill. In his plea for assistance, King emphasized this point, declaring, "I want you to join me, if necessary, in St. Johns County Jail." Hosea Williams, too, called for a renewed commitment from civil rights workers if they hoped to bring a halt to segregation in this community. "We must be willing to go to jail, we must be willing to bleed, we must be willing to die that America be free."[47]

The evening of the twelfth started clamly with civil rights marchers even pausing for a ten-minute prayer session at the slave market, but at 10:00 P.M., an unusual demonstration began. Segregationists had received a parade permit from the city to march through the black community that evening. They gathered at the slave makret, where J. B. Stoner spearheaded the march. Stoner told a crowd of 300, "Tonight we're going to find out whether white people have any rights. The coons have been parading around St. Augustine for a long time." He warmed up his audience by calling King a "longtime associate of Communists" and suggesting that King and his supporters wanted to associate with white people "because they're tired of associating with filthy, sorry niggers." The crowd applauded enthusiastically, responding "That's right," "Great," and "Tell 'em about the Jew!" Under a heavily armed police guard, the segregationists headed toward Washington Street and "niggertown."[48]

Young had promised state police officials that he would try to keep as many people "off the streets as possible," but as the group lumbered through the black community, a sizable number of local residents greeted them from the sidewalks, singing, "I love everybody, I love everybody, I love everybody in my heart." The reception had been planned by Williams, and Young agreed to support it if violence was avoided. The response by black residents caught the segregationists completely off guard but not reporters who captured the significance of the reception. Angered at being upstaged, whites tried to drown them out by singing: "She'll be comin' 'round the mountain when she comes."[49]

As the weary and deflated marchers approached Big Daddy's Blue Goose bar, several patrons wandered to the edge of the street, clapping and hollering "welcome." One man commented: "They don't need no police guard to come down here. But when we go in there . . . we're glad to have 'em." Some of the underlying anger in the black community emerged, however, when the same man continued, "I wonder how they would feel inside if we was to throw bricks and all at them." Another woman muttered, "I'd like to take a machine gun an' kill them all."[50] The segregationists concluded their march at the slave market where Stoner told them to be back the following evening at 7:00 P.M. and to bring their friends. For the next two nights the whites paraded in even larger numbers through the town, but on each occasion violence was avoided.

Despite the restraint of black residents, state police realized that they were sitting on a powder keg. Large numbers of out-of-county and out-of-state vehicles entered the city each day and the quantity of arms had increased alarmingly. State patrolmen suspected that the sheriff's deputies were returning the weapons to segregationists as quickly as they were seizing them.[51]

Reflecting the concerns of his state patrolmen, Bryant announced on June 15 that he was creating a Special Police Force to maintain peace and order in St. Augustine. The unit comprised the Florida Highway Patrol, State Board of Conservation, State Beverage Department, Florida Sheriff's Bureau, the Game and Fresh Water Fish Commission, and investigators of the governor and attorney general's offices and would report daily to the governor.[52]

Throughout this period St. Augustine was a city marked by contrasts. By day St. Augustine remained a picture of tranquility with old men playing checkers on the plaza and tourists wandering through the Castillo de San Marcos and the Flagler Hotel. From all indications this was a pleasant community surrounded by the ocean and by history. Summer was at hand and the days were exceedingly warm, but the nights usually remained balmy with a pleasant breeze coming off the ocean. SCLC conducted sit-ins on a daily basis, but they were relatively isolated and unobstrusive, interfering hardly at all with the city's daytime activities.

At night the city took on another personality as it became a seething, often violence-torn environment. The checker game in the park was replaced by a much more deadly game of "get the nigger." The peace and tranquility of St. Augustine gave way to racial epithets and hatred.[53]

A temporary lull in the crisis occurred on June 15 and 16 when several civil rights leaders left the community. King was released from jail on June 14 to receive an honorary Doctor of Laws degree at the Yale University commencement ceremonies, an occasion he used to draw attention to the harsh conditions SCLC had encountered in St. Augustine. Meanwhile, Dr. Hayling, Henry Twine, and Roscoe Halyard traveled to Washington, D.C., to participate in a march on behalf of the civil rights bill coordinated by the AFL-CIO. Hayling and his two companions took the opportunity to meet with Burke Marshall, apparently at the request of Attorney General Robert Kennedy, to discuss the deteriorating race relations in St. Augustine. They also conferred with George Sinclair, special adviser to President Johnson. Both federal officials expressed concern over recent developments but still seemed to believe that the grand jury investigation held promise for a peaceful solution.[54]

On June 16, according to Williams, SCLC began modifying its tactics to draw added attention to the worsening racial environment in St. Augustine and thereby generate additional outside pressure on local leaders. As part of this new strategy, it appears that SCLC conducted demonstrations which were intended to provoke segregationists to violence, thereby insuring greater press coverage. Williams remarked later that SCLC was convinced that reporters would tire of the daily demonstrations unless the routine was changed. Since media attention was essential to SCLC's local and national aims, the organization changed its tactics not only to accomplish its goals but also to retain press interest. Helping to shape this new strategy was the decision to abandon the tactic of filling the jails when additional jail space in nearby counties was made available to the city, thus depriving SCLC of its contention that conditions in the jails were inhumane.[55]

This new phase in SCLC's offensive began that evening when Jackie Robinson, former infielder for the Brooklyn Dodgers and the first black athlete to break the color barrier in professional baseball, arrived in St. Augustine to meet with local leaders and address

civil rights supporters. Designed to strengthen the commitment of local residents to the movement, Robinson's presence insured the largest crowd yet for an evening meeting and also provided important
national media coverage. Over 600 people, including representatives
from the major television networks and newspaper dailies, gathered
at St. Paul's A.M.E. Church to hear Robinson emphasize the importance of the work being done in St. Augustine and encourage civil
rights workers to maintain the struggle. He told his audience that the
entire nation was following events in the community.[56]

The new tactics included wade-ins at the previously segregated St. Augustine beach. Hayling had integrated the beach on
one occasion in 1963 with a small group but had not returned since
then. Reporters and cameramen were notified in advance and a large
group arrived to film the confrontation on June 17. The demonstration was conducted peacefully although there was a great deal of name
calling and police were barely able to keep segregationists away from
the civil rights group.[57]

That evening SCLC unveiled its new plans for the
marches. Andrew Young told reporters that a new route would be
taken and it would go through upper-class white residential areas.
"Many people have become immune from our struggle," he declared,
"simply by staying away from downtown. We decided we must take
our struggle past their doors."[58] Police had experienced difficulty in
protecting marchers along the old route that circled past the plaza
and returned to Central Avenue. The new route was unmistakably
more dangerous to the unstable peace. The old route and the potential violence had been confined to the public areas downtown which
were open and lighted. SCLC's new route, however, proceeded through
many "narrow streets bordered by shrubs and wooded areas without
sufficient lighting." Adding to the problems of the physical layout of
the route were reports by police that "the demonstrators have pur-
posely attempted to mislead the law enforcement officers as to their
projected routes and times of marches."[59]

The most dramatic of the new tactics employed by SCLC
occurred the following day, June 18, when several demonstrators
jumped into the pool at Monson's Motor Lodge. Hosea Williams and
SCLC aides planned the swin-in and notified reporters. The demonstration began with the arrival of an integrated group at the door-

way of Monson's restaurant at 12:39 P.M. Led by several rabbis who had come to St. Augustine at the invitation of King, they were greeted by Brock, who announced that his business was segregated and they would not be permitted in. The constant demonstrations at the motel were beginning to take their toll on Brock. Normally a mild-mannered, gregarious person, Brock appeared nervous and irritable as he greeted the integrated group. Demonstrations had been conducted almost daily at the motel for the past month and not only was Brock subjected to pressure from the civil rights forces, he was also being encouraged strongly by the white community and the segregationists not to surrender. During the previous week Brock had received several threats against his life and his business. In addition, his mother-in-law had suffered a heart attack following one demonstration at the motel.[60]

The confrontation between Brock and the rabbi-led group deteriorated quickly. The rabbis knelt to pray for Brock when he refused to admit them. As the integrationist group started praying, Brock, a deacon and superintendent of the Sunday School at the Baptist Church, suddenly lost control of himself, grabbing the rabbis and shoving them off his property.[61]

At 12:47, eight minutes after the rabbis had approached Monson's, five blacks leaped from a car that had just pulled up and jumped into Brock's swimming pool with two white men who were registered at the motel. Brock immediately left the rabbi-led group and told the two whites in the pool "You're not putting these people in my pool." These are our guests," came the reply. "We are registered here, and want these people to swim with us." Brock ran to his office and returned with a two-gallon container which he announced was acid as he poured it into the pool. During the demonstration, King, Abernathy, and their aides stood across the street on the sea wall. King was heard to say, "We are going to put Monson out of business."[62]

A group of whites had now gathered around the pool, where St. Augustine city police officer James Hewitt ordered the swimmers out of the pool, announcing that they were under arrest. Another city policeman, this one off duty, pulled off his shoes and jumped into the pool where he began pummeling one of the white swimmers. A crowd of nearly one hundred gathered around the pool and yelled at police, "Arrest them! Get the dogs!" As cameramen positioned themselves for the best shot, the swimmers slowly began coming out of the pool.[63] State police, who had arrived shortly after the demonstrations began, moved to assist with the arrest. Lt. Henry Randall was in the process of escorting one white swimmer away when auxillary Deputy Sheriff Ray Robbins came running up, grabbed the arrested man's arm, and began punching and kicking him. Despite the efforts of Randall, Robbins continued to beat the man until he was placed in the safety of a state police car.[64]

The new tactics employed by SCLC had a greater impact than even they perhaps envisioned. The demonstration at the Monson pool appeared on the evening national television news and on the front page of most of the nation's leading newspapers. It was also pictured in the foreign press, including the front page of *Izvestia.* King seized upon these developments to wire Attorney General Robert Kennedy, complaining about the "raw brutality" of local police and urging the use of federal troops.[65]

Significantly, SCLC had initiated its new tactics at the same time it appeared that peace was in the offering. State Senator Verle Pope informed the press on June 16 that he and State Attorney Dan Warren hoped to organize a biracial committee composed of local businessmen and black leaders in conjunction with the grand jury investigation. Believing that the only obstacle to a truce rested upon the establishment of a biracial committee by the city commission, Pope and Warren persuaded Wolfe to approach Shelley on this matter once again. Warren kept SCLC informed about these developments.[66] On the same day City Manager Barrier told reporters that St. Augustine's merchants would meet the following day and announce their intention of obeying the law and complying with the civil rights bill once it was enacted. According to Barrier, merchants planned to stand on their legal rights to deny service to anyone until the bill was passed.[67]

On the afternoon of June 17, 1964, St. Augustine merchants accompanied by State Senator Verle Pope promised to abide by all present and future laws. With the grand jury recommendations expected to be made public shortly, peace seemed genuinely at hand when SCLC suddenly conducted eight separate demonstrations the following day, including one in which six individuals marched loudly past the grand jury meeting room.[68]

Why had the peace initiative collapsed? Although the details are sketchy, it appears that Wolfe could not get Shelley to agree to a biracial committee unless SCLC would leave the community for a period of thirty days. In addition, the grand jury subsequently recommended that SCLC and other disruptive forces remove themselves from St. Augustine for one month after which a biracial committee, composed of five whites and five blacks, would be established. Referring to past "racial harmony" in the community, the presentment pointed to the absence of segregation in several areas of society and suggested that peace could be restored with the removal of outsiders. The report also contended that the racial situation in St. Augustine was "no greater a problem than that of many other communities throughout the entire nation," and it certainly was not as great as "shown to the nation by sensational news reporting." Continuing on in a subjective vein, the presentment alleged that "in this economic setting, with a solid background of harmonious race relations, with a past history of non-discrimination in governmental affairs, and of the more recent progress toward the integration of privately owned facilities, St. Augustine has been libeled as 'the most segregated City [sic] in America.' " The grand jury suggested that St. Augustine was "merely a symbol for the Negro civil rights movement."[69]

Had SCLC deliberately sabotaged the momentum for peace? SCLC had learned of the proposed thirty-day cooling off period on June 12 and found it unacceptable. King and Hayling declared their opposition to the proposal the following day because it asked "the Negro community to give all and the white community to give nothing." Hayling complained that the grand jury report was "based on the false assumption that St. Augustine had genuinely peaceful race relations until the Southern Christian Leadership Conference 'picked' it as a symbol before the world." He and King added that "a more honest assessment of the situation would reveal that St. Augustine has never had peaceful race relations: it may have had a negative peace which was the absence of tension, but certainly not a positive peace which is the presence of justice." King called the request to leave town and stop the demonstrations "impractical" and "immoral." Expressing their desire to end further demonstrations "if we could see a good faith move to solve Saint Augustine's racial problems," King and Hayling proposed that the grand jury appoint the biracial commission immediately and that as soon as it convened all demonstrations would be halted for a week.[70]

SCLC also appeared reluctant to accept a peace proposal at this time because the civil rights bill was being debated on the floor of the Senate, and passage, while assured, still necessitated SCLC's active involvement in King's view to keep senators and the nation alert to the problems encountered by blacks in a segregated community. Rather than simply rejecting the grand jury proposal, SCLC opted to show its dissatisfaction by conducting numerous demonstrations the day the grand jury made public its recommendations. This served two purposes: it prevented the report from getting very much publicity and thus kept the nation unaware that the white community was interested in settling the crisis; and it further publicized St. Augustine's racial problems.

Aware of King's dissatifaction with their recommendations, the grand jury criticized SCLC's demonstrations, which they felt were designed to deter them: "At the very hour we were to issue our presentment, Dr. King fostered a demonstration which could only have been planned to divert attention of the public away from our good faith effort to reach accord in this matter." Jury Foreman Aubrey Davis declared that "this Grand Jury will not be intimidated. We will not negotiate. We will not alter our presentment." Senator Verle Pope threw his hands up in frustration over the day's developments, saying, "Well, we are through. We can't understand why they hit us like this when we were working sincerely on this thing. The jury was working on a really worthwhile report. Now it's all gone." The apparent conciliatory attitude of white leaders collapsed with the day's demonstrations.[71]

Although SCLC had undermined the peace initiative, there were extenuating circumstances. In fairness to King it should be observed that local black activists had much more to lose by a thirty-day cooling off period and the withdrawal of SCLC than did the white community. The only leverage exercised by local blacks was through the threat of continued demonstrations and the national publicity which resulted from these activities, especially when King and other prominent outsiders participated.

Unwilling to accept the grand jury proposal, SCLC opted to return to the barricades and accelerate its protests. King wired several religious supporters in the North urging them to join him "in a Christian Witness in the jail" and to "point up to all the world that laws which do not respect the dignity of man are not laws at all." Although SCLC ignored the grand jury recommendation, the organization was still prepared to negotiate, and the renewed demonstrations were designed to pressure the city into accepting a biracial committee.[72]

On the evening of June 18 SCLC decided not to inform state police of the route of the march as they proceeded through the white residential areas. Williams led the group of two hundred to Monson's, where they sang, "We are not afraid." The anger of many local whites at SCLC for the renewal of the demonstrations showed itself when Sheriff Davis intercepted the marchers. Williams asked to speak privately to Davis but he refused saying, "You came out here to march, so march." When Williams refused to continue the march, Davis and his deputies jerked him from the line, clubbed him, and threw him in a car.[73] The following day SCLC conducted several sit-ins downtown and a wade-in at the beach. Violence was narrowly averted on each occasion.

Concerned about the efforts of militants to increase their numbers and escalate the violence, state police contacted several civil rights leaders on the evening of the nineteenth to learn about their route "but no accurate information could be obtained." Black leaders contended that they would march but were waiting on instructions from Dr. King. Police anxiously sought directions of the route because segregationists had been advertising that they would hold a mass rally at the slave market. But SCLC leaders seemed determined to force a confrontation with the militants that evening and refused to inform police.[74]

Approximately one thousand whites gathered in and around the plaza at 8:30 P.M. to hear J. B. Stoner and Don Cochran and Al Massey of the Jacksonville Ku Klux Klan. The meeting was alleged to be a rally of the United Florida KKK. Stoner presented his usual diatribe, arguing that "niggers want to integrate because they want our white women" and denouncing the "Communist-controlled Federal government." In an obvious attempt to copy the efforts of

SCLC, Stoner also announced that the *Thunderbolt*, a National States Rights Party newspaper, would urge white citizens to vacation in St. Augustine and participate in the white countermarches. A˙ march through the black community was planned for the next evening in which, Stoner claimed, Sheriff Davis would participate as a private citizen.[75] At 9:55 P.M., two hundred marchers paraded down Bay Street to the slave market. Despite the best efforts of Stoner, police were able to keep the two groups apart although bricks, rocks, and assorted paraphernalia filled the air. A flanking effort by one hundred whites resulted in several minor beatings, but Davis was able eventually to persuade them to turn back.[76]

After the last of the demonstrations had broken up, Major John Jourdan of the Florida State Patrol informed Governor Bryant's office that he did not believe his officers could prevent more serious violence from occurring. Jourdan's fears were borne out when a near deadly encounter took place at St. Augustine beach the following afternoon. The civil rights group encountered a substantial number of segregationists. In the ensuing confrontation several demonstrators were nearly drowned by the militants.[77]

On the morning of June 20, Mayor Shelley, Senator Pope, and other local officials, alarmed at the escalating violence, met and agreed to ask Governor Bryant to prohibit further nighttime marches. After discussing developments with advisers and State Patrol officers, Governor Bryant told Jourdan that he was banning all future marches and demonstrations in the St. Johns County and the St. Augustine area. Invoking powers granted him in times of emergency by the legislature, Bryant told the press that he thought "every opportunity" had been given for the civil rights activists to express their views" in a reasonable, lawful, and peaceful fashion." Reflecting the views of Jourdan, Bryant said that both groups—civil rights activists and segregationists—have shown a "certain lawlessness and utter disregard for the laws of Florida."[78]

Bryant was serving his final year as governor when the St. Augustine racial crisis exploded. He had been a businessman's governor who sought to make the state more attractive to northern investment through better highways, an improved school system, and construction of the Florida Barge Canal. Though an expressed segregationist, Bryant had permitted schools in the state to integrate quietly. He had not matched the leadership of his predecessor LeRoy Collins, but he governed the state efficiently if not inspirationally.[79]

The governor viewed himself as a conservative constitutionalist pledging to "maintain segregation by every honorable and Constitutional means." Although he favored utilizing every legal channel available, Bryant opposed violence and extralegal means to retain racial barriers. Unfortunately, his commitment to the law was not always clearly defined. During 1963 and 1964 Bryant led a vigorous campaign against the civil rights bill.[80] The night before he issued his proclamation halting the evening demonstrations, Bryant had spoken to the Florida Police Chief's Association, where he denounced the actions by civil rights activists and declared that: "We are living in a time when intellectuals, ministers, even national leaders encourage, even participate in what they choose to call civil disobedience." Bryant characterized this as "fancy semantics" amounting to "a crass violation of law, clothed in other language." Significantly, Bryant did not condemn the segregationists for their actions. By his actions and statements he inadvertently led the more extremist groups in St. Augustine to believe he shared his views.[81]

In announcing his curfew on night marches, Bryant informed reporters that his chief concern was to insure the maintenance of law and order. He also expressed his hope that "the Federal District Court [specifically Judge Bryan Simpson] neither has nor will enter orders that will prohibit me from discharging my duty." Simpson had ruled consistently against efforts to impede the First Amendment rights of SCLC in May and June.[82]

During the following evening, Major Jourdan notified a large crowd of segregationists gathered at the slave market of the governor's proclamation and, although disgruntled, they disbanded on learning that it applied to the civil rights demonstrations as well. The state police intercepted the civil rights marchers minutes later on Cordova Street. They too agreed to return home.[83]

On June 20 Judge Simpson stayed the governor's proclamation, ordering Bryant to show cause why he should not be held in contempt. That same day word was received that Congress had approved the civil rights bill. King was ecstatic about both developments, calling the latter a "lasting tribute to the memory of John F. Kennedy" and adding that it "might help cool things off in St. Augustine." Segregationists bitterly denounced the decisions by Simpson and Congress.[84]

Angered and frustrated by news concerning the civil rights bill and Simpson's order, segregationists now resolved to give King a good physical thrashing in St. Augustine and to discourage whites from accepting the proposed civil rights law. On the evening of June 21, militants apparently broke the windows in Senator Pope's insurance office for his efforts to end the crisis by establishing a biracial committee. Three days later Connie Lynch told a large crowd that violence appeared necessary to defend the Constitution from recent developments and warned that all "Jews and nigger lovers had better make tracks." He noted that there were rumors about three civil rights workers missing in Mississippi, which brought loud laughter and cheering from the crowd.[85]

The segregationists became further emboldened by the statements of Governor Bryant and Attorney General James Kynes and by the actions of local police. Bryant and Kynes had both criticized Congress's enactment of the civil rights bill. Kynes called it highly discriminatory because it gave "one particular class of citizens the privilege of bypassing the normal channels of justice, while insisting on the strict compliance of the law by all others."[86]

During a wade-in on June 25, the Reverend Elizabeth Miller of the American Baptist Convention, a largely white organization, described the increasing violence by Klan supporters against civil rights demonstrators. As the civil rights group arrived at the city beach, a large crowd, including several women, greeted them at the entrance. Miller asked a local black activist what the women were doing there. He responded that, "Those are the cheerleaders, you'll hear from them." As the group approached the ocean, the white women started screaming obscene remarks and taunts, urging their men "to beat the Hell out of them." The militants stood in a horseshoe pattern to block access to the ocean as the demonstrators approached. The leader of the SCLC group was immediately assaulted by a Klansman, and within seconds militants attacked others in the group, including the Reverend Miller, who had her nose broken and was nearly drowned.[87]

During this and other demonstrations police and sheriff's deputies often refused to intervene. When the Reverend Miller, for example, was assaulted, Davis' men did not arrest her attacker nor did they question her about the assault.[88] Both Davis and Stuart's men as well as the State Patrol were beginning to suffer from battle fatigue. The strain on the men began to tell as police, already sympathetic with the views of local militants, took an increasingly hostile stand against civil rights forces. A sheriff's deputy, not in uniform, was arrested by state police while heading toward a civil rights march with a crowbar. Although the man later claimed to have seized the weapon from a segregationist, he did not inform the state police that he was a deputy sheriff or how he obtained the weapon when he was arrested.[89]

State police found themselves increasingly subject to abuse not only from segregationists but also from respected members of the community for trying to keep the peace. During the pool demonstration at Monson's on June 18, Lieutenant Randall had been berated by City Attorney Robert Andreu and County Attorney Frank Howatt for not being more firm with the demonstrators. When Randall attempted to explain state patrol's policies, Andreu, Howatt, and the group with them only became more incensed, accusing him of not protecting the property and safety of white residents. At the beach demonstration on June 25, state police were criticized for using excessive force to restrain a segregationist, and a deputy sheriff and state patrolmen became involved in a shoving match over the incidents. "Those finks," a white woman shouted in disgust, "they didn't beat the niggers at all." State police found their jobs exceedingly demanding since their sympathies also lay with the white community.[90]

The thirty days of nearly constant demonstrations were beginning to tell, too, on SCLC and its out-of-state supporters who were anxious to leave St. Augustine as soon as possible. The organization was also faced with a rapidly depleting treasury and a membership suffering from battle fatigue. In an effort to facilitate its departure as well as to force a settlement, SCLC accelerated its demonstrations and its pressure on the White House and state officials.[91]

Andrew Young asked the Civil Rights Division of the Department of Justice for the assistance of federal troops. Young commented that Manucy and Stoner had been seen repeatedly at the St. Augustine jail and at the beach confrontations, and he suggested that local police and the militants were in collusion. Although Burke Marshall opposed the use of federal troops, he promised to continue to watch events in the city closely and send a negotiating team from the Community Relations Service to St Augustine once the President signed the civil rights bill into law. Young and SCLC doubted that their request for federal troops would be met, but they believed that by maintaining pressure on the federal government, they could force Washington to exert other forms of pressure on St. Augustine.[92]

Without a sufficient police force to restrain them, militants became further emboldened. On the evening of the twenty-fifth, a large white crowd, angered by the police response at the beach demonstrations that day, assembled to hear Lynch and Stoner. As the civil rights marchers walked past the Ponce de Leon toward the slave market, the segregationists engulfed them like a tidal wave. For the first time the police found that they were not immune from attack. One officer was wounded by a zip gun while others were hit by bricks, acid, and firecrackers. The violence ended only because the civil rights marchers ran swiftly and because the whites' desire for vengeance seemed satiated after thirty minutes.[93]

The following day Sheriff Davis, Major Jourdan, and Elmer Emerich, the Governor's personal investigator, informed Bryant and local leaders that they could no longer control events in the city. Bryant immediately sent another eighty state troopers to the city bringing the total to 230, but Jourdan remained unconvinced that they could prevent further violence.[94] The increased size and militancy of the segregationists had made Jourdan pessimistic. During the evening meetings at the slave market in the last week of June, over five hundred militants gathered nightly to hear Lynch, Stoner, and state Klan leaders. Moreover, their rhetoric was being increasingly directed at the FBI and State Patrol officers for allegedly harassing segregationists and protecting civil rights marchers. On the evening of June 27, Stoner accused the "Negro-loving FBI agents and the niggers" of burning "a house in Jacksonville and [blaming] it on the Klan." Despite the efforts of the FBI and the State Patrol, Stoner promised that "we will never eat with niggers, drink with them or swim with them." After Stoner's speech, the crowd attempted to march into the black community but were turned back by police.[95]

The arrest of Mrs. Malcolm Peabody (*seated, left*), mother of Governor Endicott Peabody of Massachusetts, and Mrs. John Burgess (*standing, left*), wife of the Episcopal Bishop of Massachusetts, by Sheriff L. O. Davis (*standing, right*) for attempting to integrate the restaurant at the Ponce de Leon Motor Lodge on March 31, 1964. This event received national publicity and brought the country's attention to the civil rights crusade in the nation's oldest city. From the files of the *St. Augustine Record*.

The Reverend Martin Luther King, Jr., sends pickets to protest segregation in St. Augustine. King and the Southern Christian Leadership Conference relied on the assistance of young children after many adults were arrested by Sheriff L. O. Davis and City Police Chief Virgil Stuart. From the Associated Press Wirephoto Service.

The arrest of the Reverend Martin Luther King, Jr., for trespassing on the property of the Monson Motor Lodge on June 11, 1964. The civil rights campaign in St. Augustine had begun to stagnate, and in an effort to re-kindle support and enthusiasm for the movement, King and his aides staged his arrest at the motel where most of the state and national reporters stayed. The publicity that resulted reinvigorated the movement, as he had hoped, and assisted passage of the civil rights bill through Congress. From the As-sociated Press Wirephoto Service.

Civil rights demonstrators march through downtown and around the Old Slave Market. Most of the demonstrations took place in this area which stood in the heart of the city—a particularly symbolic area for black resi-dents since slaves had once been sold in the old market building which stood on the town common. Photo by Bill Kuenzel, from the *Miami Herald*.

J. B. Stoner, Hoss Manucy, and the Reverend Connie Lynch meet the press in St. Augustine. These three were the chief spokesmen for the white militant position in St. Augustine during the demonstrations of 1964. Stoner and Lynch were closely allied to the Ku Klux Klan and other militant white organizations throughout the country, and they traveled the circuit stirring up hate and violence. Neither man was from St. Augustine. Manucy was from St. Augustine and was a friend of Sheriff L. O. Davis, having served as an auxiliary deputy on his staff. Manucy became a spokesman for the community when other white civic leaders refused to talk to the press. From the Associated Press Wirephoto Service.

White demonstrators march through St. Augustine's predominantly black residential neighborhood. In retaliation for the marches conducted by civil rights groups, white militants decided to stage their own march. Much to their surprise, they were greeted by black residents who sang, "We love everybody." Photo by Bill Kuenzel, from the *Miami Herald*.

St. Augustine police officer Henry Billitz jumps into the pool at the Monson Motor Lodge to arrest an interracial group that was swimming in an area reserved for whites. This photograph captured the creativity of the civil rights protestors and the absurdity of the St. Augustine response to the demonstrators. It was picked up by nearly every news service in the country and appeared on the front pages of most of the nation's newspapers. From the Associated Press Wirephoto Service.

Police assault civil rights demonstrators at St. Augustine Beach. Under the leadership of Hosea Williams, the civil rights forces in St. Augustine often took their protests to areas where they knew violence might result, on the theory that violence captured national attention and went far in furthering the cause of racial reform. Events proved that they were correct. This demonstration also revealed the extent of segregation in the South, where segments of the beach were divided so that the two races would not intermingle. From the Associated Press Wirephoto Service.

Blacks responded to these developments with a new militancy of their own. FBI reports referred to "a vicious mood" among black residents due to beatings by militants and harassment by police. During the segregationist demonstration at the slave market, a large number of Negroes gathered along Wahington Street and several whites were assaulted when they attempted to march into the black community. Shots were also fired by blacks and whites at one another, with two people suffering minor wounds and one home being damaged.[96]

With the increase in demonstrations by SCLC, an angry black community, a more committed group of segregationists, and an alienated white leadership, St. Augustine seemed in danger of losing all semblance of a civilized society when the federal government suddenly intervened. Responding to further appeals from Young and other SCLC leaders and anxious to have racial peace when he signed the civil rights bill into law, President Johnson asked Senator George Smathers to see if he could arrange a settlement. Smathers contacted Herbert Wolfe and Governor Bryant about forming a biracial committee, and Wolfe expressed his willingness to serve on such a committee. He also thought that Frank Harrold, president of the St. Augustine National Bank, would serve, but Wolfe refused to commit himself until he talked to others in the community and they consented to support such a committee. Wolfe contacted Mayor Shelley who arranged a meeting which included other commissioners and city leaders. Shelley immediately expressed his opposition to the plan and the others supported him, arguing that the creation of a biracial committee would be perceived locally and nationally as a victory for King. Wolfe reported the decision to Smathers and Bryant. To the surprise of all, including Wolfe, Bryant announced on June 30 that a biracial committee had been formed in St. Augustine and that the members, whom he refused to name at the time, would prepare a proposal acceptable to both sides.[97]

Bryant's announcement was ingenious, satisfying the immediate desires of both community and civil rights leaders. Despite registering their disapproval to Bryant privately, local leaders remained quiet even though they knew no such committee existed, and King, also aware of what happened, agreed to call off further demonstrations. According to States Attorney Dan Warren, Bryant's action was not his "way to get King out of there. It was King's way to get out." King had met with Warren at Dr. Puryear's office and told him, "I want out of St. Augustine but I can't go out of here a loser and will not go out of here a loser."[98]

The available evidence seems to support Warren's view. The planned signing of the civil rights bill which would desegregate St. Augustine's public facilities and the creation of the biracial committee insured the adoption of King's two major goals. Essentially this was the same plan offered by the grand jury, but, at that time, the passage of the civil rights bill was not assured. In addition, King received promises from Warren that local blacks would be protected from further violence and intimidation. The costs of the St. Augustine campaign had accelerated dramatically in the last month, encouraging SCLC to accept a settlement. Hayling estimated the campaign cost one-half million to three-quarters of a million dollars. Leaving only a few members to test the community's support of the civil rights act, SCLC withdrew from St. Augustine on July 1.[99]

White businessmen in the community, anxious to end the demonstrations and the economic decline that had resulted from them, endorsed the proposed biracial commission and the civil rights bill. When President Johnson signed the bill into law on July 2, the town's business community breathed a noticeable sigh of relief. At a meeting of eighty of the town's one hundred businessmen, they voted to comply with the public accommodations section of the new law and desegregate their businesses. James Brock commented to reporters that his colleagues unanimously opposed the measure in principle but, with only "a few dissenters," agreed to abide by it. Black leaders felt justifiably pleased by developments.[100]

To avoid the appearance of pulling out entirely from St. Augustine, SCLC announced that it would continue its efforts to obtain a pardon for all convicted civil rights participants, test compliance with the new law by the city's business leaders, and implement a variety of programs to help the black community. On July 1, SCLC established a tutorial program for students of all ages which ran through the middle of August. The school program was designed to meet the basic educational needs of the black community through courses in reading, writing, mathematics, history, and science. SCLC also sought to heighten community interest in education which the organization felt was not highly regarded by local blacks. As part of this effort, twenty-two St. Augustine students spent two weeks in Westport, Connecticut, from where they visited New York. Jackie Robinson also entertained Jo Ann Anderson and Aubrey Nell Edwards, the two girls who spent six months in the state correctional institution, for two weeks at his home in Connecticut. Additionally, SCLC established a recreation program for teenage blacks at Florida Memorial College to overcome the limited recreational opportunities for them in the community. The tutorial and recreational programs were organized by students from Yale with classes held at First Baptist Church and Florida Memorial College, and with field trips planned to St. Augustine's historical sites.[101]

Events seemed to be proceeding toward the establishment of racial peace, but no one had taken into consideration the response of the Klan members and their supporters. Allowed to assume a leadership role in the community when a vacuum was created by the unwillingness of civic officials to deal with the crisis, these elements were not now ready to comply with this hated law and permit the desegregation of St. Augustine. On the fourth of July, sixty-two robed Klansmen and Klanswomen, followed by 150 men, women, children, marched through the center of town to protest the adoption of the Civil Rights Act. Organized by Manucy, Lynch, and Stoner, white militants also began parading in front of the desegregated establishments, carrying picket signs proclaiming "Delicious Food—Eat with Niggers Here," "Niggers Sleep Here—Would You?" and "Civil Rights Has To Go."[102]

Brock, whose place was picketed daily beginning July 9, asked J. B. Stoner, who stood on the sidewalk, why he had been designated as a target. Stoner replied, "We're just trying to help you get some nigger business." Two days later Brock asked Edward Mussallem, owner of the Caravel Motel, how he managed to get the pickets removed. Mussallem told Brock that he had been in touch with Hoss Manucy, who agreed to remove the pickets provided Mussallem promised not to serve blacks. On July 16, Brock, with his business slumping badly, joined a growing list of businesses which had resegregated. Judge Simpson immediately ordered the restaurants and motels to open their doors to blacks or face fines of $500 to $1,000 a day.[103]

At a meeting with other restuarant owners on July 3, Brock announced an agreement to abide by Simpson's ruling and the Civil Rights Act. Early the following morning Brock's restaurant was hit by two Molotov cocktails that caused $3,000 in damage. One motel owner complained in the aftermath of the bombing, "We have been caught in a dilemma." Under federal law "we are forced to serve Negroes although it hurts our business. If we serve them, the white pickets run the rest of the business away."[104]

The activities of segregationists were not confined to demonstrations alone. They continued to assault and threaten blacks who sought service at motels and restaurants. Five whites with iron bars attacked Henry Twine and Robert Preiskil after they left a local motel. Even blacks who were not involved in demonstrations felt the ire of hostile whites. Six local blacks, including a forty-year-old woman, were beaten while fishing near the ocean.[105]

Many local blacks blamed SCLC for exacerbating race relations in the community and then leaving them alone to face the wrath of the segregationists. Despite King's praise of his "dedication and sacrifice to the civil rights cause," Hayling joined with those residents criticizing King and decried his decision to discontinue the demonstrations without the establishment of a legitimate biracial committee. In retrospect, there seems to be little question that King and SCLC were primarily interested in St. Augustine as a way to facilitate passage of the civil rights bill and, having accomplished this, sought to retire as soon as protection could be assured for local residents. Bryant's offer of a biracial committee and Warren's pledge provided just such an opportunity. King called Bryant's action "a demonstration of good faith," and left St. Augustine even though, the evidence suggests, he knew the biracial committee was a fraud.[106] Significantly, only one of SCLC's original demands had been agreed to by community leaders as the organization departed (see page 104).

When the biracial committee failed to meet and violence against local blacks continued through July and August, King returned briefly on July 17 and indicated he would resume mass demonstrations unless the community desegregated. He also telephoned Governor Bryant's office to protest racial developments in the city and announced his intention to request the assistance of LeRoy Collins, director of the Community Relations Service. When race relations continued to deteriorate, King threatened to return although he never did and it is doubtful that he ever intended to do so since SCLC became deeply involved in the Mississippi Freedom Summer Campaign.[107]

Reflecting on the St. Augustine campaign, Pat Watters commented: "If there is the suggestion that SCLC exploited the local Birmingham situation, the suggestion was stronger in St. Augustine." King himself observed that, "some communities, like this one, had to bear the cross." In a telegram to Hayling, King reiterated his belief that St. Augustine served a larger purpose: "Our nation responded in humble compliance to the civil rights act of 1964 largely because of the movement which you headed in our nation's oldest city."[108]

The efforts of King and civil rights aides to obtain a biracial commission and other concessions from civic leaders were complicated by the reluctance of the federal government to pursue a more consistent and vigorous role in St. Augustine. Both Presidents Kennedy and Johnson were constrained by political considerations, especially their forthcoming presidential campaigns, from pursuing such a course of action. Prior to his assassination in November 1963, Kennedy was anxious not to alienate the southern support he had received in his close election victory over Richard Nixon in 1960. Kennedy advisers also feared a bloody backlash in the South and an angry southern response in Congress. Johnson, a native southerner, wanted to keep his region in the Democratic fold and also avoid the embarrassment of being defeated in this section. Both Presidents took protection behind the argument that they could not act without federal court approval.[109]

Johnson's reluctance to intervene in St. Augustine also reflected his preoccupation with the civil rights bill. Johnson was anxious to avoid any course of action, such as mobilizing federal troops or bringing pressure on local officials in St. Augustine, that might alienate southern political leaders. Johnson's primary concern was winning passage of the bill, and he wanted as many southerners supporting the measure as possible. That would cast the region in the best possible light. He was also interested in avoiding any direct confrontation with southerners that would alarm them about the potential impact of the proposed law and induce them to resort to extremist measures to insure its defeat. Johnson perceived racism as a millstone around the neck of the South and believed that its removal would do as much to free the region as to free black southerners. These political concerns prevented both presidents and Johnson in particular from operating freely in St. Augustine.[110]

Moreover, despite the prominence of the civil rights demonstrations in St. Augustine, events there never seized the attention of either president as Birmingham dominated the civil rights scene in 1964. Lee White, Burke Marshall, and other Johnson advisers expressed concern and the federal government limited its involvement to FBI surveillance and regular reports until Johnson moved directly to end the crisis in late June prior to signing the civil rights bill.

While the St. Augustine racial crisis helped to improve conditions for blacks in other sections of the country by expediting passage of the Civil Rights Act, it left the city bitterly divided. Indeed, race relations had seldom been worse. Nearly all communication between local white and black leaders had ceased during the civil rights demonstrations, and an attempt by a grand jury to establish a genuine biracial committee in August after the governor's committee never met, collapsed when only one of five whites appointed to the committee agreed to serve.[111] Adding to the dilemma of local blacks, the media had departed with King. Black residents thus had to confront a hostile white community without benefit of a sympathetic press which had proven of great assistance in mobilizing outside support for the St. Augustine movement.

That black leaders felt abandoned and isolated should not be surprising. King, SCLC, and the media provided the local movement with a credibility and visibility it had lacked throughout 1963. The support from SCLC and the media also enabled local black leaders to gain valuable assistance from the federal government and northern public opinion in their effort to desegregate St. Augustine. The local movement not only became dependent on SCLC for leadership but also relied on it for manpower and financial assistance. Despite SCLC's pledge to continue to provide such assistance, it ended in July for all practical purposes.

Lacking sufficient funds, leadership, manpower, and media attention, the civil rights movement faced a difficult future. Furthermore, the local climate could not have been more hostile to further racial progress. Despite the passage of the 1964 Civil Rights Act and a willingness by business leaders to comply with it (see chapter 6 for further discussion of the role of businessmen), few whites willingly accepted the new era and a vigorous civil rights movement was essential if these rights were to be protected and additional racial advances made.

Chapter 5.

A Judge for the Times

Throughout 1963 and 1964, civil rights leaders repeatedly sought the assistance of the courts in their effort to desegregate St. Augustine. Despite charges by their lawyers that a "vast conspiracy" existed in the white community and numerous instances of violence and intimidation against black residents, judges at the county and federal level ruled consistently against their legal petitions. It was County Judge Charles Mathis, Jr., for example, who had ordered the four black teenagers to the state reform school in 1963. Similarly, Federal District Court Judge William McRae had dismissed the appeal of civil rights workers in November 1963, ruling that Hayling and Eubanks, not city officials, had come into court with unclean hands and had shown "a lack of restraint, common sense, and good judgment" in leading the St. Augustine movement.[1]

Following the arrest and imprisonment of Easter demonstrators in late March 1964, lawyers for SCLC had asked federal Judge Bryan J. Simpson to overturn the decisions of Judges Mathis and Grier, contending that the convictions against the demonstrators were unjust. Simpson had ruled forcefully against the SCLC appeal, and he had also refused to grant a writ of habeas corpus for those arrested during the demonstrations or consider a reduction in their bonds. When civil rights lawyers sought a temporary injunction against sheriff's deputies and police officers from interfering with "peaceful demonstrations," Simpson again responded unfavorably, telling the attorneys that the petition would have to be amended because he would not spell out any pattern for law enforcement officers to follow in pursuance of their duties.[2]

Although the federal district court bench in Jacksonville had ruled against SCLC in these instances and many of its supporters were pessimistic about the future of race relations in St. Augustine, black leaders still felt confident that the appeal's process was one avenue that promised an end to the racial turmoil in St. Augustine and an eventual improvement in conditions for local blacks. No figure loomed more important in the pursuit of this strategy than the federal district court judge. Leon Friedman observed that the federal district court judge was "the most immediate interpreter and enforcer of Federal law. Since most of the claims of Negroes against the authorities of the southern states [were] . . . based on violations of their constitutional and Federal rights—in terms of voting restrictions, segregated schools, and discriminating treatment in public accommodations or other public facilities—a Federal district court judge had the power to correct a wide range of discrimination and abuses."[3] Furthermore, federal district court judges could remove the inequities encountered by blacks swiftly, if they so desired.

This approach was not without its pitfalls, however. Southern district court judges had an "astonishingly bad" record in civil rights cases, and *Time* magazine observed that they might be "the greatest obstacle to equal rights in the South." Friedman found that some ignored precedents of superior courts, denied black rights clearly granted them, engaged in open confrontations with the Justice Department, and delayed trials of blacks for months. While civil rights leaders were well aware of the potential problems, they based their decision in part on the belief that one federal judge would see the legality of their decision. They also believed that the Fifth Circuit Court of Appeals or the United States Supreme Court would eventually rule in their behalf. Legal actions in Montgomery and Birmingham had shown civil rights lawyers that this process, while exceedingly slow, was also fruitful.[4]

Without realizing it, city leaders and Governor Farris Bryant played directly into the hands of the SCLC's legal strategists. When King and his aides inaugurated the evening marches in late May and violence erupted, city leaders sought to halt the marches rather than increase police protection for the demonstrators.[5] In another questionable development, Sheriff L. O. Davis indiscriminately hired his auxiliary deputies without regard to their attitude toward the civil rights demonstrations and without establishing guidelines for handling the evening marches. Indeed, Davis' hiring practices suggested that he had sought the most militant whites as deputies in an effort to suppress the demonstrations. Nevertheless, he did not employ his assistants on the basis of racial attitudes; rather he relied on his familiarity with them and on their prior experience when filling these positions. Not surprisingly, however, these men generally shared Davis' racial prejudices and this was reflected in their treatment of civil rights activists.[6] Governor Bryant unwittingly helped SCLC prepare its lawsuit by following a strategy almost identical to that of the city. As had civic leaders before him, Bryant held the civil rights forces responsible for the disturbances in St. Augustine, and his policies sought to end the demonstrations rather than to control the militants.[7] SCLC lawyers immediately appealed to the federal court, accusing the city and state of violating the marchers' First Amendment rights.

Into this legal battle stepped Judge Bryan Simpson once again. City leaders and county judges felt confident that Simpson would uphold their actions based upon his decision in April. But Simpson's views on desegregation were not so clear-cut, as his earlier ruling in a Jacksonville case in May 1963 had demonstrated. On that occasion Simpson had ruled against the Hyde Park Golf Club, because it had deliberately discriminated against two black applicants by requiring that two members endorse their applications.[8] Simpson's position had also been influenced by the decision of Fifth Circuit Appeals Court Justice Richard T. Rives, who had overturned Simpson's April decision and released forty-eight St. Augustine demonstrators. This decision had a dramatic effect on Simpson. Above all he was a man of the law who thought a federal judge had an obligation to follow the guidelines established by his superior court. He did not see himself as a judicial innovator. As he told one reporter, "I've never consciously tried to do anything but determine binding precedent and follow it."[9]

Simpson had come to the federal court in 1950 when President Harry Truman appointed him as United States Judge for the Southern District of Florida, which embraced the territory south of Orlando to Miami. As a federal judge, Simpson joined readily with the judicial practice of questioning witnesses personally. He would sit at his bench, idly whittling away at a piece of wood, a habit he had developed during his early years as a judge, periodically interrupting a witness or a lawyer to seek clarification of a particular point. In one of his first civil cases, the attorney representing the plaintiff had completed questioning a key witness when Simpson began asking his own questions along the lines the defense attorney had tried unsuccessfully to pursue. The plaintiff's attorney quickly jumped to his feet, "Your honor, you can't do that." Red-faced, Simpson replied, "You're right, I guess I can't."[10] It did not take Simpson long, however, to realize what he could and could not do. In 1961 he became chief judge of the Southern District and later in the same year he changed districts to assume the same position for the Middle District of Florida, which included the area north of Orlando to Jacksonville.

Tall at 6'2" with white hair and a courtly manner, Simpson looked and acted like a judge. Lawyers found him to be very workmanlike, articulate, and insightful but also very down to earth—a lawyer's judge. He was also described as a judge who "looked beyond the law to the parties involved in the cases." Throughout his judicial career, Simpson evinced a concern for the individual and was determined that no injustice be committed in his court.[11]

Simpson handled his first case concerning racial discrimination while sitting on the state circuit court in 1948. The case involved a black couple who had changed trains in Jacksonville and sat in the white waiting room during the layover. When they refused to leave, the police arrived upon a complaint from the stationmaster and arrested them. They were subsequently found guilty of violating the state's segregation law and fined $100 in municipal court. After paying the fine, they appealed the case to the circuit court. Simpson heard the case, but ruled that the couple had no appeal since they had already paid the fine. He later commented that he was glad at the time that he did not have to decide on the case since he was running for reelection that year.[12]

After being appointed to the Federal District Court, he heard a case in which a group of black citizens in Daytona Beach asked for the right to attend concerts at the city auditorium. Simpson ruled in their favor but delayed the decision for sixty days to allow the city time to install separate toilets and other segregated facilities. Simpson's decision reflected a very gradual shift away from a segregationist view of American society. Aiding him in this transition were the decisions by the Supreme Court in *Henderson* v. *United States* (1950), which invalidated racial discrimination in railroad dining cars, and *Brown* v. *Board of Education of Topeka* (1954) and, according to Simpson, the greater latitude he enjoyed as a federal court judge who did not have to face reelection. Simpson's views were also influenced by his perception of his oath of office; as he told a reporter: "When you take an oath, it means something." To Simpson, in particular, the oath meant that he had a responsibility to be as informed as possible about a case and see that the rights of all individuals were properly protected.[13]

Simpson's sense of duty and his racial moderation strongly reflected his personal background. His family had played a very prominent role in the development of Florida—his grandfather served five terms in the state House of Representatives and his two uncles sat in the United States Senate. While not the wealthiest of families, it was certainly one of the most influential. The northern origins and the pro-Union sentiments of the Simpsons during the Civil War had served to undermine any racial extremism in the family. Neither his mother's nor his father's family had been strong supporters of racism during Reconstruction, and Judge Simpson felt no emotional bond with racism and segregation.[14]

In the midst of the St. Augustine civil rights cases, Simpson's critics alleged that he sided with the civil rights proponents because he had been promised a seat on the Fifth Circuit Court of Appeals by the Attorney General and the President.[15] Simpson was, in fact, appointed to the Fifth Circuit Court in New Orleans in 1966 after the events in St. Augustine had quieted. Nevertheless, despite the contention of his critics, it is very unlikely that he was promoted for other than legitimate reasons, and no evidence exists to support such a view. Certainly the attention he received and the reputation he gained by his handling of the St. Augustine cases greatly enhanced his place in the judicial community. It does not appear, however, that his appointment came as the result of a bargain worked out in advance with the federal government.

Simpson heard the first of SCLC's appeals on June 1. The

civil rights organization sought to overturn the city's ban on juveniles participating in evening marches and a prohibition against automobiles in the downtown area between 9:00 P.M. and 5:00 A.M.[16] During the course of the three-day hearing, Simpson asked Sheriff L. O. Davis to remain seated so that he could cross-examine him following his questioning by SCLC counsel William Kunstler. FBI field investigators had notified Simpson that a number of Davis' deputies and special deputies belonged to Klan or Klanlike organizations in St. Augustine. On the basis of this information, Simpson asked Davis, "Are you a member of the Ku Klux Klan?" Clearly surprised by the question, Davis replied that he was not. Simpson then asked Davis if he recruited his special deputies from the Klan. Davis declared emphatically, "No, sir." Still unsatisfied, Simpson continued, "What is the Ancient City Gun Club? . . . Isn't the club another name for the Klan?" Davis said he did not think it was. Simpson suggested to the sheriff, "Haven't you neglected to look into the background of men before deputizing them?" Unnerved by Simpson's questioning, Davis responded, "I didn't have time."[17]

Simpson ordered Davis to return to court the following day with a complete list of his deputies. When Davis returned on June 3, Simpson read the names out loud, pausing at Holstead Richard Manucy. "Isn't he a bootlegger?" Simpson asked. Without waiting for Davis to reply, Simpson declared that this man "is a convicted felon in this court. . . . Has he had his rights of citizenship restored?" "Not that I know of, I don't know," Davis replied. "He's good enough to be a deputy sheriff?" asked Simpson. Davis had to admit that he was not. Simpson concluded by cautioning Davis that "as a law enforcement officer, you can appreciate the danger in a situation like this when you have members of the Klan and allied organizations in your organization as deputies."[18]

Lawyers for SCLC asked Judge Simpson to remove the ban on night demonstrations by Stuart, Davis, and city officials on the basis of the First Amendment rights of assembly, speech, and petition. City leaders contended that the violence in St. Augustine could be halted only by keeping both white and black youths off the street. The parking ban, they declared, was designed to prevent troublemakers from coming from other communities.[19] Simpson asked SCLC officials if they would refrain from evening demonstrations while he reviewed the arguments. Satisfied with Simpson's handling of the case to this point and not wishing to alienate him, Andrew Young agreed to do so.

In preparing his findings, Simpson observed that Davis had an overwhelming force available to protect the marchers and "that no 'clear and present danger' existed in and around St. Augustine, Florida, at any of the times pertinent to these proceedings." Noting that important individual freedoms of speech, assembly, and petition were at stake, Simpson argued that "prior restraint against their exercise casts a heavy burden upon the defendants to demonstrate" such a danger. "This burden the defendants failed to meet," he concluded in setting aside the ban.[20] Simpson's decision was based on several precedents including the recent *CORE* v. *Douglas* case in which the Fifth Circuit Court overturned a lower court decision prohibiting CORE from conducting sit-ins and protest demonstrations.[21] It also reflected disapproval of the course taken by Davis in hiring his special deputies and the violent methods they employed against civil rights demonstrators.

Simpson's ruling did not put to rest the issue of the evening marches, however. With the resumption of the nightly protest demonstrations on June 9, violence escalated dramatically. City police and sheriff's deputies, aided by state police, were hard pressed to prevent massive rioting. To ease the crisis, Governor Bryant, on the advice of his state patrol and States Attorney Dan Warren, established a special law enforcement district in St. Johns County and sent eighty additional state troopers to assist local law enforcement officers.[22] The governor's intervention led to a temporary truce on June 16 and 17, but violence again erupted on June 18, beginning with the confrontation between James Brock and several rabbis.

City and state officials led by Senator Verle Pope appealed publicly to Governor Bryant to take steps to stop the escalating violence. The state police commander also informed Bryant that his men could not control events in the city. Warren, who had witnessed the violence on June 19 when five hundred white militants assaulted one hundred and fifty civil rights marchers with bricks, bottles, and other debris, also thought the situation was extremely dangerous and warranted more forceful action by the governor.[23] In response to these appeals, Bryant issued his second proclamation on

June 20 in which he banned all demonstrations between 8:30 P.M. and 5:00 A.M. because of "certain lawlessness and utter disregard for the laws of Florida exhibited by the demonstrators and counter-demonstrators." SCLC immediately appealed the governor's executive order to Judge Simpson contending that it conflicted with his order of June 9 elaborated upon on June 13.[24]

Simpson asked Attorney General James Kynes' office to explain why Governor Bryant should not be held in contempt for violating his decision. In response, Kynes asserted that Bryant had the authority as governor and under the state constitution and statutes of Florida to issue such a ban. He also noted that the governor was not among those restrained by the judge's previous injunction; that the governor's order of June 20 was not prohibited by that injunction; that the governor's action was motivated by a concern for the citizens of St. Augustine and St. Johns County; and that Bryant had the "dominant interest" in preventing violence and disorder. Kynes' argument, furthermore, questioned a contempt citation as a "misconceived, improper, and inadequate means" to challenge the sovereign power of the governor. Simpson, however, had no doubt about his legal authority. He instructed Kynes to appear in court on June 22.[25]

Kynes testified that both sides were to blame for the violence, but Simpson remained unconvinced. "It's a question of taking the view that, when somebody gets socked in the eye, he's just as guilty as the man that's on the fist," he said. Somewhat later during the testimony he reemphasized this point: "If one group is entitled to march peacefully and to the right of freedom of assembly and to the right of freedom of speech and the right of petition guaranteed by the First Amendment, it doesn't seem to me at all that a corresponding freedom to attack with physical violence goes to another group."[26]

Under questioning from Simpson, Elmer Emerich, the governor's adviser on St. Augustine, was forced to admit that the trouble came from "the lawless elements" who were young white militants and not civil rights demonstrators. Once the state admitted that the militants were the source of the violence, Simpson suggested that more forceful steps be taken to restrain them: "There was no restraint by this Court on whatever action the law enforcement officers wanted to take with respect to this lawless element."[27]

Anticipating that Judge Simpson might find Governor Bryant in contempt, Attorney General Kynes and Bryant huddled over what alternative might be available to the governor. Bryant believed Simpson's action was ill-conceived and that it could well cause considerable bloodshed. The governor told Kynes that he would "not condone violence on any scale and appropriate action . . . [would] be taken to prevent it," even if it meant a direct clash with Simpson. He also informed the attorney general that he "would not hesitate to exercise every power available to me as Governor to insure that law and order prevail."[28] Kynes's office developed two possible arguments the governor might employ to sidestep a possible contempt citation, but neither seemed to offer Bryant a viable option. The first relied on the decision by former Governor Fuller Warren (1948–1952) not to appear before the United States Senate Committee on Organized Crime in Interstate Commerce, chaired by Senator Estes Kefauver. Warren argued that as the chief executive of Florida he was not subject to the demands of a congressional subcommittee. While Warren successfully avoided appearing before Kefauver's committee, Bryant and Kynes both knew that Warren's decision had cost him considerable support among the Florida electorate and state political leaders. In addition, the St. Augustine crisis that confronted Bryant and Warren's refusal to appear before the Kefauver subcommittee had few similarities.[29] Kynes' second proposal seemed more appropriate but hardly more attractive. It was based upon Governor Orval Faubus' decision to use the state National Guard to prevent the desegregation of Little Rock's white high school. Kynes pointed out to Bryant, however, that the federal court had ordered Faubus to comply immediately with the court-ordered desegregation plan and President Dwight Eisenhower had sent in elements of the 101st Airborne Division to see that the court order was obeyed.[30]

Not anxious for a showdown that could damage his political future and disrupt the state, Bryant instructed Kynes and States Attorney Dan Warren to tell Simpson that he would comply with his wish to enforce the law more vigorously. Kynes promised Simpson that "people arrested won't be put into the jail by the State officers through the front door and released out the side door by the local officials; and . . . the weapons won't be turned in by the State officers and released back to the offenders by the local people."[31]

Simpson also sought to avoid a confrontation with Bryant that would exacerbate the crisis. No doubt influencing his decision was the fact that he and Bryant had known one another for many years and were quite friendly. The judge had also received information from the FBI, which he had requested, indicating that conditions were very dangerous in St. Augustine. With the promise from Attorney General Kynes and States Attorney Warren that more forceful steps would be taken to halt the violence and that the state would assume principal responsibility for maintaining law and order, Simpson decided not to hold Bryant in contempt. Instead he withheld his decision pending the outcome of the governor's efforts but did set aside his ban on evening demonstrations. Simpson also had been informed that Bryant planned to try to establish a biracial committee in St. Augustine to mediate the crisis. In addition, the civil rights bill was within days of enactment and it would most likely resolve the crisis if all else failed.[32]

In the midst of his imbroglio with Governor Bryant, Simpson heard an appeal from several civil rights demonstrators who alleged that Davis, Stuart, and Judge Mathis had levied excessive bail and confined them in quarters that were unfit for human beings. Davis and Mathis had originally fined demonstrators $100 for each violation with most bail amounts averaging $300. As the demonstrations escalated in May and June, these two men, apparently in collusion, began assessing people $500, and in some cases $1,000, per violation. Their aim was to discourage further protests by forcing the demonstrators to pay huge fines or spend several days in jail. In addition, they also sought to deplete SCLC's treasury which usually paid the bonds.[33]

Davis and Mathis' new bond rates dramatically increased the number of prisoners, forcing Davis to build a compound outside the jail to be used by the prisoners during the day. Instead of designing the compound to allow prisoners more space, Davis and his deputies utilized it to intimidate the demonstrators. The compound received direct afternoon sun which in Florida in June meant that the temperature invariably rose above 90 degrees. Davis also left the demonstrators out in the yard during one severe afternoon thunderstorm.

Testimony also revealed that Davis and his deputies had threatened and mistreated civil rights workers in their cells. When the demonstrators sang freedom songs at night, Davis had the nine men confined in a 7' by 8' concrete "sweatbox" overnight. On another occasion Davis made twenty-one females, including a polio victim, Georgia Mae Reed, who could not walk without crutches, spend one hour and twenty minutes standing in a small circular cell, ten feet in diameter. On removing the women Deputy Wade Turner declared that someone "should take a rifle and kill all those damn Negroes."[34]

During the course of the hearing before Simpson, Davis claimed that he alone was responsible for the high bail rates: "I raised them because I wanted to." Somewhat later he alleged that Mathis had set the bail. Irritated by his conflicting responses, Simpson asked Davis, "Well, are you taking any of the responsibility for the size of these, or are you putting it all on Mathis?" Angered by Simpson's question, Davis responded, "I'm not putting it off on anyone. I'll take my share of responsibility." Simpson interjected, "Well, what is your share?" "All of it," Davis blurted out in frustration. "I was the one who posted the bonds."[35]

Simpson was clearly irked by Davis' comments as well as by what he suspected was collusion by Davis and Mathis to use their offices to hinder the civil rights effort. No doubt Simpson had also been moved by the testimony of Georgia Mae Reed, whose infirmity was apparent to all in the courtroom. The Judge ordered Davis and Mathis to reduce bail for all demonstrators to a maximum of $300. He also ordered Davis to release all the children in jail to their parents and to cease placing prisoners in a sweatbox, padded cell, or open pen when it was 90 degrees.[36]

Simpson did not stop there, however. He went on to portray Davis' handling of the prisoners as "more than cruel and unusual punishment. Here is exposed in its raw ugliness, studied and cynical brutality deliberated and contrived to break men, physically and mentally." He also berated Mathis' handling of juveniles, calling "their detention without bond or release . . . an arbitrary and capricious act of harassment." While Simpson's criticism of the county's two leading law enforcement officers appeared designed to maintain legal standards, he also sought to discourage St. Augustine's white leadership from continuing its opposition to the civil rights movement.[37]

Shortly after Simpson's decision in this case, President

Johnson signed the Civil Rights Act on July 2 and nearly all businesses voluntarily complied with the new desegregation law. It was at this point that SCLC began withdrawing its forces from St. Augustine, assuming incorrectly that peace and desegregation had been achieved. But many businesses had resegregated by the middle of the month after J. B. Stoner and Hoss Manucy began their counterdemonstrations. When Fred Martin of SCLC asked Police Chief Stuart for protection, he replied, "We are not going to be at any test sites. It is a Federal law. Call the FBI."[38]

One of the first businessmen to bar blacks was William Chew, manager of the Palms Congress Inn and an ardent segregationist. Chew had been very vocal in his criticism of the civil rights movement from the outset and needed little prodding from Stoner to resegregate. On August 12, Arthur Funderberk, a local black resident, acting on behalf of SCLC, attempted to register at the Palms, but was informed that the Inn did not register local residents. On August 14, Lester Tate, a native of Clewiston and a student at Florida Memorial College, successfully registered at the Palms without difficulty. Tate had been brought in deliberately by SCLC after Funderberk had been turned away, and while spending the night at the Palms he had entertained several guests including Funderberk. On the 15th Tate tried to go swimming with his friends in the Inn pool but found it had been closed for cleaning.[39]

Lawyers for SCLC immediately charged Chew with violating the equal access provision of the new civil rights law, and the case was heard in Judge Simpson's court on August 20. Funderberk testified that sheriff's deputy Charles Lance, Jr., had attempted to discourage him from conducting further desegregation tests at the Palms Congress Inn. As he and two friends were leaving the Palms restaurant on August 11, Lance entered and called the three men "black bastards." Lance then followed Funderberk in his police car, driving very close to his rear bumper until Funderberk, concerned for his safety, stopped at the SCLC office on Washington Street.[40] On August 14 when Funderberk dropped two people off at the Palms Inn to register, Lance again followed him. During further testimony before Simpson, Lance alleged that he followed Funderberk and his friends to "protect them." During the cross-examination, however, Lance admitted that he had not followed Funderberk on August 11, even though two white militants stood across from the Palms restaurant and harassed him as he got into his car.[41] Additional evidence disclosed that Lance and Chew were good friends, that Lance ate lunch and drank coffee at the Palms each day, and that Lance, his wife, and friends went swimming regularly at the Palms Inn pool.[42] The latter point seemed quite significant in light of Chew's contention that the Inn did not cater to local residents.

Earlier testimony revealed that Davis had hired his appointed and auxiliary deputies without investigation, although he had informed all his assistants of Judge Simpson's injunction protecting blacks against threats and violence and admitting them to places of public accommodation. Lance stated that he had been told of this injunction by Sheriff Davis. Paul Greenburg, attorney for Funderberk, remarked to Sheriff Davis during his cross-examination, "I understand he [Lance] is rather bitter about enforcing the law." Davis replied angrily, "All of us are."[43]

During conferences between lawyers for both sides and Simpson, Chew's counsel admitted that he had been "one of the more recalcitrant original defendants" in the case brought against local business leaders by SCLC prior to the passage of the Civil Rights Act. Since Chew and Lance were close friends and personally opposed to desegregation, Simpson observed "that regardless of their denying it that these matters were the subject of considerable discussion between Mr. Chew and Mr. Lance."[44] Simpson found both men guilty of civil contempt.

He then discussed at some length what options he had available to him to insure that Chew obeyed the law. He noted that he had not been asked to have the Palms Inn admit Funderberk, simply that it comply with the new law. Instead Simpson chose to require Chew to admit local blacks on the same basis as local whites, declaring that Chew had been using his policy regarding local guests with such discretion that black residents had been consistently turned away whereas local whites had not. To ensure that Chew obeyed his order, Simpson asked his lawyer to submit to him within twenty days a list of the Negro guests, local and nonlocal, who had been admitted and who had been turned away. He also ordered sixteen other motels and restaurants to desegregate within thirty days in compliance with the Civil Rights Act.[45]

After completing his response to the central issues in the case, Simpson turned to Lance's role in recent events and announced to the great surprise of all present, "I would require a report from Mr. Lance . . . within 20 days, that he has resigned his, whatever it takes to get off the Sheriff's force, resigned his commission, turned in his star or turned in whatever County equipment he owns, and that he no longer holds himself out as an officer." In concluding the case, Simpson ordered Lance and Chew to pay the attorney's fees and taxable costs for Funderberk's lawyers.[46] Simpson also warned Manucy and other members of the Ancient City Gun Club against "intimidating, threatening or coercing" blacks who sought service at restaurants or motels in St. Augustine. Martin Luther King, Jr., immediately praised Simpson's decision and remarked that it should put an end to a "rule of terror" in St. Augustine.[47]

The response to Simpson's removal of Lance from the sheriff's department, however, was largely critical, involving scores of protests from local, state, and federal officials. Sheriff Davis commented that deputies could not be expected to treat integrationists "with a glad heart" when there was not $5 left in the entire city. Still smarting from his own legal encounter with Simpson, Governor Bryant told reporters that "my initial reaction is unfavorable but I am not familiar with the circumstances and I have not read the order." The most outspoken critic of the decision was Senator Strom Thurmond from South Carolina who said that the decision proved his point about the Civil Rights Act of 1964: "This legislation provides an unbridled license for judicial dictatorship in this country."[48]

Lance's lawyer, Frank Upchurch, Jr., announced in September his intention of appealing Simpson's decision regarding Lance's position as deputy, and two weeks later the state joined with Lance's appeal. Attorney General James Kynes commented that "the federal courts should not be in the position of dictating and controlling the personnel policies of local law enforcement agencies." Simpson welcomed the appeal but noted that he did not seek to administer police affairs but only to remove a policeman who violated his oath of office. He added that he had not interfered with Lance's livelihood since he was fully employed in the lumber and service station business and he served as an unsalaried deputy.[49]

The Fifth Circuit Court of Appeals upheld Simpson's decision in December 1965 with one amendment. The court ruled that the order prohibiting Lance from serving as a deputy sheriff could be lifted if "he should satisfy trial court that he was no longer in violation of orders and would in good faith thereafter comply with [them]." Lance never responded to the court's decision and never served as a deputy sheriff again.[50]

Chew resigned his position as manager of the Palms Congress Inn rather than accept Simpson's decision and initiated steps in September to establish a St. Augustine branch of the White Citizens' Council with himself serving as chairman. In encouraging residents to join the new organization, Chew stated that "a group of civic leaders in St. Augustine, concerned about the menace of racial integration which now threatens our state and local community, have been meeting together to find a solution to the problem."[51]

Few local citizens responded to Chew's appeal, perhaps because they realized that the Citizens' Council did not offer the community a viable solution to its racial problems. Judge Simpson had informed city leaders and local businessmen that he would not permit them to resegregate. The only avenue available to residents was to accept racial change as a matter beyond their control and begin the process of resurrecting the tourist trade and preparing for the 400th anniversary. This was essentially the path they pursued, although not without seriously weighing tactics to undermine Simpson's position.

Simpson's opponents fell into two categories: those who witnessed events in St. Augustine on the television news or through the newspapers and berated him through the mails; and those who were intimately involved in the racial turmoil and had appeared in court before Simpson. The former suggested he had "treated the white citizens of St. Augustine like criminals" and threatened to beat him "to a pulp," or to kill him.[52] The latter pursued a more sophisticated course of action which was designed to impugn his reputation and undermine his credibility.

Five of his chief critics, Judge Mathis, whom Simpson had overruled on several occasions, Sheriff Davis, Mayor Shelley, City Attorney Andreu, and Dr. Norris, met privately in late June to discuss how they could counteract the rulings of Simpson. They were motivated by what they viewed as an effort by the federal judiciary to destroy the fundamental values of their community. All five men believed strongly in segregation and regarded the civil rights movement as Communist inspired and Communist led. They saw themselves as leaders of the community and representatives of its best interests, and genuinely thought that segregation was best for white and black citizens. Unlike Klansmen and other extremists, they followed legitimate channels in trying to block racial change.[53]

At the meeting Mayor Shelley proposed that they get lawyers to examine the testimony before Simpson and his subsequent decisions and then move to have him impeached. Norris agreed and also recommended that a brochure be put together and presented to the people of the area and to the state legislative committee, which had been recently appointed to examine the crisis, to convince them of Simpson's bias. In addition, Norris suggested that a few billboards on the highway between here and Jacksonville would impeach Judge Simpson. To head up the impeachment effort, the group proposed that an ad hoc committee led by themselves with representatives from St. Johns, Putnam, Flagler, and Marion County be created. Norris declared that what they needed was "a front organization, like the Communists [have]."[54]

The five men were convinced that Simpson's decisions were unconstitutional and biased. Shelley contended that every time Simon or Kunstler failed to address a point adequately in their questioning, Simpson would intervene. Endorsing Shelley's view, Andreu added that on each occasion he entered Simpson's chambers he found the Judge discussing some point with Simon and Kunstler. Both asserted that during one such meeting, Simpson had literally begged Kunstler and Simon to have their clients stop the sit-ins and marches while he ruled on a point of law. Shelley claimed if he was a lawyer, the first thing he would do would be to move to disqualify Simpson. Andreu agreed and indicated that he would move to disqualify Simpson from further cases. For some reason, Andreu believed that Simpson wanted to be removed from these cases and would be glad to have himself challenged off the cases.[55]

They viewed Simpson's decision to remove all cases from Mathis' court as a miscarriage of justice. Mathis told the others that Simpson would never try these cases and that the defendants would never have to pay their fines or court costs. This especially irked

Shelley who believed that none of them were residents of Florida and they should therefore have to pay for their meddling. Arrest records, however, disclosed that a majority of those jailed were not only citizens of Florida but also residents of St. Augustine.[56]

Perceiving himself as the resident intellectual of the group, Norris called the civil rights movement "a revolutionary aspect of our society, and he [Simpson] has made himself a party to this revolution. . . . He has joined sides." Norris was convinced that Simpson was trying to usurp authority from the legitimately elected city officials in order to foist the civil rights movement on St. Augustine. Shelley agreed, adding that Simpson was doing this because he felt there was a "vast conspiracy in St. Augustine" to suppress the rights of local blacks.[57]

Reflecting the views of the others present as well as many residents, Shelley called for Simpson's impeachment, declaring: "It was obvious up there that Judge Simpson had been made a promise by the President of the United States that he'd be promoted." He was "bought and paid for by Lyndon Johnson," Shelley asserted. While noting that Simpson had been fair in his initial handling of the civil rights cases, Mathis pointed out that he had since listened only to those he wanted to hear from. Mathis believed that, after the Easter demonstrations, every case heard by Simpson was "a loaded case." These five men tried to solicit support for their impeachment effort, but Governor Bryant's announcement establishing a biracial committee followed by the adoption of the Civil Rights Act on July 2 completely eroded support for their position. Frustrated and angry, they finally abandoned their attempt to impeach Simpson with considerable reluctance.[58]

Despite the opposition to his decisions and the repeated threats on his life, Simpson remained unwavering in his insistence that St. Augustine desegregate. He cooperated closely with lawyers for SCLC, meeting privately with Al Bronstein, for example, and informing him that he would "allow attorneys fees in any case brought under the Civil Rights Act." During this same discussion, Simpson suggested to Bronstein that he would like to see a broad suit entered against the Klan and the National States Rights Party "to prevent any of their members from violating the Civil Rights Act." While stepping beyond the bounds of judicial propriety in this instance,

Simpson had apparently decided that the crisis would only be ended if he assumed the responsibility for removing the white militant factions. In mid-August 1964, he gave Flagler Hospital thirty days to remove racial barriers or face the loss of over $6 million in federal funds. The hospital maintained racially segregated dining rooms, toilet facilities, rooms, and wards.[59]

Despite Simpson's involvement, black residents continued to encounter difficulty in gaining access to restaurants, motels, and beaches; schools remained largely segregated; and economic opportunity continued to be inaccessible to black residents. Moreover, the intervention of SCLC, northern whites, and the media, and the activism of local black citizens had so alienated white residents that few willingly accepted the new order in race relations. Indeed, few whites bothered to hide their resentment toward local blacks for developments of the past spring and summer.

In December 1965, Simpson ended the legal question involving the crisis of 1964 by dismissing charges against 400 demonstrators. His decision went beyond the request of civil rights attorneys who had expressed a willingness to remand twenty-five cases to state courts because they did not involve issues covered by the 1964 Civil Rights Act. Simpson asserted, however, that developments since 1964 had shown the position taken by civil rights activists to be correct and he saw no point in continuing the legal controversy.[60] Simpson thus made it clear to St. Augustinians that there was no hope of returning to the past and suggested that they would be wise to accept the new racial patterns.

In the last analysis, the federal court, encouraged by an SCLC-led civil rights movement, moved to resolve the crisis by mandating desegregation. But it had taken an extraordinary judge who was willing to interject himself directly into the crisis to prevent Klan and Citizens' Council forces from carrying the day. With President Johnson unwilling to allow the government to intervene directly, it was crucial for civil rights forces to gain the support of the federal courts if they hoped to remove the racial barriers in St. Augustine. Simpson emerged as a figure sympathetic to the efforts of SCLC. Leon Friedman has written that Simpson was one southern "district court judge who . . . exceeded all others in his speed in enforcing the law and in his willingness to embark on new legal territory to protect Negro rights." A black lawyer for the NAACP called him a "man for that time" who "fully understood what was going on."[61] Simpson's intervention had also proven crucial for the community, for it resulted in the removal of outside white militants from St. Augustine and enabled the more law-abiding elements, led by businessmen, to reestablish political control.

Chapter 6.

Every Job Had a Name
and a Face

No group in St. Augustine remained immune to the civil rights developments of 1963 and 1964, certainly not the business community. Although the city was known principally for its historical past and several historic buildings stood in the heart of the city, the ten-story Exchange Bank physically dominated the town square. The presence of the bank was important in understanding the life of the community; for in spite of the city's commitment to preserving its heritage, St. Augustine remained first and foremost a business community bent on profiting from its location, history, and tourist economy.

Business leaders constituted the most active and effective special interest group in St. Augustine. The small size of St. Augustine and the heavy involvement of most businessmen in tourism facilitated a closer relationship among business leaders than existed in many other communities in the North or South. While it would be erroneous to perceive businessmen in St. Augustine as a monolithic group, they were inclined to share a common perspective—that the future of St. Augustine was tied closely to the economic success of their enterprises. Their business progressivism colored their view of city politics, social relations, and cultural activities. On the question of the Negro's place in St. Augustine, business leaders supported the prevailing status quo; they never questioned the segregation barriers that had been erected in the city during the 1890s or the racial assumptions which had prevailed since the days of slavery. This attitude toward race relations reflected their own biases as well as their desire to maintain stable social relations, thereby assuring an environment that would benefit their business activities.[1]

Given the extent of their influence and their desire to avoid controversy, what role could business leaders in St. Augustine be expected to play in the post-*Brown* era? And were their responses typical of businessmen elsewhere in the South?

Several historians and journalists have contended that businessmen in a number of southern cities acted as a force for racial moderation and insured a gradual reordering of race relations in the South following the *Brown* decision. Harry Ashmore first enunciated this view, suggesting that many business leaders recognized "that the South is still painfully short of risk capital, and that its economic development depends primarily upon the great national corporations and the expanding smaller companies seeking plant sites outside the older industrial concentrations." To encourage business relocation into their state and city, chambers of commerce downplayed racial hostility to portray "a favorable climate for industry."[2]

Ashmore's views were largely ignored in the immediate post-*Brown* era as writers focused their attention on the militant responses of the white community led by the White Citizens' Councils and the Ku Klux Klan. But in 1963 Claude Sitton of the *New York Times* commented on the important role business leaders played in ameliorating a racial crisis in Cambridge, Maryland. Sitton fund that "the effective pressure to end the crisis came from within the business community" and added that similar developments had occurred in Little Rock, Birmingham, Atlanta, and other southern communities. He concluded that "economic self-interest frequently leads to racial change in situations where other factors seemingly have little influence." Analyzing events in Little Rock and New Orleans two years after Sitton's story, Reed Sarratt declared that when violence erupted "businessmen began to act in their accustomed role as community leaders." He also observed that in Dallas and Atlanta "businessmen successfully exerted their influence to prevent disorder before it developed. Recent studies of racial developments in Dallas, Columbia, Jackson, Little Rock, and Norfolk have largely confirmed this view, especially after businessmen witnessed "the fearful blow that defiance and chaos had dealt Arkansas' industrial development."[3]

Not all writers, however, have agreed entirely with the picture painted of the South's economic leaders. While acknowledging that business leaders "tended to be somewhat more tolerant on racial issues than the population at large," Numan Bartley has argued that the businessmen of the South did not react uniformly to racial developments in the post-*Brown* era. In fact, Bartley saw three different responses emanating from the business community. Economic leaders in such Old South cities as Charleston and New Orleans "tended to be profoundly reactionary" when confronted with social change. Tradition, respect for old customs, and an elitist viewpoint shaped their outlook. A second response came from the South's nouveaux riches in communities such as Jackson, Birmingham, Shreveport, and Monroe, Louisiana, and veered toward ultraconservatism. "Members of this group frequently were lower class in socioeconomic background and fundamentalist in religious training" and exhibited "little awareness of social responsibility." In contrast to the first group, businessmen in the second group were prepared to resort to violence if necessary to preserve segregation. According to Bartley, the sole progressive position among the South's economic leaders was occupied by a third group who were involved in capital-intensive, scientific, and nationally oriented businesses. These elites resided largely in the New South cities of Atlanta, Miami, Houston, and Baton Rouge. "While they were normally quite conservative in outlook, they placed far greater value on progress and economic advancement than on white supremacy." Despite the varying responses from these three groups, Bartley concluded: "most of all, southern business sought to avoid involvement in the controversy altogether."[4]

At first glance, St. Augustine's business leadership would appear to fall within Bartley's first category. St. Augustine had a highly structured, tradition-bound society. The older business leaders, especially, evinced a concern for a style of social life and a respect for traditional ways that often guided their economic activities. Their attitudes and those of their colleagues reflected the relative stability of St. Augustine during the post—World War II period. The economy prospered due to a resurgent tourist trade but otherwise the community seemed little changed from the prewar era. The majority of newcomers who arrived seemed to come chiefly to retire, reenforcing the town's traditional values.[5] In the postwar era business leaders often deliberately blocked industrial development which threatened the character of St. Augustine. One local businessman alleged that Exchange Bank President Herbert Wolfe "didn't want any outsiders and he could keep them out since he used to own a lot of land along with his cronies." Another small businessman argued that "the only time the power men in town have supported industry is when it served their own interests."[6]

Reinforcing their commitment to maintaining the status quo was the involvement of several senior businessmen in the St. Augustine Historical Society.[7] Most prominent business leaders participated in planning for the 400th anniversary since it would highlight the community's heritage and also promised to be a large moneymaking enterprise. Much like their counterparts in other small communities, businessmen thus tended to have a narrow world view, often motivated by their own self-interest.

But St. Augustine also depended for its very existence on the appeal it offered vacationing northerners and midwesterners. An estimated 85 percent of the community's wealth came from the tourist trade. In this economic setting, the business leaders generally tried to moderate the city's internal problems to avoid alienating their northern guests. One historian and former resident commented that the business community consistently sought "to keep social order and peace."[8] For economic reasons, it thus appeared that St. Augustine's business leaders would act as a moderating force in any racial crisis, much like those found in Bartley's third group.

Nevertheless, during the initial stages of the civil rights movement in 1963, St. Augustine's business community simply ignored the sporadic demonstrations as symptomatic of demonstrations occurring throughout the South. Most felt, no doubt, that if they ignored the protests they would end. Those who paid attention to the demonstrations chose to disregard them because they appeared to be the work of a radical dentist who was not from St. Augustine and some vocal black teenagers. The absence of older black residents from the demonstrations confirmed in the minds of many the lack of support for the movement in the black community and the unreasonableness of the demands. Although Howard Johnson's, Woolworth's, and McCrory's desegregated during the summer, they seemed to respond as much to pressure being exerted upon their establishments elsewhere in the South as to the events in St. Augustine. When the protests continued throughout the summer, however, individual business leaders moved to discourage them by threatening black workers with the loss of their jobs if they continued to demonstrate.[9] Businessmen in St. Augustine thus displayed a remarkable similarity in their initial response to the civil rights protests as their colleagues in such traditional southern communities as New Orleans and Charleston. When the demonstrations began to increase in number, their views generally hardened.

The opposition of business leaders to racial accommodation reflected their personal prejudices as well as those of their friends and neighbors. Typifying the views of many in the business community, Herbert Wolfe regarded blacks as socially inferior to whites and generally opposed changes which would promote equality between the races. A story he occasionally recounted to close friends underscored his racial views: As a young man he was preparing his father's land for planting when an old black man, who was whiling away his time on a fence overlooking the land, told young Wolfe he was doing the plowing all wrong. The old-timer then proceeded to tell him how to do it correctly. Wolfe listened for a moment then dropped the plow and walked off, deciding he would never do anything again "that a nigger could do better."[10]

While Wolfe had pronounced racial views, he was no extremist. His vast business interests in banking, construction, and farming led him to seek an easing of tensions during the racial crisis of 1964. Wolfe's wealth, no doubt, also influenced his more charitable views. He could afford to separate himself fully from the town's black citizens and they posed no threat to his economic and social position.

Frank Harrold, the other major banking figure in town, shared most of Wolfe's views. Generally perceived as the most respected man in town because of his success and concern for others, Harrold was not sufficiently committed to segregation to jeopardize his banking responsibilities or the stability of the community he had helped develop. Harrold, Wolfe, and the business managers of the Fairchild Stratos Corporation also came to realize that their businesses could be adversely affected by a hostile federal government through federal contracts and loan policies.[11]

Because of the importance of their banks and their

prominence in St. Augustine, Wolfe and Harrold enjoyed considerably more influence within the community than did other businessmen. Most were caught up in the day-to-day concerns of running their
small businesses and had little opportunity to reflect upon community development for more than a twenty-four hour period. Involved
in the daily preoccupations of their businesses and their relationships
with neighbors and fellow businessmen, they tended to accept certain commonly held views, and, generally, to follow the attitudes
which prevailed in the community. Ordinarily, these men could be
expected to look to Wolfe and Harrold for leadership and advice on
controversial issues. But race relations was not an issue on which St.
Augustine willingly accepted the wisdom of others, especially when
it flew in the face of accepted norms. Furthermore, Wolfe and Harrold gave every indication of holding racial views consistent with
segregation prior to the racial crisis of 1964. They thus found themselves in a very difficult position when they sought to effect a compromise with civil rights leaders in 1964.[12]

The John Birch Society acted as a brake against racial
moderation. Despite the relative smallness of the organization, its views
seemed to enjoy a widespread following in the community and, in
particular, among businessmen. State Senator Verle Pope claimed that
"there was a very active group who might be said to be of a John
Birch variety, who were very prominent and very strong. They were
the leaders in the Kiwanis Club. They were on the vestries in the
churches. Wherever you turned it was the same small group of people who were in power in the various organizations."[13] The evidence
suggests that Pope's comments were exaggerated and reflected the
frustration he experienced in attempting to negotiate a peaceful settlement in 1964. Nevertheless, the philosophy enunciated by the John
Birch Society reached a large group of people in St. Augustine who
believed that Communism threatened the nation's democratic fabric
and its capitalist heritage.

Since most of the key Birch sympathizers had resided in
St. Augustine for many years, they knew one another on a "first name"
basis. Most were close friends who lunched together periodically, shared
a round of golf, and saw each other at business and social gatherings.
The relative smallness and stability of St. Augustine and the close
contact between Birch supporters and other leading citizens made it

unlikely that any businessman would express publicly a different viewpoint. Hamilton Upchurch, Frank Upchurch's son and president of the Chamber of Commerce in 1965, commented that during the racial crisis of 1964 the Birch sympathizers made a conciliatory position untenable. Upchurch observed that the close relations between members of the community severely limited a businessman's freedom of action—"every job had a name and a face."[14]

Despite the continuation of demonstrations throughout the summer of 1963, the business community remained generally unaffected by the protests. Profits and tourism continued to accelerate beyond 1962 levels. With the exception of representatives from the Fairchild Corporation, businessmen in St. Augustine boycotted the hearing conducted by the Florida Advisory Committee to the U.S. Commission on Civil Rights, contending that the civil rights problems were a local matter and that the committee was composed of civil rights sympathizers. In addition, most perceived the conflict as one between militant whites and blacks.[15]

Business leaders wholeheartedly endorsed Governor Bryant's property rights argument against the proposed civil rights bill. In their minds, the real issue concerned "property rights" and who should make the final determination about these rights: the man who earned them or "the man who covets that which he has not earned." Business leaders in St. Augustine and, perhaps, elsewhere in the South looked upon property rights as more important than the civil rights of local blacks. The idea that black citizens had to receive service if they sought it was totally foreign to their experience and value system. Wolfe commented, "Under our system, which I think is the best in the world, a man has the right to choose who he will buy from and sell to. As for me, I will try to do my best to keep it that way."[16]

The prominence of business in the day-to-day life of St. Augustine and the possibility of exploiting that dependence dawned slowly on local civil rights activists. Dr. Hayling had first suggested that the NAACP seek to block the use of federal funds for the city's 400th anniversary. While this effort threatened to have economic repercussions for businessmen, black leaders were primarily interested in showing civic leaders that their continued support for segregation could undermine the city's 400th anniversary.[17]

The realization that tourism was the Achilles heel of St.

Augustine struck SCLC leaders almost immediately, since they had tried to bring Birmingham to its knees using similar tactics. Harry Boyte pointed out: "This is the first time we've been able to put things on such a firm economic basis. In Birmingham the downtown merchants were hurt but we couldn't shut down U.S. Steel. Here it's a total community effort."[18] The economic figures for 1963 showed how vulnerable St. Augustine really was. Over 400,000 people had visited the community in the preceeding twelve months, pumping nearly $7 million into the economy. King quickly exploited this situation, urging northerners to spend their vacation in some other community. While SCLC conducted the demonstrations at Easter for publicity reasons, the organization also sought to demonstrate to businessmen and the community the impact such protests could have on the economic life of the community. Significantly, the Easter demonstrations did not negatively affect economic conditions in the city because they were so brief. Reports from the Tourist Information Center and the more reliable Castillo de San Marcos disclosed that tourism had increased by 50 percent over the figures for Easter week of 1963. Businessmen who opposed the civil rights demands of SCLC were pleased by this news.[19]

In the aftermath of the Easter demonstrations, SCLC decided to accelerate its economic efforts against the city as a way to break down segregation barriers. Mrs. Peabody urged northern tourists to avoid the city in their travels into Florida and the Reverend William Sloan Coffin made a similar appeal in a letter to the editor of the *New York Times*. Local leaders in the SCLC also sent a letter to the executive director of the Organization of American States asking that no funds be provided for the 400th anniversary. Finally, King wired Secretary of Defense Robert McNamara complaining about the intimidation of black employees at the Fairchild Stratos plant and urging the suspension of all federal contracts to the company.[20]

The use of economic pressure to force the city to reconsider its racial stance angered St. Augustine's businessmen initially. When Harry Boyte approached Herbert Wolfe at the beginning of June and asked him to use his influence to stem the mounting violence, Wolfe refused to do so. He told Boyte that he saw nothing wrong with the status of Negroes in St. Augustine and expressed support for a local editorial which accused King of being a troublemaker, who was turning the city into a battleground for no apparent reason.[21] Two other business leaders who opposed any compromise, reflected the views of many of their collegaues, when they argued that "the sole reason for this movement is that local public officials will not force owners of private business to integrate their facilities in direct opposition to the 13th Amendment to the United States Constitution which outlaws involuntary servitude."[22]

The economic consequences of the second wave of protests beginning in late May did not become apparent until the middle of June so that no businessmen were willing to yield to the civil rights demands. Thus even the motel and restaurant owners who bore the brunt of the demonstrations resisted the economic pressures to desegregate until "a federal court orders us to." Nearly all agreed with Herbert Wolfe who told a reporter, "I'm just opposed to establishing a precedent of yielding to intimidation and that's what it would be if we throw in the towel."[23] Business leaders did not meet as a group to plot strategy, although one prominent businessman observed that they resented being invaded to the point that they unanimously opposed a settlement. Several other leaders commented that the press increased their resentment by constantly misquoting them and portraying St. Augustine as a racist community.[24]

After one month of demonstrations and boycott of local businesses, the economic toll began to make itself felt. People like James Bradd, a railroad teletypewriter from Muncie, Indiana, decided to delay their vacation trip to Florida. Bradd had originally planned to spend a portion of his vacation in St. Augustine, "but we're skipping St. Augustine now—it looks like the farther away you stay, the better." Most northern whites chose to stay away because they either feared violence or were sympathetic to black efforts to desegregate the community. One motel owner complained that "I've gotten as many cancellations as reservations this week. I just want all this to end." James A. Kalivar of Chimes Restaurant claimed his business was off 60 percent. Captain Francis F. Usina, who ran a sightseeing vessel, grumbled that his business was running 50 percent behind a year ago. "If Martin Luther King doesn't stay away, the whole summer will be lost," he said. The National Park Service reported that attendance at the Castillo de San Marcos had fallen 30 percent behind the previous year's total. The fort's historian commented: "If it keeps up, there's no doubt the decline will get bigger."[25]

The figures proved especially startling to business leaders

who anticipated that tourism would be up significantly in 1964 with the city receiving considerable publicity on the eve of its 400th anniversary. One resident remarked that the demonstrations had had such a devastating effect on tourism that "you could fire a cannon down the street and hit nothing."[26]

All businesses, not just those directly involved in tourism, felt the effects of the ongoing demonstrations. A hairdresser whose business stood near the old slave market observed: "Business is terrible. I guess it will be as long as the Ku Kluxers and white trash are coming into town to stir up trouble." The owner of a pastry shop commented that he was "closing at 6 P.M. instead of 8 P.M. or 9 P.M. People are afraid to get out on the streets—they might get caught in a demonstration."[27]

Despite the decline in tourism, few business leaders proposed that elected officials seek a reconciliation with civil rights activists. Instead, they joined with their neighbors in condemning King for creating a racial crisis where none had existed before and for using events in the city to further his own ends. W. I. Drysdale reflected the stubborness of many businessmen when he stated angrily, "We're not going to call off the celebration even if we just have a little parade or something." Some local blacks contended that a few businessmen had even resorted to brandishing clubs and chains against them.[28]

Adding to the resolve of business leaders was the pressure that continued to be placed upon them by the John Birch Society and Ku Klux Klan. Norris and Birch members told motel and restaurant owners that surrendering to King would mean a victory for Communism. The organization also took out a two-page advertisement alleging that SCLC was substantially under the control of the Communist Party."[29] Supporters of the Klan used far less subtle tactics. Hoss Manucy, J. B. Stoner, and other Klan members visited restaurants and motels to make sure no owners served blacks. No threats were made, but they did encourage owners to keep "the niggers out." Few owners doubted, however, that threats and violence would be forthcoming should they decide to allow blacks on the premises.[30]

By the third week in June as the violence continued and business losses escalated, the motel owners met at the urging of State Senator Verle Pope to discuss ways to end the crisis. The assembly

included representatives from many of the restaurant and motel facilities as well as officers in the Chamber of Commerce, City Manager Charles Barrier, and Herbert Wolfe. The discussions did not lead
to a compromise proposal, however. Rather, the group through Pope
denounced all outsiders for desecrating St. Augustine "for some un-
known reason." They also refused to meet with Dr. Robert Hayling
under any circumstances because of his threat to arm himself and for
allegedly threatening to rub white faces in the dirt for the years of
racism.[31]

Business leaders did agree "to continue to operate their
businesses in accordance with present and future laws." The impli-
cation was clear. They would abide by the civil rights bill if and when
it was passed by Congress. But when reporters asked Pope if the businessmen were proposing a compromise, he replied, "I don't think so.
We are simply trying to advise the outside world that these problems
are difficult to solve and conditions are much different than they might
have been led to believe." Business leaders hoped King would accept
their promise to obey the pending civil rights bill and withdraw. In
making the announcement to the national media they also sought to
convince tourists that businessmen in St. Augustine were quite progressive and that conditions had not deteriorated as dramatically as
the press had implied.[32]

SCLC viewed the statement of business leaders with mixed
reactions. The Reverend Fred Shuttlesworth characterized the announcement as "segregationist" in tone and declared that it did "not
show much evolution." He promised that SCLC would "keep our
present program."[33] But the organization had been tiring of the constant violence and the expense involved. With passage of the civil
rights bill imminent, Dr. King decided to keep the lines of communication open. He reported that he had heard several business leaders were willing to desegregate, hire blacks, and drop charges against
the demonstrators if a compromise could be arranged. "Some businessmen told us that they were afraid of violence from Klan and
Klanlike elements in the community," King added.[34] Where King received his information is unclear. It appears extremely doubtful that
several businessmen stood ready to desegregate. The overwhelming
majority wanted the Klan and SCLC out of St. Augustine, but this
did not mean they favored desegregation. If given a choice, busi-

nessmen would have opted for a continuation of the racial policies of the past.

When businessmen failed to open discussions with SCLC, the organization decided to conduct the dramatic demonstration on June 18 including the swim-in at the Monson Motor Lodge, a development that thoroughly alienated leaders like Pope and Wolfe, who had favored some racial adjustments. All talk about a peace initiative among business leaders ended. Brock, who supported Pope's efforts, conceded his attitude had changed as had those of his colleagues in the motel business.[35]

The economic picture continued to worsen for St. Augustine's business community as July began. The National Park Service disclosed that tourism at the Castillo had declined by nearly 50 percent for the month of June. Most other businesses reported reductions of over 60 percent. H. B. Chitty, executive director of the St. Augustine Chamber of Commerce, said that the city stood to lose $5 million and might lose as much as $8 million if the racial crisis continued.[36]

With the community on the verge of catastrophe, Wolfe and Governor Bryant received a telephone call from Senator George Smathers seeking their support for a biracial committee. Wolfe contacted Frank Harrold who expressed his support for the establishment of such a committee and indicated his willingness to serve on it if necessary.[37] In their positions as bankers, both men realized St. Augustine could ill afford a continuation of the racial crisis. Despite their prominence in the community, neither man was willing to take a position that ran contrary to the attitudes that prevailed in the community. Both had to live in St. Augustine long after the civil rights crisis had passed, and they had to see these people at social functions and business meetings. As a consequence, when Mayor Shelley and other leading citizens met at his house and bitterly opposed Smathers' proposal, Wolfe and Harrold refused to act alone.

It seems likely, however, that Governor Bryant informed Wolfe of his decision to announce the establishment of a biracial committee and that Wolfe viewed it as an effective way to calm local tempers. The governor's announcement enabled businessmen to sidestep the pressures being exerted upon them by Birch and Klan sympathizers without facing retribution.

Seizing upon Bryant's initiative, Edward Mussallem and James Brock contacted others in the motel and restaurant business to discuss ways to end the crisis. While none of the owners favored the civil rights bill, they agreed that they would support it. The chamber of commerce opted to abide by the decision of the group and "to inform the public or our necessity to comply."[38] By emphasizing the need to obey the proposed law, business leaders hoped to prevent Birch and Klan followers from responding hostilely. Two days later Lyndon Johnson signed the civil rights bill into law.

Following Johnson's action, Frank Upchurch, representing the city, and Tobias Simon, representing SCLC, met and agreed that Upchurch would speak to the Restaurant Association to find out which owners would abide by the Civil Rights Act and would provide Simon with the names of those who refused to comply. SCLC planned to visit those who agreed to comply with the provision of the law no more than twice a week, while those who refused would be visited daily and prosecuted. SCLC officials compiled a list of all restaurants and motels in the community and recorded their response to the desegregation tests. In the following days SCLC members fanned out across the city to test the business community's compliance with the law. Initially, black groups received service at all but two restaurants.[39]

After nearly two months of racial violence and near economic collapse, businessmen thought the crisis had passed when Klansmen suddenly began their counterdemonstrations. In addition to the protests, several owners received telephone threats against their businesses. Manucy claimed, "The picketing was being done on a volunteer basis in the name of the White Citizens' Council. Nobody is getting paid. When a businessman tells us they will refuse to serve Negroes the pickets are removed."[40]

As the threats and demonstrations continued through the middle of July, business leaders began gradually resegregating their facilities, in order to hold onto their white customers. SCLC reports showed that by July 16, most restaurants were refusing to serve black groups. The devastating slump continued throughout this period as businessmen groped for a solution. Individual restaurant owners took to pleading with Manucy to remove the picketers. Motel owners met with Hamilton Upchurch on the evening of July 23 at the Monson

Motel to discuss legal steps available to them. Upchurch persuaded the owners to consent "to the entry of an injunction against you to obey the law," contending that this might also persuade the courts to stop further picketing.[41] Early the following morning two white men, responding to news of the decision, threw a Molotov cocktail into the Monson restaurant badly damaging the interior. During the day, those businessmen who had not begun turning blacks away now did.[42]

State Attorney General James Kynes, who viewed most of the crisis from Tallahassee but had been periodically sent to St. Augustine at the request of the governor, had little sympathy for the plight of the business community. When blacks were conducting sit-ins, Kynes observed, merchants allowed young white toughs to set the mood of the town with little or no resistance to their actions. Now, he noted, the businessmen found they could not take back control when it no longer suited their purpose to have gangs of whites roaming the streets.[43] Kynes was correct in his assessment; business and civic leaders had indeed helped to create a monster which now ran amok in their city.

The momentum to break down the new segregation barriers and to prevent the segregationists from interfering in the desegregation process came from Judge Simpson. His intervention was critical for it led to the removal of outside militants from the community and allowed business and civic leaders to reassert control.[44]

Simpson's actions did not immediately restore normalcy to community life or permanently end the violence, since many white residents were still incensed over the intervention of King and SCLC into "their peaceful community." Though the Restaurant Association adopted a resolution reluctantly agreeing to integrate, the statement did not stop there. It went on to say, "We deplore the action of the Congress and the Courts in enforcing integration" and "that integration of places of accommodation is obnoxious to us." Once again owners emphasized their obligation to "comply or suffer the penalty of the law" to keep from incurring the wrath of segregationists. Several restaurant owners also put signs above their cash registers stating that all money spent by integrationists in their establishment would be used to aid Barry Goldwater's 1964 presidential campaign because of his opposition to the Civil Rights Act.[45] In a speech before a local civic group, Harold Colee, head of the state Chamber of Commerce and a native St. Augustinian, reflected the views of many when he remarked derisively how the recent racial crisis could be marketed to attract more tourists: "You may interestingly point out just where a certain prominent New England lady—a professional bleeding heart—was standing when she posed for cameramen of the national news media, working from a prepared script, in the year 1964."[46]

By the middle of 1965, blacks were still unsure about their place in St. Augustine and few were willing to dine in white restaurants or register at white motels. One black citizen who could afford to eat at such restaurants commented: "You can be pretty sure that if you eat at a white restaurant and they know who you are, your boss will be told that you're trying to stir up trouble. If they don't know you, you might be arrested after you leave so they can find out about you."[47]

Despite such circumstances, the business community had substantially altered its racial policies if not its racial attitudes by the spring of 1965. The impact of the racial crisis on the tourist industry in St. Augustine had gradually awakened business leaders to the consequences of their actions during the past year. By the end of 1964 tourism was off 40 to 60 percent in virtually all businesses from the 1963 levels.[48] No one in the community could afford a repetition of the decline experienced in 1964.

With the 400th anniversary about to be celebrated in September 1965, and SCLC promising renewed demonstrations if the violence did not cease, businessmen organized to block further resistance. They viewed the anniversary celebration as an opportunity to recoup the losses of 1964 and were particularly anxious that nothing be done to jeopardize this event. Twenty businessmen began meeting in the spring to find ways to improve the city's image. They also appointed a five-man executive committee which met with five black leaders to seek solutions to the community's racial problems. After several discussions, the white executive committee agreed to support a Jaycee-sponsored voter education drive and an integrated public sunrise Easter service. White committee members also acknowledged black criticism of the police and the courts and agreed to assist blacks in upgrading the quality of the city's law enforcement agencies. In related events businessmen sought unsuccessfully to persuade Flagler Hospital to desegregate its facilities. And, in an overture to the black community, the *St. Augustine Record* ran a favorable front page story of Mrs. Rosalie Gordon's campaign for a seat on the city council.[49] Through these steps, business leaders successfully undercut opposition in the black community and, despite minor protests, the anniversary celebration was an economic success.

Unfortunately, the advances made in racial communication and understanding came to a halt in the wake of the celebration. Several business leaders did write the city commission, requesting that they be appointed to meet with leaders of the black community. However, Shelley persuaded his fellow commissioners to defeat this proposal because he viewed it as simply another name for a biracial committee, which he and the commission dogmatically opposed in 1964. With this setback, contact between the business community and black leaders came to a halt.[50]

In assessing the business community's response to the racial crisis in St. Augustine, it seems clear that it had a great deal in common with that found in such Old South cities as Charleston and New Orleans. "Tradition, respect for old wealth, concern for the style of social life, and an elitist outlook acted as barriers to changes in social and ideological outlook," Bartley observed. An Episcopal clergyman found the businessmen in the city to be "independently minded" and "sufficiently committed to what they believed . . . to jeopardize their businesses."[51] Perhaps even more important, however, were the pressures exerted upon business leaders by a relatively small, interpersonal society and an influential John Birch organization which tended to discourage views that supported negotiation. These people were friends, neighbors and, in some cases, business partners. An alternative course of action proved to be untenable in such a society where opposition to the civil rights movement was so deeply ingrained.

The businessmen in St. Augustine thus had to be forced to abandon the racial traditions of the past by a vigorous civil rights effort, the federal courts, and the federal government. Only when civic and business leaders realized that there was no turning back, and the community's economic well-being and the celebration of the 400th anniversary were tied to the amelioration of the crisis did they oppose the reemergence of racial violence.

In marked contrast to the era of Reconstruction, the federal pressure to desegregate St. Augustine remained unwavering throughout the 1960s. Without such urging, the business community in this historic city would have unhesitatingly trod along the segregationist path it was so accustomed to. A social transformation did occur in St. Augustine, but it did not emanate from the business leadership in the community, as Claude Sitton and Reed Sarratt have suggested. The passage of time, a vocal black minority, the persistent threat of federal intervention, and a decline in the influence of the Birch Society (see chapter 8) gradually brought about the acceptance of a desegregated society by the city's businessmen in the late 1960s. If the response of St. Augustine's economic leaders was typical of those in highly personal, tradition-bound, and Birch-influenced southern communities, then such places did not willingly accept the racial developments of the 1950s. On the contrary, a national government, encouraged to act by the courts, civil rights group, and a sympathetic North, mandated these social changes.

In the aftermath of the racial crisis, businessmen largely removed themselves from the civil rights debate. The rapid decline of the civil rights movement with the final departure of SCLC and the decision by Dr. Hayling to move to south Florida in 1967 facilitated the withdrawal of business leaders from racial deliberations. With the racial crisis at an end, businessmen readily returned to their chief concern, their own enterprises.

When the school crisis emerged in 1969 (see chapter 8), most businessmen watched the Birch supporters and their opponents square off. Few were anxious to jeopardize their businesses by taking sides or getting in the middle of this fight. In recent years, businessmen have avoided becoming involved in civil rights developments altogether. Black leaders have largely ignored the private sector during this period, choosing instead to concentrate their efforts on the public sector in an effort to improve job opportunities for local residents and public services for black neighborhoods. Never anxious to be in the limelight on social issues which did not directly affect their enterprises, businessmen have been content to stay in the background and ignore recent racial concerns. Without the involvement of this most influential group, however, real economic opportunity for black St. Augustinians has not been possible and black gains since 1965 have been largely limited to the social and political arenas.

Chapter 7.

The Most Segregated Hour
in America

On the surface, at least, the church appeared to be a potent force for racial change in the South and in St. Augustine. Doctrinally, the Protestant and Catholic churches and Jewish synagogues did not discriminate between the souls of white and black southerners. In addition, as Weldon James noted, ministers provided "perhaps the greatest threat to the unity sought by organized segregationists" because they frequently voiced anti–Jim Crow views.[1] The independence of the clergy was no more apparent than in the aftermath of the *Brown* decision when the central governing bodies of the major religious denominations in the South spoke out unanimously in support of the Supreme Court ruling. Within three days of the pronouncement, the Catholic Interracial Council called it "a logical step in the expansion and perfection of American democracy. The next step is the creation and practice of community educational patterns consistent with the spirit and intent of the Court decision."[2]

The major Protestant denominations in the South soon echoed the views expressed by the Catholic Interracial Council. Reflecting its post–World War II concern with social issues, the Southern Baptist Convention led the way, urging "all Christians to conduct themselves in this period of adjustment in the spirit of Christ" and declaring support for the public school system with the hope that it "shall not be impaired." The statements by other denominations varied in tone and strength of commitment but generally recommended that Christians abide by the Court's decision. The Episcopal General Convention meeting in 1955 made, perhaps, the strongest commitment, asking that "all the clergy and people of this church accept and support this ruling of the Supreme Court." It also encouraged the establishment of a dialogue "between the races concerned in each diocese and community." The Florida Council of Churches added to the chorus of religious voices by "urging the people . . . to remember their obligation as a people 'under God' and to act in charity, tolerance and wisdom in bringing this state into conformity with the will of the conscience of the nation as expressed" by the Supreme Court.[3] The churches had thus expressed themselves unequivocally on the *Brown* decision.

Nevertheless, despite these statements and recommendations by the General Convention and Assemblies of the various denominations, few Florida parishes and no St. Augustine churches took steps to promote school desegregation or to open the doors of the respective churches to blacks. Frank Loescher's observation in 1948 was still applicable during the period 1955 to 1964, especially in St. Augustine: "Protestantism [Catholicism as well], by its policies and practices far from helping to integrate the Negro in American life, is actually contributing to the segregation of Negro Americans."[4]

It was relatively easy for church leaders at a general convention to express support for the *Brown* decision, but to implement such a policy at the local level in the South was fraught with difficulties. As religious historian Samuel Hill noted in 1964, "Involvement by church officials in support of integration would cost their churches dearly in loss of members and offerings."[5] Furthermore, for the Protestant denominations which lacked an ecclesiastical hierarchy and where control was vested in the local congregation, ministerial leaders could be removed from their positions if they advocated racial views contrary to those of the congregation. In the day-to-day world of the church, they served as employees subject to the whims of their employers—the parishioners.[6] In an environment of racial hostility and "intense feelings of Christian laymen," few ministers stood prepared to exert leadership on an issue that promised few temporal benefits and seemed certain to disrupt drastically the life of the church. Some, of course, shared the prejudices of their church members. In commenting on the integration resolutions adopted by the Southern Baptists, one man declared: "They were just a little bit exalted. When they got back with the home folks, a lot of 'em wondered how they did it."[7] Martin Luther King's contention, "If ever the White ministers of the South decide to declare in a united voice the truth of the gospel on the question of race, the transition from a segregated to an integrated society will be infinitely smoother," was certainly correct, but despite the statement of the South's central religious bodies, such a united voice appeared to be a long way off in 1956.[8]

The Catholic Church, which did have the hierarchical structure to protect local clergy from congregational whims, was not a major force for racial change in the South. The Church sought to avoid controversy to keep from further isolating itself from the mainstream of southern life. Historically, the South had been slow to accept the Catholic Church and anti-Catholic sentiment reached its apogee in the twentieth century. Adding to the Church's malaise in the South was the absence, save in New Orleans, of dynamic, young Catholic priests who typically served elsewhere.[9]

As was true of the South generally, religion formed a central part of community life in St. Augustine. St. Augustinians were very active churchgoers and virtually all community leaders played a prominent role in one of the local churches. In addition to being attracted to the church as a source of spiritual and moral guidance, many St. Augustinians were interested in the church's social activities.[10] While the involvement of St. Augustinians in religious affairs had not diminished, by 1960 a qualitative change in their relationship with the church seemed in the process of taking place. Because of the prosperity enjoyed by white St. Augustinians in the post–World War II period, they were increasingly caught up in worldly matters, especially with ways to spend their recently acquired wealth. They were less dependent on the church and less in need of the security it offered; consequently, they were less likely to turn to it for guidance and direction on days other than Sunday.[11]

The major religious denominations in St. Augustine in 1960 were much like those found in other southern towns and included Baptist, Presbyterian, Episcopal, and Methodist. But in contrast to most southern communities, St. Augustine had (and continues to have) a very large Catholic population, which comprised nearly one-third of the citizens, many of whom were of Minorcan descent. St. Augustine also served as the episcopal see for Catholic Florida, then under the direction of Archbishop Joseph P. Hurley; the Cathedral of St. Augustine sat directly on the site where it had been constructed initially in 1797. Twenty to twenty-five percent of the town's population attended several Baptist churches in the community. Episcopalians, Presbyterians, and Methodists constituted nearly one-third of St. Augustine's religious population. Episcopalians worshiped at the historic Trinity Episcopal Church, while Presbyterians attended the First Presbyterian Church, built by Henry M. Flagler in 1889. Methodists attended two churches in the city, Grace Methodist and First Methodist.

Of these five major denominations, only two ministered to the needs of the black residents of St. Augustine. Both the Catholic and Episcopal churches provided separate missions with small churches for black communicants, inviting them periodically to take part in special religious festivities and ceremonies at the main church. Generally, however, no black communicants attended regular services at any "white" church.[12] The other Protestant churches in St. Augustine had no black members and provided no missions to members of the black community. While there were Baptist and Methodist churches ministering to the needs of blacks, they operated in complete isolation from their counterparts in the white community.[13] King's observation that "eleven o'clock on Sunday morning . . . is the most segregated hour of America, and the Sunday School is the most segregated school of the week" could not be disclaimed by St. Augustinians.[14] The condition described by King made it extraordinarily difficult for ministers to support integration in the public schools and elsewhere in society. Indeed, the segregation that existed at church provided moral and spiritual support for the segregation that pervaded society. Not insignificantly, this segregation persisted even while the community's black ministers welcomed people of other races to their services and were willing to have white ministers preach to their congregations.

In the years between the *Brown* decision and the racial crisis of 1963 and 1964, St. Augustine's religious leaders took no steps to prepare their congregations and the community for the racial changes that were to come. Very little was said about the "equality" of all people in the eyes of God.[15] Thus, when the racial crisis began in 1963, not one white church and none of the communicants was prepared to cope with the issues from a religious perspective. The laxness of the religious leaders is explained in part by the absence of any dialogue between white and black churchmen. The ministerial alliance "talked an awful lot about meeting with the blacks but never got around to it," one minister remarked.[16]

Further undermining the influence of the church in societal matters was the weakness of the ministerial alliance. According to one prominent white minister, the relationship between the religious leaders in the white churches was not sufficiently healthy to create a united ministerial front working for racial betterment. He noted that the priests at the cathedral would not even "speak to me on the streets" while the Baptist ministers refused to "associate in any way with blacks."[17] They were the two largest and most influential denominations in St. Augustine. Lutheran and Methodist ministers remained in the community for only a brief period according to church custom, making it difficult to develop any continuity on racial policy and preventing the development of an effective stance against segregation.

Throughout the troubled summer and fall of 1963, the white churches in St. Augustine remained noticeably aloof toward the efforts of the black civil rights leaders. Robert W. Saunders of Tampa, field secretary of the NAACP, asked Archbishop Hurley to "assume the responsibility of establishing communication so that the racial discrimination and segregation can be ended without violence." Saunders never received a reply from the archbishop. Instead, the Catholic Church chose to ignore the racial crisis which engulfed the community and the demonstrations that took place at the footsteps of the cathedral.[18]

More than any other church in St. Augustine, the Catholic Church had the greatest opportunity to influence the racial response of the community. Catholicism had been intimately connected with the history of the community and commanded the religious loyalties of the greatest number of people. In addition, because of its organizational structure, the priest was freer than his Protestant counterparts to speak on religious, moral, and social matters without being subject to the disaffection of his congregation. The presence of the archbishop gave the Catholic Church in St. Augustine an added bit of prestige and influence in the lives of its people.

The Church, however, failed to take advantage of its unique role in the community to halt the crisis or to initiate a compromise. Not insignificantly, Mayor Joseph Shelley was a devout Catholic who might have been persuaded to abandon his opposition to a biracial committee if encouraged to do so by the archbishop. The Church's racial conservatism was further revealed when it did not integrate its parochial school system until a year after the public schools began token integration and two months after the racial crisis ended.[19]

The failure of the Catholic Church to intervene in the racial crisis reflected in large measure the human frailties of Archbishop Joseph P. Hurley, whose meteoric rise in the Catholic Church had ended dramatically with his return to St. Augustine in 1950. Hurley had been born on January 21, 1894, in Cleveland, and as with many of the eldest sons of good Irish Catholic families, he attended parochial schools and was groomed for the priesthood. After pursuing philosophical studies at St. Bernard's Seminary in Rochester and theological studies at St. Mary's Seminary in Cleveland, he was ordained on May 29, 1919, and served as assistant pastor in Youngstown and Cleveland. In the late 1920s this extraordinarily bright and articulate young priest caught the interest of Bishop Edward Mooney of Cleveland who chose Hurley as his secretary when he became apostolic delegate to India in 1928. The paths of the two men became intertwined for the next several years as Hurley accompanied Mooney to India and then succeeded him as chargé d'affaires of the Apostolic Delegation in Japan, 1933–34, and as head of the American desk at the Secretary of State's office in the Vatican, 1934–1940.[20]

In October 1940 Hurley was consecrated as a bishop and sent to St. Augustine. A priest attached to the diocese at the time recalled that "it was the expectation of the American church that he was going to be the new great American churchman."[21] Hurley quickly led many to believe that this impression was correct. Under his guidance two important National Catholic Conferences on Family Life were held at Catholic University in Washington. In addition, Hurley, who believed the American Catholic Church had been woefully shortsighted in its failure to criticize Hitler, addressed Floridians in May and the nation in July about the menace of Nazism to world peace. In the latter address on "The Catholic Hour" he labeled the Nazis "enemy number 1 of America and the world." Both addresses were strongly criticized by Irish-Americans who saw the German threat to England as a boon to the Irish dream of an independent Ireland. Many Irish churchmen echoed Hurley's critics, including the Bishop of Buffalo who referred to it as the "Mein Führer Roosevelt" address. [22]

Following the war, the man he had worked for as papal secretary of state in Rome became Pope Pius XII and he named Hurley apostolic nuncio to Belgrade, Yugoslavia, in November 1945. Hurley received considerable credit for defending the Church against attacks by Marshall Tito, coming to the assistance of the imprisoned Cardinal Aloysius Stepinac, and providing relief to millions of starving Yugoslavians. For all this he incurred the undying enmity of Tito. [23]

During this period, Hurley continued to serve as bishop of St. Augustine with the Reverend Thomas McDonough acting as auxiliary bishop in his absence. Correspondence between the two over developments in the Florida diocese proved exceedingly difficult because of Tito's suppression of the mails. As a consequence, Hurley asked McDonough to meet with him in Locarno, Switzerland, to discuss developments in the diocese. The two met there in the summer of 1950, but when, following their discussions, Hurley attempted to reenter Yugoslavia, he found the border closed to him. Tito refused to let him be readmitted and Hurley eventually returned to Rome. Furious at Hurley for leaving Yugoslavia without his permission and at losing the Church's leading spokesman in this Communist nation, Pope Pius XII would not meet with him, and for several months Hurley remained in Rome without assignment. Finally, Pius made him archbishop ad persona, meaning he was an archbishop in title and rank but without having an archbishop's authority or territory, and sent him back to St. Augustine.

Pius' action permitted Hurley to return to the United States with a measure of respectability, but Hurley knew his advancement within the church had come to an end. [24] The impact of this development on the archbishop was devastating according to an assistant. Thereafter, Hurley confined his duties to matters pertaining to the diocese of St. Augustine and played little role in the life of the Church outside the state.[25]

During the height of the civil rights crisis in St. Augustine in 1964, Hurley arrived on an airplane at Imeson airfield in Jacksonville. Stepping down from another plane a few minutes later was Martin Luther King, Jr. According to one observer, Hurley saw King approaching and, rather than greet him, deliberately hid behind a pillar to avoid having to discuss racial developments in St. Augustine.[26] Hurley's action symbolized the role played by the Catholic Church under his leadership throughout the crisis. He and the other priests remained hidden behind the doors of the cathedral to avoid involving themselves in the racial crisis which occurred adjacent to and, on some occasions, on church grounds.

Hurley subsequently wrote a speech that Monsignor John Burns read to the congregation and the press, explaining the Church's position on the racial crisis. Unfortunately, it came near the end of the third month of the crisis and merely expressed in vague generalities the view that "Catholic people [ought to] abstain from any actions which might occasion or increase disorder . . . in our city." A similar statement was made by the chancellor of the Diocese of St. Augustine, who wrote that "the Catholic Church in St. Augustine has used its influence consistently to achieve equal justice under law and Christian Fraternity among people of different races." "The best interests of Saint Augustine will be served in the difficult period of transition," he concluded, "by refraining from any act which might occasion or perpetuate ill will or hatred among our people." Hurley's address and the views expressed by his aides failed to indicate any new initiatives to be undertaken by the church to alleviate the crisis, merely that "we shall gladly work with others of like mind and purpose."[27]

The Catholic Church did not stand alone in its ineffectiveness, although it stood out more noticeably than the other churches because of its prominence in the community. During the Easter demonstrations mixed groups attempted to integrate several churches. Most of the groups were turned away and not allowed to attend religious services. The Reverend W. W. Fountain, pastor of Calvary Baptist Church, wondered aloud, "If God doesn't force himself on you or me, is it Christian to force yourself on others?" He insisted that in normal times local blacks would be seated in his church. Fountain criticized northern clergymen, who, he asserted, had done less to solve racial difficulties in their own cities than local ministers in St. Augustine. Even moderate religious leaders, such as Dr. J. E. McKinley, pastor at First Methodist Church and secretary of the local Ministerial Alliance, argued that race relations were proceeding smoothly until Mrs. Peabody came to town. Those who preached to fundamentalist, nondenominational sects in the county generally denounced the civil rights movement and the evils of race mixing.[28]

Religious leaders who were inclined to support desegregation decided against doing so when they saw what happened to others. The Reverend Howard W. Lee of Flagler Memorial Presbyterian Church opened the doors of his church to demonstrators after they had been denied entrance on Easter Sunday by lay leaders. Lee and two ministers at First Methodist Church, who had also supported the desegregation effort, were subsequently removed by their congregations because they were considered "too liberal." One northern white minister who marched with the Negroes, and who was beaten and put in jail, said in an interview, "I am appalled at the lack of action on the part of local ministers—I can't understand why the city's leaders sit back and say nothing."[29]

During the racial crisis, however, no church experienced the furor over desegregation that Trinity Episcopal Church did. In many ways, the civil rights struggle was fought out in microcosm within that church and the controversy that engulfed Trinity pointed out in dramatic fashion how difficult it had become to steer a middle course during the crisis. At the onset of the racial crisis, Trinity Episcopal Church had a membership of nearly five hundred. It was led by the Reverend Charles Seymour, parish rector for nearly fifteen years, and the Reverend Stanley Bullock, his recently hired assistant. The communicants came largely from the middle and upper class in St. Augustine and some traced their lineage back to the British period. Seymour described the congregation as "not necessarily the upper crust in the community but often times those of better socioeconomic standing in the community . . . [who enjoyed] white collar jobs, education, and travel."[30]

Although he found several able and committed Christians in the church, Seymour felt from his first years "that there was

a certain built-in selfishness about the people in Trinity." He remarked that they "were satisfied with themselves and what they had
and not too concerned about outside." This smugness permeated the
outreach programs of the church. The congregation had little interest in giving for any local nonchurch matters and for diocesan programs. In areas they considered to be peripheral to the Episcopal
Church, such as race relations, they had absolutely no concern and
no desire for the church to participate.[31]

  The vestry of Trinity Episcopal Church, which met
monthly with the ministers to discuss church policy, tended, to be
"a younger crowd" in 1964, and sympathetic to the views of "the
White Citizens' Council." Of the twelve vestrymen serving in the
spring of 1964, eight were businessmen, one worked for the county,
one served as editor for the St. Augustine Record, one was active in
the National Guard, and another independently wealthy. In reflecting upon the composition of the vestry, Seymour contended that
Clayton Stratton, senior warden, did not know the congregation or
church too well and that Kenneth Barrett, junior warden, and A. H.
Tebeault, Jr., two of Seymour's more vocal critics, "knew less than
that." Seymour's comment about Stratton seems particularly unusual
since the minister in the Episcopal Church personally designates the
senior warden and most ministers select older members, who they can
work with and who are familiar with past church policies. Nevertheless, Seymour said he chose Stratton because he thought Stratton was
someone he could trust and a person who would be likely to agree
with him on various policy matters. Seymour went on to say that all
but one vestryman had "no use for blacks." Tebeault, a young, articulate, and very conservative sort, generally carried three others with
him in any discussion. Tebeault had few doubts about his own abilities and felt very confident about his knowledge of the church and
race relations. He and Barrett exhibited no hesitancy in expressing
themselves on any religious or social matter.[32]

  Trinity's involvement in the racial crisis began when word
was received that Mrs. Peabody planned to visit St. Augustine in
support of the desegregation effort. The Reverend Hamilton West,
bishop of the Diocese of Florida of the Episcopal church, telephoned
her husband, Bishop Malcolm Peabody, to ask that he and his wife
reconsider her participation both for personal and religious reasons.

West feared for her safety, but also believed her involvement would suggest that the Episcopal church in New England and perhaps else-where supported an activist desegregation movement. His appeal came to nought.[33]

On March 30, the day after her arrival, Mrs. Peabody led a large group of young blacks seeking to integrate the ten o'clock Tuesday morning service at Trinity, despite a request from Seymour that she refrain from coming if she intended to demonstrate. As the group walked down St. George Street from Central Avenue, a sizable number of young whites stood waiting for them across from Trinity Church on the plaza. Seymour was in his office when Charles Walker, treasurer of the church, told him about Mrs. Peabody's plans and the threat of violence. Within a matter of minutes several vestrymen en-tered Seymour's office, asking the rector what he intended to do. Some others went to the rear of the church and locked the exterior doors to prevent Mrs. Peabody from entering. When Mrs. Peabody and her group failed to gain entrance to the church, she asked for directions to the church office.[34] She and a small group from Massachusetts met Seymour, Bullock, and several vestrymen in the outer area of the church as they walked toward the church for the scheduled session. Mrs. Peabody asked the church leaders to admit the blacks in her group. One vestryman responded that "we do not want any demon-strations of any kind." Mrs. Peabody criticized the vestry for "not trying to solve your problems." "Integration and civil rights are American problems," she declared. A vestryman accused her of setting civil rights "back five years down here." "The Negroes have waited a hundred years," retorted Mrs. Peabody. When another vestryman grumbled about "do-gooders," the high-spirited Mrs. Peabody admitted, "That's exactly what we are, or what we hope we are." The meeting came to a close with both sides still at loggerheads.[35]

The failure of Mrs. Peabody to gain entrance to Trinity Parish received considerable national publicity and generated wide-spread criticism of Seymour. The press highlighted the fact that the doors of the church had been locked when her group tried to enter and implied that Seymour was responsible for this step. Bullock re-called that several Episcopal ministers called Seymour less than a priest for permitting the doors to be locked.[36] Others suggested that he be removed from the church.

After the Peabody incident, several groups of demonstrators attempted to integrate Trinity parish but were turned away repeatedly by ushers who were "almost invariably members of the vestry." On one occasion, Julian Brown, an Episcopal preministerial student, entered a side door at Trinity accompanied by three teenage black girls. They planned to attend the 11:00 A.M. service but were early and seated themselves during the recessional which marked the end of the previous service. As the people left, an usher approached them and announced, "You're not welcome here." He told Brown to leave and added, "Don't you ever come back here."[37] According to Stanley Bullock, the vestry "had determined that they were not going to receive into the church persons who were specifically there for the purpose of demonstrations." Bullock and Seymour both claimed they were "not aware" of what was happening since they were with the choir or in their vesting rooms preparing for the service.[38]

As a result of the controversy surrounding the Peabody demonstration and their dissatisfaction with the vestry's opposition to desegregation, Seymour and Bullock in consultation with Bishop West decided that they would assist efforts to integrate the church. This decision came on the heels of the vestry's declaration that they did not want the church involved in the racial crisis or the "use of our facility . . . for any purpose of demonstration or public display."[39]

During the first week in April, Bishop West ordered all churches in the Diocese of Florida to open church doors to anyone who wished to attend services. On April 12, in what appeared to be a carefully orchestrated move, five local black Episcopalians attended the Sunday morning service at Trinity. Seymour told reporters that "the Negroes came in just like anybody else and they took their seats just like everybody else. Nobody paid attention."[40] Seymour's observation was not entirely accurate. The vestrymen and members of the church had followed closely the development on April 12. As one vestryman remarked, "The vestry had been opposed for some time to demonstrators attending services at Trinity; however, Bishop West had taken the matters out of our hands and nullified our decision."[41]

West had become bishop of the North Florida Diocese in 1956 after serving eight years as bishop coadjutor in charge of clergy promotions and diocesan work in colleges. Reported to be an able pastor, administrator, and missionary, West had been selected without much controversy. His career had been solid if unspectacular with considerable work at the parish level in Utah and Florida before his years as coadjutor. He had also been active in interdenominational work and served as president of the Florida Council of Churches. In this capacity he supported the desegregation of Protestant churches but was not an outspoken advocate of civil rights.[42]

Despite the announcement of the bishop and the action of the clergy, members of the Trinity vestry refused to step aside quietly. During the two weeks following the events of April 12, the vestry met and drafted a resolution to the bishop censuring the National Council of the Episcopal Church for its position on civil rights. In the resolution, the vestry asked each parish in the diocese to join with them in "deploring the participation of Church officials and laity in any activities, [or] demonstrations . . . which violate or willfully ignore the law, or which disregard the property rights of others, or . . . make a mockery of the Church by using it as a tool."[43] The action by the vestry deliberately contravened the position held by Bishop West and the Reverend Seymour. Though nothing further came of this development, it became clear that the vestry stood prepared to challenge the authority of their bishop and rector should the crisis worsen. The vestry did not take any more radical action at this time apparently because the crisis in the community seemed to have run its course with the departure of Mrs. Peabody and SCLC. In addition, it had not yet become certain that SCLC would reenter St. Augustine.

Caught in the middle between the progressive views of the national church and the racist views of Trinity's vestry and some members of the congregation was the Reverend Seymour. He had become rector of Trinity parish in 1949. Described as a minister who viewed the church as an important spiritual and secular institution in the lives of its members, Seymour had entered the ministry in 1935 at the age of twenty-five.[44] In 1949 he accepted a call from Trinity Episcopal Church to become its rector because it was a large church which offered him a better salary and because it had greater possibilities for growth and development than the South Carolina parish he had served during World War II. During his early years at Trinity he guided the construction of a parish house and the remodeling of the church. He also encouraged communicants to follow the example of Christ by caring for the poor and the infirm. Trinity thus grew physically and spiritually under Seymour's guiding hand.

Seymour never encountered any serious racial problems in St. Augustine until 1963, although the issue of race was always present. "Unfortunately, this was solved, so to speak, in many areas by having a separate [Episcopal] church for the black," Seymour recalled.[45] Black Episcopalians attended St. Cyprian's, a small mission which was ministered by the assistant at Trinity or by a young minister from Jacksonville. Black Episcopalians were "always welcomed at services of the whites," Seymour contended. In saying this, however, he meant that blacks were not expected to attend Trinity except on such special occasions as weddings, funerals, and special days. Although Episcopalians in the South tended to be liberal and well educated, they showed no particular interest in sharing the Sunday morning worship hour with blacks even if they shared the same faith.

Although Trinity profited by Seymour's leadership, the church was not without its internal problems. Several conservatives in the church led by A. H. Tebeault, Jr., Dr. Hardgrove Norris, and E. W. Trice, expressed dissatisfaction with Seymour's ministry. Norris characterized Seymour "as very weak" and felt he was too willing to follow the liberal policies of the national church. Tebeault echoed Norris' view, criticizing Seymour and the Episcopal Church, in general, for its excessive concern with the secular world.[46] The controversy that swirled around Trinity Episcopal Church in the spring and early summer of 1964 saw the two issues of discontent with Seymour by certain members of the congregation and of anger over the racial crisis come together, resulting in a bitter confrontation between the clergy and members of the vestry.

The renewal of demonstrations in mid-May by SCLC, assisted by financial support from the National Council of Churches, heightened tensions within Trinity. On May 19 the vestry decided 9 to 3 to hold all funds pledged to the diocese in escrow until "the Diocese withdraws complete support from the National Council of Churches." This amounted to a sum of $2,400. The vestry also drafted a resolution explaining their version of the events that had unfolded at Trinity and sent copies to all vestrymen in the diocese. The three-page letter blamed "racial agitators" for all the problems at Trinity.

It criticized Bishop West for his order admitting blacks to church services and singled out the National Council of Churches for its support of a wide variety of civil rights activities. "We feel we cannot condone the orders of the National Council of Churches or the National Council of the Episcopal Church, in support of racial agitation, demonstration and their policy of de-segregation of life in the Church," the vestry declared.[47]

The vestry resolution was also published in the church bulletin along with highly critical comments by Seymour. Seymour stated that the purpose of the vestry letter was to cause the Episcopal Church to withdraw from the National Council of the Churches of Christ. Such action, Seymour observed, could only be accomplished by the General Convention of the Episcopal Church. He suggested that, if Trinity Parish desired to be a part of the Episcopal Church, it had to accept all its policies, not just those it agreed with, and it had an obligation to support the work of the diocese.[48]

During the week of June 14 Seymour invited the Reverend Wayne Buchanan from St. Luke's Church in Hot Springs, Arkansas, who was visiting his daughter in St. Augustine, to preach for him at the 11 A.M. service on June 21. On Saturday, Seymour and Bullock received word from an Episcopal priest, the Reverend Henri Stines from Atlanta, that he was going to lead a mixed group into Trinity for the 11 A.M. service and wanted Seymour to be aware of his plans. Seymour suggested to Stines that he lead the group himself, and bring just a small group of Episcopalians. He asked that he come at the 8 A.M. service because Buchanan would be preaching at 11 and because the congregation would be smaller, creating less chance for confrontation. Stines gave his initial approval but said he had to clear it with the other black organizers of the demonstration.[49]

Both Seymour and Bullock waited at the back of the church prior to the 8 A.M. service on June 21 to make sure the biracial group was not accosted or locked out by the vestry, but no one arrived. Seymour received a telephone call from Stines after the service informing Seymour that his fellow demonstrators would not accept Seymour's stipulations. Instead, they arrived at the 11 A.M. service, accompanied by newsmen and television cameras. By this time, news of the attempt to desegregate the church had also reached the vestry and several vestrymen gathered at the sidewalk gate to the church grounds. The members of the vestry informed Stines and his group that they were not welcome and urged them to leave. Seymour and Bullock both stood in the lobby of the church to the right of the entrance with a good view of the front gate. On seeing what the vestrymen were attempting to do, both ministers walked to the gate and Seymour asked the vestry to step aside, in order to allow the Stines group to enter the church. Bullock meanwhile tried in vain to get the newsmen and cameramen to leave, telling them they were complicating an already difficult situation.[50]

Over the protests of the vestry, Seymour and Bullock escorted the Stines group past the incensed vestrymen. Jim Alexander had posted himself at the front of the procession, however, where he refused to move. Seymour told him he would have to step aside. Alexander replied that "I'll be damned if that's so." When Seymour persisted Alexander threw the church bulletins on the ground in disgust, and walked off in the company of his fellow vestrymen. Stines and his group then entered the church.[51]

The following day, Seymour went to Jacksonville to discuss developments within the church with Bishop Hamilton West. Seymour also sought to get a temporary respite from the severe criticism he had received from several members of the congregation following his handling of the demonstration. In private conversation, West expressed his complete support for Seymour.[52]

On June 23, with Seymour still in Jacksonville, the vestry held an emergency meeting with the Reverend Bullock present. After a lengthy discussion with Bullock participating and defending Seymour, the vestry voted 9 to 1 to ask Seymour to resign due to a "disagreement over certain policy decisions." The vestry also established a committee to solicit letters from the congregation in support of their action. During the following week the church received forty-three letters expressing dissatisfaction with Seymour and concurring with the vestry's decision. When Seymour refused to resign, the vestry, as permitted by canon law, asked Bishop West to remove Seymour from Trinity Episcopal Church because of irreconcilable differences between the congregation and the rector.[53]

On July 1 Bishop West drove the thirty miles from Jacksonville to St. Augustine to confront the rebellious vestry. With Seymour and Bullock present, West read a letter responding to the vestry's request for Seymour's removal. In forceful terms, he expressed his complete support for Seymour, declaring "that the Diocese of Florida thoroughly disapproves of your action" and that the vestrymen would face excommunication if they did not change their stance. West also announced that the diocese had established "a ministers' relief fund" to prevent Seymour from being intimidated by the vestry's plan to freeze payment of his salary if he did not resign.[54]

The members of the vestry had apparently not expected such a strong statement from the bishop and their initial response was one of confusion. Objections were made to the bishop's charge that vestrymen used obscene language during the confrontation with Stines and that Stines had been struck. Other vestrymen objected to the tone of the letter and asked for a paragraph by paragraph discussion. Tebeault referred to the forty-three letters supporting vestry action.[55]

After several confusing minutes, Bill Craig, a local businessman, raised the issue of admitting blacks into the service: "It seems that this Vestry is going to continue stopping these demonstrators . . . I'm going to . . . and we're subject to excommunication; is that right?" The bishop responded without hesitation, "That's right." Craig replied angrily: "Then you had better start excommunicating."

Several vestrymen quickly tried to temper Craig's comments by pointing out that other churches in St. Augustine had refused to admit demonstrators. Kenneth Barrett drew attention to the problems that existed between the vestry and Seymour and that the "integrating thing" was only one part of the problem. Tebeault, who had been relatively quiet to this point, interrupted Charles Walker's summary of the demonstrations at Monson's Motor Lodge and elsewhere to ask if "the Clergy must enforce entrance of Negroes to the Church?" West replied unequivocally, "Yes."

Tebeault declared: "Well, we're at an impasse because it won't happen. I must decide between being an American or an Episcopalian." West quickly interjected that "the Vestry is wrong and you have taken the wrong position."

Tebeault: "Must we provoke you to excommunicate?"

West: "Either that or be converted; not to my point of view but by reading Matthew, Mark, Luke, and John."

West informed the vestry that the Episcopal Church had

always been open to all races although it had pursued this policy strongly only during the last ten to fifteen years. He attempted to bring the acrimonious meeting to a close by announcing that "The Diocese is firm in its position, and the Vestry is firm in its position; a change is needed. You must alter your ways." "You do not accept our decision?" Tebeault asked. "We do not," the bishop declared. Kenneth Barrett offered his resignation from the vestry and West accepted it. Tebeault moved that the vestry withdraw from the Episcopal Church, taking all properties and monies with them. This proposal was rejected with only Tebeault and Alexander supporting it. Both Bill Craig and Tebeault resigned from the vestry. The meeting then adjourned with Seymour still serving as priest but in a church that was bitterly divided.[56]

Gradually, over the next two months as the racial crisis abated in the community, hostilities at Trinity lessened, but relations between Seymour and many parishioners continued to be cool at best. For the well-being of the church and himself, Seymour accepted the call of Canon Bill Turner, rector of Trinity Episcopal Church in New Orleans, the largest in Louisiana, to serve as his assistant, effective October 1. "It was a good time for a change of leadership," Seymour recalled.[57]

Stanley Bullock took over as priest-in-charge at Bishop West's request. West thought that since Bullock was from nearby Jacksonville, he understood the views of the Trinity congregation and would be able to work with the members, despite his support of Seymour during the crisis. The bishop's selection of Bullock proved to be a good one, but the tensions in the church had already been eased by the departure of Seymour and Martin Luther King's nonviolent army.

As the examples of Trinity Episcopal and the Catholic Church make clear, the role of the churches in preparing St. Augustine for a new era in race relations following the *Brown* decision and in seeking to alleviate the racial tensions of 1963 and 1964 can only be characterized as inadequate. This failure seems attributable largely to the absence of a strong ministerial alliance. No church, with the possible exception of the Catholic Church, was influential enough in the community to change racial attitudes alone. Indeed, without the cooperation of the Catholic Church and Archbishop Joseph Hurley, the most important religious figure in the community, even a vigorous ministerial alliance would have had difficulty in persuading local citizens to follow a different path. Also undermining the influence of the ministerial leaders was their failure to establish a working relationship with their black counterparts. Communication between the two was nonexistent, with the exception of the two black missions provided by the Catholic and Episcopal churches.

Additionally, local blacks seemed content with their own churches and satisfied merely to have access to white churches. Indeed, those activists who took part in church demonstrations generally came from outside St. Augustine. Black religious institutions occupied a special place in the community and, despite the desire of nearly all black citizens to desegregate the community's schools and public facilities, few desired to desegregate their churches which had provided the bond that held the community together and gave their life special meaning during the worst days of segregation.[58]

When a few ministers at white churches tried to open their doors to blacks in the spring of 1964, they found little or no support. Such a step seemed precipitous to their congregations since the ministers had not prepared them previously for this development. As previously noted, these congregations responded by removing their ministers. Only Trinity Episcopal parish found itself engulfed by the crisis. The controversy in the church was aggravated by the presence of several lay leaders who also served as community leaders and had been outspoken in their opposition to the civil rights movement. Adding to the church's difficulty in confronting the crisis was the tenuous position of Seymour who found himself caught between the orders of the bishop and the sentiments of the congregation. As the person who implemented the unpopular policy decisions of his bishop and the national church, Seymour was obliged to confront the vestry and the congregation. The Reverend Seymour's difficulties were further exacerbated by the relative absence of controversy in other churches. As a result, it seemed to many in the church and the community that Trinity's problems were due to the racial liberalism of its pastor.

In the aftermath of the racial crisis, several ministerial leaders, who were concerned about shortcomings of the religious community, began meeting informally early in 1965 to break down past racial barriers and seek ways to improve race relations in the community. During the first few meetings, all were afraid to say something that might offend the others with the result that nothing of substance was discussed. Finally, a black clergyman broke the tension, declaring: "Look we ain't going to get nothing done until you can call me a nigger if you want to, cause that's what you usually call me and I can call you a powderface, cause that's what I usually call you."[59] After all enjoyed a hearty laugh, the group began discussing plans to lessen racial animosities. They also began involving key community leaders like Herbert Wolfe in the deliberations, thereby broadening their influence.

Despite the leadership of Bullock and several black ministers, however, the ministerial meeting, like other biracial efforts, collapsed. Opposition from community leaders, especially within the white congregations, forced the white ministers to resign from the group. The efforts of the ministerial group were also frustrated during the Easter holidays in 1965 when an interracial group was denied admission to services at Grace Methodist and the Ancient City Baptist churches. The same group did gain entrance to Trinity Episcopal Church, but were pelted with eggs by white teenagers when they left the service. In addition, Bishop Hurley refused to allow Catholic priests to take part in the ministerial discussions and without the Catholic Church this religious effort had only a slight chance of success.[60]

The Catholic Church did desegregate its parochial schools and religious services under Hurley's direction in the fall of 1964. While not insignificant, the desegregation of parochial schools followed one year after the county had desegregated its public schools. Moreover, few blacks were Catholic and the desegregation effort saw very little change in the racial composition of the parochial schools or religious services.[61]

The position of the Catholic Church remained perplexing after the Reverend Michael Gannon, a priest at the Mission de Nombre de Dios and a long-time resident of the community, drafted a "Declaration of Good Will" with local leader Earle Newton in an effort to end the crisis. The declaration decried "the disastrous extremes of left and right," the violence "carried on last summer by belligerent racists," and the recalcitrance of local leaders who seemed bent on prolonging the crisis. The resolution urged an end to the

rancor and the beginning of a serious dialogue to ease the racial hostilities. Gannon received no assistance from Bishop Hurley in the
preparation of his proposal, however, and the effort collapsed when
city leaders, led by Mayor Shelley, refused to support it.

In February 1965, the Community Relations Service
(CRS) sent Harold Hunton to St. Augustine as a conciliator because
of his involvement in the Catholic Interracial movement. Hunton
was asked to "get hold of the Catholic aspects of this problem" and
meet with the bishop and Catholic lay leaders. After several visits,
he urged CRS leaders to explore ways to convince Bishop Hurley to
make a positive statement concerning race relations. Hunton wrote
that the Catholic Church had invested large sums of money in restoration projects, especially a Catholic shrine commemorating the
Spanish arrival, and warned that the accessibility of these projects to
the public would be hampered by the racial climate. Hunton added
that it was not clear that Hurley "shares this view or fully under-
stands this situation in St. Augustine." By the end of 1965 Hunton
had received little cooperation from the Catholic religious hierarchy
which severely compromised his efforts to influence the attitudes of
Catholic lay leaders.[62]

While the churches were not a greater obstacle to desegregation than other institutions in St. Augustine, they had failed to
provide the moral and spiritual leadership generally expected of them.
By their hesitancy (or unwillingness in some cases) to address this
issue, the churches helped provide the opportunity for militant groups
to speak in behalf of the community. The response of the local
churches differed little from religious institutions throughout the South.
With very few exceptions, the churches, whether fundamentalist or
hierarchical, remained passive at best and resistant at worst to the
civil rights developments of the 1950s and 1960s. The religious community thus remained aloof to much of the racial crisis, reflecting in
microcosm the forces at work in the larger community.

Chapter 8.

No Real Controversies

I n the period from 1965 to 1980, the white leadership in St. Augustine continually refused to address racial problems in a systematic manner. They responded to black requests for change only when civil rights demonstrations threatened the economic vitality of the community. Although the ad hoc nature of their response occasionally led to an easing of racial tensions and the appearance of progress, it never fully resolved black concerns and, perhaps more importantly, it never led to the establishment of an agenda that would end racial discrimination. Such a development may well have been impossible in a community that had experienced a racial crisis as severe as St. Augustine had in 1964; nevertheless, the white leadership never even tried. Complicating the efforts of black residents to effect change was the growing split in the black community between activists who favored renewed demonstrations and moderates who did not.

In the immediate aftermath of the summer's crisis, efforts at conciliation continued to be frustrated by white leaders. Andrew Young tried to calm white concerns about a vengeful black community by pledging that blacks would not use the civil rights law to "force our rights down someone else's throat."[1] A grand jury led by Judge Horace Riegle and States Attorney Dan Warren also attempted to reduce the tensions between the races by establishing a genuine biracial committee. The grand jury named five white residents including Andrew J. McGhin, Jr., president of the St. Augustine and the

St. Johns County Chambers of Commerce; and five blacks, including Dr. R. W. Puryear of Florida Memorial College; Mrs. Elzora Martin, member of the local NAACP executive board; and Otis Mason, principal of Hastings High School. The biracial committee seemed to offer the community an opportunity to reestablish communications between both groups and avoid further repercussions from the violence of the summer months.[2]

Shortly after the names had been made public in August, however, four white members led by McGhin announced that they would be unable to serve because of a variety of health, business, and community concerns. The evidence suggests that considerable pressure had been brought to bear on these men by friends and neighbors who opposed a reconciliation between the races. Few civic leaders and businessmen had recovered sufficiently from the demonstrations and the unfavorable publicity of the summer, as well as the recent court-ordered changes, to support an effort to improve race relations. When these men refused to serve, no others could be found to replace them and the biracial committee collapsed.[3] Another opportunity to bring the community together had been rejected by the white leadership.

Governor Bryant encouraged white recalcitrance by announcing that he would seek to provide St. Augustine with economic aid after its dismal tourist season.[4] Nothing ever came of this offer, largely because Bryant shortly left office and also because of the questionable constitutionality of such assistance when the community had not been struck by a natural disaster. Nevertheless, the governor's promise seemed to sanction the policies pursued by city leaders during the summer. Bryant placed an additional obstacle in the path toward peace in the community when he opposed the efforts of the Community Relations Service to intercede in August to help restore racial cooperation. Though the newly established agency did not need state government permission to enter a community, the organization was reluctant to intervene without gubernatorial cooperation.[5]

The Community Relations Service had been created by the 1964 Civil Rights Act to help communities defuse racial hostilities before they exploded into violence, and LeRoy Collins, governor of Florida from 1954 to 1960, had been selected by President Johnson to head the agency. A southern moderate who had guided the state peacefully through the tumultuous 1950s, Collins would perform yeoman work for CRS, especially during the Selma, Alabama, crisis of 1965. Unfortunately for St. Augustine, the agency was initially prevented from intervening in local affairs because Bryant and community leaders refused Collins' offer of assistance.[6]

Bryant had never been particularly friendly with Collins and the relationship grew more strained during Bryant's unsuccessful gubernatorial campaign against Collins in 1956 and during the 1960 campaign when Collins openly endorsed Bryant's opponent. Collins viewed Bryant as a political opportunist who would undermine the racial progress achieved in Florida during his administration. Bryant perceived Collins as a potential rival for his planned U.S. senatorial bid in 1966 and had no desire to enhance Collins' visibility by allowing him to intervene in the St. Augustine crisis.[7] Though Collins expressed deep concern about St. Augustine, he believed that his agency could help it through the difficult transition period. Bryant responded irritably to Collins' initiative, stating that he did not "anticipate calling them in any instance." Shelley and several other community leaders endorsed Bryant's decision.[8]

Without a dialogue between the black and white communities, racial violence and intimidation continued to plague the city throughout the fall of 1964 and into 1965. After ordering coffee and a hamburger at a fast food stand, a black student at Florida Memorial College received a bad beating from a white man with brass knuckles. When police took the student, John Phillips, to Flagler Hospital for treatment, Dr. Norris refused to treat him, claiming that he was going off duty. A second doctor did not arrive to examine Phillips for more than an hour. In another racial incident, fifteen to twenty white youths attacked a similar number of black youths after taunting them at the local theater.[9]

Black youths and civil rights activists refused to be intimidated, however. Encouraged by the demonstrations of the spring and summer, they asserted their new self-awareness in several ways. During the confrontation between black and white teenagers, the black youths had exchanged blow for blow. In a more traditional fashion, SCLC aides and local leaders conducted an extensive voter registration drive, expanding upon the efforts of the NAACP in the previous year. SCLC hoped to unify the black community behind the civil rights movement and to organize blacks into an effective political force. Since the NAACP had successfully registered over 80 percent of St. Augustine blacks the previous year, SCLC aides concentrated their drive in the county. Black leaders also established block captains and an informational network to encourage blacks to vote and to pinpoint issues and candidates. Harry Boyte reported that the black vote had "no pattern" to it previously and, as a consequence, had failed to defeat officials like Sheriff Davis in the past. The registration drive proved quite successful when over five hundred blacks were added to the rolls in two weeks. Whites, however, still outnumbered blacks in the county 2 to 1.[10]

Other signs of a changed racial environment also appeared. The Florida Park Service announced its decision to integrate all state parks, a decision apparently influenced by events in St. Augustine. Near the end of August, Governor Bryant removed the last of his special state police units from St. Augustine, remarking that "the situation is well in hand." In September a record number of black parents petitioned the school board to send their children to white schools (only twenty-two transfers were approved, however).[11]

Despite these developments, the local civil rights movement remained beset by difficulties that stymied the attempts of activists to combat white hostility throughout this period. In a report to SCLC on September 20, Fred Martin, SCLC representative, identified two problems plaguing the local movement—the shortage of funds and the sharp decline of adult participation. Because of the economic and social pressure exerted by white residents and widespread opposition to further civil rights demonstrations, many older black residents refused to support SCLC. Several of these black citizens also felt that further protests were unnecessary with the passage of the civil rights law. Without the assistance of older blacks, Hayling and Twine sought to resuscitate the movement and to reduce the organization's debt by appealing to northern allies. Martin also proposed to SCLC officials that prominent figures be sent to St. Augustine to dramatize events in the community. SCLC would pursue this idea during the Easter celebration in 1965.[12]

With racial conditions still unsettled in the late fall, the Community Relations Service decided to send a field representative into St. Augustine "to stimulate biracial discussions and encourage projects to promote racial harmony" despite continued opposition by Governor Bryant and civic leaders to CRS's involvement. Harold Hunton met with community leaders on three separate occasions between October 1964 and April 1965 with only limited results.[13] On his first visit, Hunton reported that peaceful negotiations were unlikely because the white community remained very bitter and, as Martin had also observed, the "leadership in the Negro community was somewhat fractured and exhausted" after the summer demonstrations. Hunton, however, persuaded a few moderate leaders in the black and white communities to meet separately and seek to develop an agenda for improved relations. During the following months the white committee members framed a manifesto of their intentions and sought signatures from other members of the community endorsing their proposals. Herbert Wolfe was among the first asked to sign the document. He apparently consulted Senator George Smathers who told him, "if you sign anything you will be pinned to the wall." When Wolfe refused to sign, no one else would either and the project was abandoned.[14]

Despite this setback, Hunton and the Community Relations Service were able to make some headway, arranging a meeting between black leaders and city officials, developing an effective working relationship with Governor Haydon Burns and his staff, and serving as a primary channel of communication among all parties. Hunton also persuaded local chain stores to hire more blacks and obtained support from the Southern Education Foundation for Florida Memorial College to encourage twenty black high school students in the community to attend college. After six months work, however, Hunton acknowledged that few substantive changes had occurred in community attitudes. "The more concerned liberal members of the white community seem somewhat depressed and subdued, pessimistic about getting anything accomplished," he wrote. Blacks still complained about inequities in the court system and in the police department. Whites who harangued and assaulted blacks were still being released after a lecture from police and sheriff's officers.[15] Frustrated himself, Hunton noted in August that the situation had "deteriorated since our last visit." He saw Mayor Shelley as a major obstacle to peace and added "that the newspaper coverage and attitude of the publishers continue to be pro-segregationist."[16]

States Attorney Dan Warren echoed Hunton's assessment in an address before faculty and students at Boston University in February. Criticizing local leaders for failing to understand the desire of blacks to share fully in the heritage and opportunities of the community, Warren declared that "good, conscientious" people remained silent and allowed the world to continue to believe that the Lynches and Stoners spoke for St. Augustine.[17]

Mayor Shelley quickly responded to Warren's comments, asserting that Judge Simpson had prevented the police department from halting such "rabble rousers as Stoner, Lynch, and King." He also accused Simpson of allowing events to get out of hand when he and other leaders could have kept this from occurring.[18] Throughout 1964 and 1965 Shelley continued to be a major obstacle to all peace initiatives. He refused to acknowledge that he might have erred in his opposition to a biracial committee and he remained convinced that the civil rights movement was communist inspired. Members of the city commission never seriously challenged Shelley's leadership on racial matters.

Shelley's position received additional reinforcement from the state investigation commission which had been appointed by the state legislature to examine the causes of the summer crisis. The commission released its report in December 1964, blaming the crisis on outsiders, especially Martin Luther King, Jr. Throughout the report, the committee made much of King's alleged Communist sympathies and accused him "and his trained army of provocateurs" of destroying "inter-racial relations." The report also singled out Ku Klux Klan elements and biased news reporting for the "distorted picture of what was happening in St. Augustine." The report placed no blame on local officials for the turmoil; rather, it simply restated the views expressed repeatedly by local leaders. Shelley and the other commissioners as well as most white residents saw the report as a vindication of the commission's position in 1964.[19]

A legacy of bitterness continued to pervade the community throughout the post-1964 period. B. C. Roberts, superintendent of the Castillo de San Marcos National Monument told a reporter, "If they [civil rights leaders] come again, they would be met with the same reaction. The attitudes haven't changed." Black residents alleged that relations had seldom been worse in St. Augustine.[20]

Although the city had become doubly dependent on a highly successful 400th anniversary celebration to recoup its losses following the civil rights crisis, chances for such an economic boost appeared small. W. I. Drysdale, chairman of the 400th Anniversary Corporation, observed that "some of the people who were ready to help us with enthusiasm have turned lukewarm now."[21] Civil rights groups led by Roy Wilkins of the NAACP discouraged outside support for the quadricentennial. Wilkins accused St. Augustine of having the "oldest ideas on race relations in the United States" and recommended that "the economic screws" be put to the community. Responding to Wilkins' appeal, Edward Litchfield, president of the University of Pittsburgh and a member of the Quadricentennial Commission, declared that holding "a nation and even international celebration in a community in which any of our people are denied the unmistakable full measure of citizenship" would be a repudiation of our culture which values "the dignity and therefore the quality of all men."[22]

Within this cauldron of developments that swirled in and around St. Augustine in early 1965, black residents urged local leaders to reopen lines of communication. R. W. Puryear and other black leaders maintained that a biracial commission was the answer. "The real need is for responsible citizens who will talk and trust and understand each other," Puryear said. "I long to work with them." City leaders ignored their petition.[23]

As evidence of this persistent racism, students from Bates College in Maine, who visited Florida Memorial College during Easter vacation 1965 under an exchange established by SCLC, were subjected to physical intimidation and verbal abuse by white residents. During their stay in St. Augustine, the Bates' students shared rooms with FMC students or stayed with residents and attended seminars and colloquia on Lent and the Christian experience. Susan Smith, a Bates student, noted that "the friendliness, openness, and generosity of the students and faculty at Florida Memorial were in sharp contrast to the hostility and lack of courtesy shown us by many of the white townspeople in St. Augustine."[24] When several members of the group stopped one day at a Kentucky Fried Chicken restaurant, the owner attacked them verbally for testing his place. One FMC student responded: "We're not testing. These are Maine students visiting us . . . and we just felt like eating fried chicken." While the students stood inside the restaurant, fifteen whites gathered outside, daring them to come out and shouting obscene remarks at them. When the students tried to exit through a side door and run for their car, the white youths grabbed one black student from FMC and tried to pull him from the car. His friends held fast, however, and managed to get him and themselves away from the mob although they were followed the entire distance to the college campus.[25]

Commenting on her St. Augustine experience, Miss Smith wrote in the Bates college newspaper that: "In ways perhaps it was a very valuable, though very frightening, introduction for all of us from Bates to a type of harassment that is a normal part of our life for our friends at FMC and for Negroes throughout the South." Though overstated, Miss Smith's observations were not inaccurate.[26]

Smith's experiences also reemphasized the continuing efforts of white militants to stymie the aims of the 1964 Civil Rights Act and to keep black residents in their place with little interference from local officials. During the Easter celebration in 1965, a group of 100 white men and teenagers, led by J. B. Stoner and Warren Folks of the Jacksonville States Rights Party, taunted a black Jacksonville high-school band that marched in St. Augustine's parade and threw eggs at band members. Only two whites, both teenagers, were arrested by city police and they were later released into the custody of their parents.[27]

The egg-throwing incident, however, caused many white St. Augustinians to question for the first time the ongoing violence and the continued presence of militants from outside the city. Blacks had participated in the parade for as long as anyone could remember, including in 1964, without being abused. The fact that most of the militants came from Jacksonville made it easier for white moderates to condemn the violence.[28]

Whites may also have been encouraged to reach some accommodation with local blacks because of increasing signs of the determination of blacks, moderates and activists alike, not to accept a return to the old ways. Symbolizing this new attitude was the candidacy of two local blacks for seats on the city commission. Oscar

Turner, vice-president of the NAACP and a resident of St. Augustine for forty years, and Rosalie Gordon, school teacher, widow of Dr. Gordon, and also a long-time resident of the community, campaigned against six whites for three seats on the five-member commission, marking the first time since the formation of the commission-manager form of government that blacks had sought this position.

The candidacy of the two also reflected, however, a continued split between moderate and activist blacks in the community. The moderates were led by Dr. R. W. Puryear, Otis Mason, black school teachers, and several ministers. They favored an end to all demonstrations and the formation of a moderate group to establish a dialogue with the white community. They also opposed further protests against the quadricentennial celebration which they felt would greatly alienate white residents and polarize the races. Activists participated in the NAACP and SCLC and were led by Mrs. Plummer and Dr. Hayling. They continued to insist upon the establishment of a biracial commission, demonstrations against the city for its refusal to appoint such a commission, and more jobs in city government for blacks. Black activists decried Gordon's candidacy, claiming it would split the black community, but moderates argued that only Gordon had a real chance of being elected because her moderation would help her obtain essential support from segments of the white community.[29]

Though Gordon received little support from civil rights activists, she enjoyed the endorsement of many white residents who respected her moderation and her leadership as president of the St. Johns County Teachers Association. Mrs. Gordon emphasized her moderate views during the campaign, promising "to improve the image of St. Augustine, to the nation and the world." Playing down the racial difficulties of the previous year, she chose instead to talk about the future of the city. Turner's affiliation with the NAACP gave him visibility in the black community but also assured him the opposition of nearly all white voters. Turner talked about the need to improve "human relations in our city" during his campaign, which whites interpreted as a desire to accelerate integration.[30] Of the 6,421 registered voters in St. Augustine, 1,160 or 17 percent were black. Even if all blacks supported Gordon or Turner, this was insufficient to elect them. Mrs. Gordon ran a surprisingly strong campaign, finishing fifth in an eight-person field with 923 votes. Not so surprisingly, Turner ran a dismal last. About 20 percent of Mrs. Gordon's support came from whites while Turner received less than 5 percent. Mrs. Gordon qualified for the runoff for the three commission seats and managed to receive 1,100 votes, but she still finished fifth behind four white, male candidates.[31]

Following the election black activists continued to push for a more open society. SCLC sent several letters to President Johnson, Community Relations Service Director LeRoy Collins, and other federal officials in July, complaining about the repeated acts of violence against local residents. The letters made particular reference to a kerosene soaked burlap sack found under the 100-gallon gasoline tank in Mrs. Plummer's house. Mention was also made of discrimination encountered at Flagler Hospital and at the beach. Thus, despite divisions within the black community, activists and moderates alike showed no willingness to accept a return to the racial traditions of the past.[32]

With the four hundredth anniversary fast approaching, civic leaders, fearing renewed demonstrations, moved to reach an agreement with black leaders without commission approval. A biracial committee of twenty leaders designated five representatives from each side to begin discussions on the quadricentennial. The membership did not include black civil rights leaders, however, and the committee chose to focus only on the quadricentennial celebrations. After two meetings, Dr. R. W. Puryear told reporters that he had encountered "an amicable feeling and a wholesome interest" in which leaders agreed to include black representatives in all the festivities.[33]

Aiding this initiative, Justice of the Peace G. Marvin Grier had adopted a tough policy for dealing with anyone who attempted to disrupt the fragile peace. When a white youth walked onto the junior high school grounds and struck a black student, Grier sentenced the youth to six months in jail. The physical intimidation of black citizens did not stop, however. During the summer months blacks who chose to go swimming in what had once been the white section of the beach found themselves harassed.[34]

In contrast to the previous summer when no members of the white community came to the defense of black residents, however, support came from a variety of quarters in 1965. In addition to action taken by Judge Grier, grand juries brought charges against whites who assaulted blacks at the beach. Furthermore, when twelve to twenty whites threw sand at a biracial group of swimmers and attacked them, Sheriff Davis asked that a restraining order used in 1964 be extended to block such assaults in the future. More importantly, Davis urged calm, noting that the beaches "are big enough to adequately serve all. Our citizens must be big enough and wise enough to ward off any attempts to use our county as a stage for the racial agitators to play." Davis still had no sympathy for civil rights demonstrators, but business and civic leaders had been urging him to tone down his rhetoric and emphasize law and order. He warned local residents not to engage in violence, pointing out that "regardless of the individual likes or dislikes concerning the passage of the Civil Rights Act, it is now the law of the land and we must live with it."[35] On the following day, City Manager Charles Barrier, who had become convinced that the city had to make some accommodation to a new racial order, called on parents to keep teenagers away from all demonstrations. He reiterated Davis' pronouncement that the civil rights law "is the law of the land and must be obeyed." NAACP officials praised the statements of both men.[36]

Throughout this period, civil rights leaders pressed city officials for additional government employment of local blacks. SCLC asked Barrier to hire four black policemen, five firemen, and four clerical workers. They also insisted on naming them. Barrier pointed out that 20 percent of all city jobs were held by black residents which corresponded to the percentage of blacks residing in St. Augustine.[37] But, as black leaders noted, the highest ranking black city employee was a water crew foreman. If SCLC had serious hopes of increasing the number of black employees, they erred in demanding that they name them, however. Even moderate whites in local government could not accept this, and it only helped reinforce the views expressed repeatedly by Mayor Shelley that SCLC was a militant, extremist organization.

When civic leaders turned down this request, several black representatives including Dr. Hayling, Lucille Plummer, the Reverend C. K. Steele, and Dr. B. J. Johnson, who represented Martin Luther King, Jr., continued their drive to desegregate St. Augustine by meeting with Governor Haydon Burns to discuss the black community's concerns about conditions there. They told Burns that they were prepared to renew demonstrations if conditions did not improve quickly. Burns, who had promised to see that the civil rights law was enforced and who had appointed several blacks to state office in the first months of his administration, still frowned upon the idea of renewed protests. "I don't want to see this happen again and I remind you that I am not as mild mannered as Governor Bryant," Burns told the group.[38] Burns seemed to be referring to his heavy-handed treatment of the massive civil rights protests in Jacksonville in the spring of 1964. At that time Burns, mayor of Jacksonville and campaigning for the office of governor, called out police and firemen to put down the protests, which they did with impunity.[39]

In responding to Governor Burns, these black leaders refused to be intimidated by his threat to employ force. Hayling spoke first, telling the governor that "things are impossible in St. Augustine for Negro citizens," and that civil rights protests were their only effective means to improve race relations. B. J. Johnson of SCLC echoed Hayling and added: "If need be, we intend to go back to the streets to expose the evils of St. Augustine." SCLC, however, had no desire to reenter this historic community and appeared to hope that through a policy resembling brinksmanship (threats of intervention and of additional demonstrations) it could avoid having to involve itself and still improve conditions for local blacks. Angered by Johnson's response, Burns ended the meeting by telling the group: "If I have to put so many National Guardsmen there that there won't be enough room for the demonstrators to walk, I'm prepared to do it."[40]

St. Augustine officials were even more anxious than the governor to avoid a renewal of the demonstrations. To offset the threat of further protests, quadricentennial officials followed the advice of the biracial committee and included blacks in all preparations for the celebration. Dr. Puryear served on the Coordinating Committee with nineteen white residents and one local black resident sat on the official welcoming committee of five. In addition, the Historical Society had involved students at Florida Memorial College in preparing for the ceremonies launching the celebration. At the governor's luncheon on September 4 which initiated the week-long festivities, blacks received twenty out of the two hundred invitations. Dr. Puryear also took part in the opening ceremonies on the following day.

While in general agreement that racial conditions in St. Augustine still needed improvement, black leaders disagreed on how best this could be done with regard to the quadricentennial. The split became apparent during the celebration when SCLC, led by Hayling and Lucille Plummer, posted signs around the plaza with captions entitled: "The Federal Government Participates Hand in Hand with the Celebration—400 Years of Bigotry and Hate." The following day twenty-five blacks picketed several events with signs stating "Visit the Poverty Area of the City" and "Local Negroes on Tax List but Not on Celebration List." When a reporter asked Mrs. Plummer why her group was demonstrating at the festivities while Puryear sat on the dais with other prominent officials, she replied churlishly, "We [SCLC] bitterly protest the lack of Negroes in the quadricentennial celebration. The Negroes who were invited are not considered leaders by us because they don't participate in the civil rights movement." Puryear and his supporters opposed further demonstrations, believing that the protests only alienated white residents and blocked racial progress.[41]

The Community Relations Service sent field representative Hunton back to St. Augustine to help defuse the division within the black community as well as the ongoing conflict with the white community. Hayling told Hunton that "plenty of people are ready to demonstrate." According to Hayling, SCLC demands included adequate representation on all bodies dealing with the celebration, fair representation on all city and county appointive boards, a biracial committee (Hayling claimed that white leaders were "willing to talk to the Negroes but not with the Negroes"), fair employment practices by the city and county, substantial integration of public schools, equal protection of the law for Negro citizens, and an improved attitude and behavior of the white community toward Negroes. Hunton urged Hayling to moderate SCLC's position to improve the chances for compromise. But Hayling told Hunton that unless these demands were met demonstrations would take place.

Hayling had mixed feelings about the role of Hunton and the involvement of the Community Relations Service in St. Augustine, and refused to abide by their wishes. He believed that the agency "tended to disband and break up the movement" by organizing a group of black moderates who had not been involved in the civil rights effort and designating this group as the representative of the black community.[42] Disregarding Hunton's suggestion, Hayling wrote a letter to President Johnson urging that the federal government withhold funds for the quadricentennial, and he also asked Secretary of the Interior Stewart Udall to refrain from participating as a speaker in the opening ceremonies. In addition, Hayling sought to use the federal government to force local leaders to accept SCLC demands.[43] Failing in this effort, Hayling and his colleagues nevertheless succeeded in blocking the use of federal funds and in limiting national publicity for the anniversary. Local leaders of the celebration recalled that "not one cent" of federal money was received by St. Augustine and a story on the celebration which was scheduled to appear in *National Geographic* prior to the quadricentennial was not published until the spring of 1966.[44]

Hayling and Plummer received assistance from SCLC throughout this period, but the organization's involvement only underscored the declining influence of the civil rights movement in St. Augustine. Although Benjamin Van Clarke of SCLC persuaded eighteen of twenty invited blacks not to attend Governor Burns' luncheon, he received very little assistance from local residents in planning or conducting the protests. Only five to ten black residents appeared at the demonstrations. In addition, despite several attempts by SCLC to discourage his participation, Secretary of the Interior Stewart Udall did appear at the opening ceremonies, lending a measure of federal sanction to the celebration. Lucille Plummer wrote King, noting that civil rights activists were "working very hard to keep the movement alive in St. Augustine," but added that everyone is saying, "Dr. King needs to come here just one more time and conditions will be better."[45]

The black community was sharply divided, however, about King's participation in renewed demonstrations. One moderate local leader commented: "I don't want him back here now. He left us with a sick city and his coming back would kill it."[46] A large majority of local blacks thought the events of 1964 had been productive, but now believed that the community had to try to resolve its differences without further protests or black residents would receive few benefits from the changes of the past year.

The division within the black community over suitable

tactics to desegregate St. Augustine gravely handicapped the chances of further racial gains. The Reverend Charles D. Dixon, pastor of St. Paul's A.M.E. Church, which had the largest black congregation in St. Augustine, reflected the views of many moderates when he opposed demonstrations. "We want freedom, but we think there is a better way to obtain it," he explained. "I believe that if we have a law, we ought to abide by it. I felt that with the civil rights bill working, it would be the answer to our demands."[47] Moderates led by Puryear, Otis Mason, black school teachers, and several clergymen had the largest following, but the activists had the greatest visibility as well as the greatest credibility among the young people. This division enabled the opponents of change such as Mayor Shelley and the Birch Society to block all proposals for compromise, including those coming from moderates in the white community.

In an effort to heal the split in the black community, to prevent the initiatives of 1964 from slipping away, and to demonstrate to city leaders that they would not accept a return to racial customs of the past, several leading black residents established a Concerned Citizens Association. In a highly significant gesture to the white leadership in the community, the group chose Otis Mason as its chairman rather than Dr. Robert Hayling. The association was anxious to establish a dialogue with white leaders and many thought this would be difficult if Hayling served as chairman. They also wanted to demonstrate that moderates in the black community felt strongly about civil rights issues. White leaders had alleged during the crisis that most moderate blacks did not support the efforts of Dr. King and had used this as an excuse to avoid talking to him. The black members did not shun Hayling merely because they disapproved of his alleged radicalism. Rather they took a pragmatic step which they hoped would better their chances of success in dealing with the white community. Mason's acceptability to the white community had been made clear not only by his school administration position but also by his recent appointment to a seat on the Quadricentennial Commission, making him one of only two blacks to hold such a position (Puryear was the other).[48]

At the organizational meeting of the association, members agreed upon an agenda which sought additional changes in the racial attitudes and policies of city fathers, including: equal police protection, a comprehensive plan to combat poverty, improved streets and lighting in black neighborhoods, job opportunities and appointments to city boards, a biracial committee, an urban renewal program, additional black participation in the quadricentennial, and better city ordinances concerning minors. Mrs. Lucille Plummer also reported to the group that only one black man had been hired by the sheriff's department. Although he was a college graduate, she noted, he did not hold a civil service position as did other members of the force. Though the group agreed on a common agenda, there was still widespread disagreement about what tactics should be utilized to achieve these aims. This dispute would go unresolved and seriously impede black desegregation efforts.[49]

Despite the formation of this group, race relations continued along a rocky road in the postquadricentennial period. On September 12, 1965, two white youths slashed a Negro youth with a knife. The two then drove through the black section of St. Augustine, shouting threats and insults as they passed three young blacks. When the three youths shouted back, the two whites turned their car around and chased the three men, cutting one with a knife. Police arrived shortly after the incident and barely prevented a melee between a crowd of blacks and whites gathered at the scene. Hayling, the Reverend Robert Lovett of First Baptist Church, and Willie Bolden, a King lieutenant, assisted police in restraining the angry black crowd, several of whom shouted: "We're tired of this nonviolent stuff."[50] The courts helped maintain calm in the black community by consistently finding such perpetrators guilty and imposing stiff sentences in marked contrast to legal developments in 1964.

In an attempt to persuade local leaders to move off dead center and meet black concerns, SCLC brought several outsiders into the community as it had done in 1964. Former Governor of Massachusetts Endicott Peabody, son of Mrs. Malcolm Peabody, and several other prominent New Englanders visited St. Augustine in December. During their brief stay, Peabody and his fellow visitors expressed support for more black participation in local government. Rather than aiding the civil rights cause, however, the visit greatly angered city officials, who deeply resented the interference of outsiders, especially after Mrs. Peabody's presence in 1964. Many white residents were also irritated by Governor Peabody's suggestion that

Mrs. Plummer had lost her job because of her civil rights activities.[51]

Despite what black activists viewed as worsening race relations, a final legal blow to segregation in St. Augustine came when Judge Bryan Simpson dismissed all but twenty-nine cases (over 1,000 altogether) against those demonstrators whose cases had not yet been tried in the wake of the 1964 protests. Of particular interest among these cases were the ones involving Andrew Young and Martin Luther King, Jr., who were charged with contributing to the delinquency of minors when they advised black children to disobey their parents and teachers "if they felt it would enable them to obtain their constitutional rights." In dismissing the charges against Young and King, Simpson wrote that it was "ironic to me that the people of St. Johns County should light on this charge against people who are trying to help them find a better life."[52]

Although conditions had improved in the legal system for local blacks, developments which seemed to offer promise of future improvements, even amidst the continuing violence of 1965, the pessimism of black activists, and the recalcitrance of civic leaders, ultimately collapsed. The Fairchild-Hiller Corporation had completely replaced its administrators at the St. Augustine plant, and it had distributed a handbook to every employee stating that all of its employees must be in compliance with the Equal Employment Opportunity program both on and off duty. "Violation of the federal law, on or off duty . . . [would] constitute grounds for dismissal," the handbook stated. Though James Hauser, a civil rights activist, still found discrimination existed at the plant, he admitted that changes had been made for the better. Publicly, a moderate group of approximately thirty white leaders representing many of the most prominent businessmen in the community, had been meeting to see how conditions could be changed to prevent a recurrence of the demonstrations. The group had yet to meet with local blacks, but it had interceded with the city to reduce tensions. An interracial ministerial group had also continued to meet throughout the year to open lines of communication among the community's churches and to assist in easing racial hostilities where possible.[53]

By the end of 1965, Harold Hunton reported to superiors at the Community Relations Service that, despite certain improvements in race relations, many problems remained. In a positive vein, he referred specifically to the increased employment of blacks in chain stores, black participation in the quadricentennial celebration, interracial participation in a mental health workshop, the appearance of the mayor at a Negro Methodist State Conference, and the naming of a recreation center after a black Army veteran who had been killed in Vietnam. But Hunton was also frank (and somewhat frustrated) to admit that the political leadership was "doing no more than absolutely necessary." He noted that no black citizens had been appointed to significant municipal policy-making boards, no recognizable group in the white community had been formed to consider the community's social problems; the city leaders had rejected assistance from the Community Action Program; and the sheriff had hired a black deputy who had a history of felony convictions. With progress severely restricted by civic leaders, and black moderates and activists unable to agree on tactics to facilitate change, Hunton found that "a great deal of apathy" existed in the black community.[54]

A development which seemed only peripherally related to civil rights concerns appeared, nevertheless, to offer the entire community some hope for a more progressive future at the beginning of the new year. In January 1966, the John Birch Society tried to take over the Parent-Teachers Association at St. Augustine High School. The Birch Society members and supporters wanted St. Augustine High School's PTA to withdraw from the national PTA because the national organization had lost its "grass roots control." As subsequent letters to the editor of the *St. Augustine Record* revealed, however, the debate went well beyond this issue, with Birchers arguing that the national PTA favored such Communist causes as one worldism. Mrs. Clair Dobbs wrote in a letter to the editor that "in 1954 Herbert Philbrick, undercover agent for the FBI, announced that the Communist Party had issued special instructions to infiltrate P-TA." Describing the methods Communists attempted to use, Mrs. Dobbs concluded: "Knowing the dedication of any communist, we can easily imagine the job they have done in these past ten years!" Mrs. Frank Helm, Jr., another Birch spokesman, contended that the PTA by supporting the United Nations endorsed an institution that violated the "United States Constitution . . . at least fifteen times!" She went on to note that "The U.N. charter, written by such men as Russian-born Dr. Leo Pasvolsky and Alger Hiss, convicted traitor, completely omits all references to man's dependence on a God."[55]

Although the attack upon the PTA caught leaders of the association and teachers at St. Augustine High School unprepared, they quickly joined forces to defend the organization. J. Wilton Davis, the president, initially tried to deny Birch sympathizers the floor at the January meeting once their intention became clear. When Birch supporters accused him of employing Communist methods, Davis and the teachers decided to appeal to the parents for support. He urged all parents interested in their children's education to attend the February PTA meeting. Davis also accused opponents of the PTA of playing "on emotions of their followers by making false ridiculous charges that the P-TA is controlled by traitors bent on destroying America."

At the February meeting, the subject of the PTA was avoided, but it became clear that the PTA supporters had effectively marshaled their forces to the point that they could outvote the Birch followers. Letters continued to appear in the editorial page criticizing the PTA, but the tide had been turned and the Birch Society, realizing it had taken on a struggle it could not win, gave up the battle. It marked the first defeat for the Birch Society in St. Augustine. Its members did not take it gracefully, however. Criticism of individual opponents over the PTA issue was maintained until several left the community because of the "loss of business and [personal] ostracism."[56]

Following the conflict between the PTA and the Birch society, the Florida Advisory Committee to the U.S. Commission on Civil Rights sent its regional consultant, Courtney Siceloff, to St. Augustine in December 1966, to determine whether the Committee should hold a public hearing there. Siceloff began his report by observing that "there is much that needs to be done in St. Augustine," alluding particularly to the fact that most of the impetus for change had come from the courts. Siceloff found, for example, that the city council was "made up of five persons, ranging from a moderate conservative to a strong conservative or racist [Shelley]." These men, Siceloff observed, had blocked the establishment of a poverty program, the creation of a biracial commission, and the appointment of

blacks to official boards. He also commented that acts of intimidation, the use of the YMCA to house a private, segregated school,
segregated restrooms in the post office, and the limitations on black
employment all were signs of the community's reluctance to accept a
new era in race relations.[57]

Nevertheless, Siceloff found that progress had been made
in a number of areas which he thought offered hope for better relations in the future. He noted the formation of a moderate white group,
the defeat of the Birch Society on the PTA issue, the statements of
Davis and Barrier during the summer, and improved police protection for black citizens. Siceloff also made reference to the integration
of Flagler Hospital, the more progressive editorial policy of the *St.
Augustine Record*, the inclusion of the Negro news with the rest of
the paper, the integration of adult evening classes at the high school,
and the merger of the white and black Catholic schools. Siceloff declared that race relations had advanced despite the efforts of members of the John Birch Society who took "action against any attempts
to change the status quo."[58]

Siceloff recommended that the Florida Advisory Committee not meet in St. Augustine in the near future because "there
were not sufficient violations to 'expose' the city." He wrote percep-
tively that "if white moderates who are making some progress would
be willing to appear before the committee to tell their story, there
might be a point in holding a meeting for this purpose. However, in
discussion with the moderates, all indicate that they are unwilling to
appear before the Committee, feeling that their own usefulness would
come to an end, and what progress is now being made would be
stopped abruptly."[59]

Siceloff's comments indicated just how tenuous race relations were in St. Augustine. Although some small progress had been
achieved, it was clear that efforts at further improvements could be
quickly dashed. Moreover, white moderates were so insecure about
their position that they would not speak out publicly.

In the post-1966 period race relations failed to achieve
Siceloff's hoped-for progress. The passing of the quadricentennial observance, increasing divisions in the black community, and the de-

parture of key black leaders all eroded support for and interest in racial issues. Only school desegregation dominated the interests of black
and white residents, and this was due to action taken by the federal
courts and the federal government. City leaders continued to balk at
the establishment of a biracial committee, and black demands for more
jobs in city government and further desegregation of public and private facilities fell on unreceptive ears. Race relations in St. Augustine also suffered a setback when riots erupted in cities throughout
the nation during the period 1966–68. These violent protests polar-
ized racial feelings nationally and convinced conservative leaders in
St. Augustine that the racial changes of the early sixties threatened
the welfare of the nation.

The local movement suffered crippling blows with the
departure of Dr. Robert Hayling, Mrs. Lucille Plummer, and the
Reverend Goldie Eubanks, as well as Dr. R. W. Puryear and Florida
Memorial College. Hayling moved to Ft. Lauderdale in 1966 because
of continued threats against his family and himself and the loss of his
white dental business which left him in difficult financial shape. Mrs.
Plummer and the Reverend Eubanks left St. Augustine for economic
and religious reasons. According to Puryear, the decision to relocate
the college had been discussed for several years and had been decided
prior to the racial crisis in 1964. Puryear recalled that a foundation
executive had suggested to him in the early 1960s that the college
would be better able to serve the black community in a more met-
ropolitan area like Miami and that foundation support would no doubt
increase following such a move. Puryear said the departure in August
1968, however, had also been influenced by the failure of black grad-
uates to find jobs in St. Augustine following the racial crisis.[60]

Hayling, Plummer, and Eubanks had been major spokes-
men for the local civil rights movement since 1963 and their loss was
acutely felt. The departure of Florida Memorial students similarly undermined the movement by taking away its manpower. The moderate position suffered as well with the loss of the college faculty and
Puryear, who had worked diligently to reopen lines of communication with the white community. The college had also offered social
and cultural activities to the black community which were sorely
missed.

With the departure of these activists, civil rights leaders

in St. Augustine decided to concentrate their efforts against the segregated school system. The school desegregation struggle in St. Augustine had been a slow and onerous one for black residents. In 1965
only thirty black children attended desegregated schools, and this figure increased slightly throughout the next four years. During the
summer of 1969, the Department of Health, Education, and Welfare
told St. Johns County's Superintendent of Instruction Douglas Hartley
that the county school system must have an acceptable desegregation
plan for the 1969/70 school year. HEW put the county on a deferred
status, which meant that federal funds would still be available for school
programs but would not be authorized for new programs. Accord-
ingly, Hartley prepared a desegregation plan which was to be sub-
mitted to the school board on July 8.[61]

Five days before the meeting, President Richard Nixon
issued a press release announcing that school desegregation would be
enforced throughout the South, but with a caveat permitting schools
with "serious shortages of necessary physical facilities, financial resources or faculty" to postpone implementing the desegregation
guidelines in 1969. Civil rights leaders denounced the new guidelines
as a boon to segregated schools, contending that most southern communities would use the change to maintain segregation.[62]

The impact of the new guidelines was quickly felt in St.
Augustine. The school board officials voted 3–1–1 to reject the desegregation plans drawn up by Hartley and, instead, to continue operating the schools during 1969/70 as they had in 1968/69. Thus, the
county would retain a freedom-of-choice segregated school system.
Seeking clarification of the school board's intent, Hartley asked, "In
other words the local board now has no plan to submit to Washington." "That's right," was the reply. When Hartley asked if he should
contact HEW, the board members suggested he wait until HEW contacted the county.[63] School Board Commissioner Arthur Powers, Sr.,
cautioned that "If we don't adopt some new plan HEW will cut off
federal assistance and then force us to comply with their guidelines
in court anyway." But Commissioner Bill Green responded, "I think
the Negro community as well as the white community has the right
to identify with their schools." In fact, a number of black families,
especially those in Hastings, an agricultural community near St. Augustine, expressed concern about closing neighborhood elementary

schools and busing children. Green had exploited this minority opinion for his own purposes. "We don't have the right to oppose the will of the people," Green concluded, adding that "the will of the people is the law according to my terminology."[64]

The board members met again the following evening and heard several citizens criticize their decision. Powers once again questioned the wisdom of rejecting the desegregation plan, and the Reverend Thomas DeSue of St. Paul's A.M.E. Church urged the board to try a plan acceptable to HEW "before we cry so loudly that it can't be done." School board member Charles Stanton, however, called the plan unacceptable, noting that in Hastings, for example, integration would lead to a school system that would be 65 percent black and 35 percent white. White residents, he declared, would move before they would permit such a development. Mrs. Rosalie Gordon pointed out that she had been but one black out of 1,180 students attending a university. "It did not seem so terrible to me," she stated. Powers moved that the board accept Hartley's desegregation proposal, but the motion died for lack of a second. After listening to further debate, the board adjourned without reconsidering its decision.[65]

In less than two months, the movement to prevent the desegration of St. Johns County schools suffered a serious setback. On September 2, HEW informed St. Johns County school board officials that the freedom-of-choice plan was unacceptable and that the county would lose nearly $75 million in federal aid if it did not submit a more suitable desegregation proposal. Impetus for desegregation followed quickly from an unexpected source. The following day, Governor Claude Kirk announced that the state had agreed to support a desegregated state school system. Perhaps even more persuasive, the Nixon administration pursued a more aggressive desegregation plan; HEW Secretary Elliott Richardson announced that federal funds would be cut off to schools failing to integrate. The federal government also declared that it would have the Internal Revenue Service remove the tax-exempt status of segregated private schools.[66]

Pressure on school board officials to desegregate county schools also came from legal developments in south Florida in the spring of 1970. United States District Court Judge Ben Krentzman ordered Manatee County school officials to begin busing to achieve a ratio of 80 percent white and 20 percent black students in each school. When school officials implemented the judge's order on April 6, Governor Claude Kirk abruptly suspended both the school board and Superintendent of Schools Jack L. Davidson, and personally seized control of the schools. Kirk apparently sought to bolster his gubernatorial reelection bid in 1970 and to test President Nixon's statement criticizing busing. Judge Krentzman immediately ordered the governor to return the schools to county school officials and to appear before him to explain his actions. Kirk refused to appear, claiming Krentzman had "overstepped his bounds." He also defied the court by again suspending both educational bodies and warned federal officials that there might be a loss of life if they attempted to serve him with a subpoena. On April 11, Krentzman found Kirk guilty of contempt and fined him $10,000 a day until he surrendered control of Manatee County's schools. The following day Kirk bowed to the judge's demands and directed the school board to implement Krentzman's desegregation order. This confrontation convinced St. Johns County school officials that they could not avoid school desegregation by appealing to the governor.[67]

Resigned to desegregation, St. Johns County officials implemented a school integration plan for 1970 that was essentially the same plan prepared by School Superintendent Hartley the previous year. It provided for full desegregation with the exception of Webster Elementary School, which would remain all black. HEW rejected the plan in June because of the Webster situation, which enabled the other elementary schools to remain overwhelmingly white. Telling the school board he "would not recommend any further busing," Hartley called HEW "very arbitrary in their decision." The school board endorsed Hartley's proposal and the county appealed HEW's decision to the Federal District Court.[68] HEW and the Justice Department recommended that Webster become 35 percent white. Judge Charles R. Scott, however, upheld the St. Johns' plan, calling it the "best plan presently available for a unitary system." Local officials were elated with the decision and the schools opened on August 31 without incident.[69]

In August 1970, however, the Fifth Circuit Court of Appeals overturned Judge Scott's decision and remanded the case to his court, ordering him to effect desegregation of Webster Elementary.

Scott's decision not only covered Webster's status but also required the superintendent to file reports on October 1 and March 1, reporting on the number of students by race in each school and in the school district, the number of teachers by race, the requests and results which have accrued by race, the number of interdistrict transfers by race, the extent of desegregation in all facilities and in the transportation system, description of expansion plans, and the creation of a biracial advisory subcommittee to the school board.[70] Once again St. Augustine had to be coerced by the federal courts into accepting racial change. Residents had yet to be persuaded that a new era had dawned and the community would be best served by accommodating itself to it.

Indeed, in an examination of St. Augustine in 1971, the men identified as the most prominent leaders in the community did not list race relations or school desegregation as one of the major issues facing the community. Instead they ranked such issues as the sightseeing franchise, bridge construction, zoning, tourism, bond issues, and industrial development as the critical issues confronting the city. When asked about the accuracy of this report, A. H. Tebeault, editor of the newspaper, said "Those . . . you've got listed just about sum it up. Not too much else has happened around here. No real controversies."[71]

Race relations continued to be a source of great concern to black leaders, however. With the advent of school integration, they turned their efforts to improving employment opportunities in city government for black residents. They also sought recreation facilities and additional city services for the black community. During this era, leadership came principally from Henry Twine, a prominent NAACP leader, and the Reverend Thomas DeSue of St. Paul's A.M.E. Church.

As a result of the increased political orientation of the black community, Arnett Chase, manager of the Leo Chase funeral home, announced his candidacy for a seat on the City Commission in the spring of 1973, marking the first time since 1965 that a black citizen had sought local office. Using as his slogan "Be a part of the solution, rather than part of the problem," Chase emphasized a moderate approach to civic leadership throughout the campaign. He ignored black concerns about jobs, urging instead citywide traffic improvements, sewer treatment development, and a coordinated water supply program.[72]

Stressing the importance of improving the city's tourist economy throughout his campaign, Chase won the endorsement of several businessmen and the local Democratic party. In addition, he conducted an extensive mailing and telephone campaign to the city's 6,000 voters. His campaign also benefited from the lackadasical effort of his opponent James Lindsley, who had served on the commission for twelve years and anticipated little problem in being reelected. Although Chase did not discuss Lindsley's past experience, many people felt that it was time for a change in leadership. With strong backing from black organizations, Chase defeated Lindsley by 300 votes, carrying both black wards with over 80 percent of the vote and narrowly losing the five predominantly white wards by 200 votes.[73]

Chase's election seemed to offer promise of a new era in race relations. But Chase's victory failed to change the status quo, in part because he was only one commissioner on a five-member commission. In addition, Chase showed little interest in being a spokesman for black concerns and his tenure on the commission was marked by a preoccupation with business and historical redevelopment problems. Chase served but two years on the commission and then chose not to run again. It appears that he was subject to constant pressure from black activists to represent their interests. When he proved reluctant to do so, he came under sharp criticism from the black community which ultimately led to his retirement from office.[74]

By the mid-1970s, a variety of factors indicated that there had been remarkably little change in the lives of black residents since 1950. The census figures for 1970 disclosed that black family median income stood at $4,282 per year, up by less than $800 from 1960; the mean income was $4,902. Nearly 237 black families with fathers present earned less than $3,000 per year, while only 42 black families received more than $10,000 per year and none earned more than $25,000. By contrast, white family median income stood at $6,874 and the mean at $8,561. Eight hundred and seventy-three white families earned over $10,000. The educational differences were also revealing: the median education level for blacks was 8.8 years compared to 11.8 years for whites. Only 66 black males over twenty-five years of age in the community had attended college as compared to

640 white males. Though blacks could eat at white restaurants, they seldom did because few could afford it, and the country club remained segregated.[75]

Because of the heavy dependence on tourism, black residents continued to work in largely unskilled, service-oriented positions during the 1970s. Nearly 80 percent of all black women and 35 percent of the men were engaged in service work. The closing of the Fairchild-Hiller aircraft plant in 1972 further reduced employment opportunities for blacks outside the tourist industry. One black leader described the job opportunities as pretty much waiting on others or "pick and shovel." Hamilton Upchurch observed in 1978 that there were still "no blacks in responsible jobs" in city government. Black parents were particularly concerned about the departure of their children to other cities where greater employment opportunities existed.[76]

Jobs which offered more than menial wages and limited opportunity for advancement thus became the major concern of black leaders in the 1970s and into the 1980s. Blacks have focused their demands on the city, seeking more jobs in government, especially in the police department and fire department. Presently, only one black is employed by the police department, where Virgil Stuart still serves as police chief, and none is employed by the fire department. Black employment has increased steadily in city government during the 1970s, but the jobs have been almost exclusively in the blue collar and secretarial ranks.[77]

Only in the school system have blacks been able to obtain white collar positions in large numbers, and this has been a carryover in large measure from the days of segregation. Even here, however, the number of black teachers has declined as they retired or resigned and were frequently replaced by white teachers.

A few militants still remain in St. Augustine and Hoss Manucy continues to refer to blacks as "niggers." "They are, aren't they?" he asked a reporter. Manucy, like many others, believes he was right in 1964: "I thought we was right. I still think so. We was trying to tell people. It was white fools who voted civil rights in, not niggers." But even Manucy has lost his zeal for the struggle and in a subdued fashion acknowledges certain changes. "There are niggers and whites in my neighborhood. And kids of both races are bused off to schools somewhere else. I definitely wouldn't object if the niggers and whites in this neighborhood were allowed to go to school together in this neighborhood." [78]

Though many whites still regard the racial changes with displeasure and grumble about school desegregation, they seldom discuss racial matters. In fact, most St. Augustinians have consciously tried to forget the events of 1964 and the racial difficulties of the past. Two ninth grade girls (one black and one white) who sipped Cokes at a soda fountain were asked by a reporter about events of 1964. Reflecting the efforts of most whites who have tried to suppress this part of the community's past rather than deal with it constructively, the white girl replied, "My parents were living here then but I've never heard them mention it." Not insignificantly, her companion remarked that she also never heard her parents talk about 1964. Most black parents seemed to believe that there was little to be gained by reviving memories of this bitter struggle. Police Chief Virgil Stuart told the same reporter, "I don't hear anybody talking about it." [79]

Conclusion

In reflecting upon the changes in St. Augustine since 1964, many black residents, including former civil rights activists, believe conditions have improved, and some think they have advanced significantly. Black citizens such as Clyde Jenkins, who had become involved in civil rights demonstrations in 1963, refer generally to "much better race relations" and specifically to desegregated schools, equal access to public facilities, and voting rights. Rosalie Gordon-Mills points to the election of Arnett Chase to the city commission and the selection of Otis Mason as assistant superintendent of schools as a sign of a new era in race relations. This attitude which pervades much of the black community is particularly noticeable among those middle-aged and older. Only those few still active in the local civil rights cause today and the young people question such assumptions. These widespread perceptions help account, in part, for the decline of civil rights concerns among black residents and the spread of apathy in the black community in the 1980s.[1]

An examination of St. Augustine's racial heritage discloses, however, that even though the legal barriers of Jim Crow have been removed, many of the racial patterns established at the turn of the century persist. The "civility" that William Chafe observed in relations between the races in Greensboro throughout the twentieth century has also typified those in St. Augustine. A cordiality and a respectfulness within the bounds of segregation have pervaded racial patterns in the nation's oldest city. Similarly, the economic restrictions encountered by black residents in the nineteenth century have continued into the twentieth century.[2]

During the period following Reconstruction, black residents were continually reminded of their place by a variety of barriers, including the segregation of public facilities and schools and severely limited economic opportunities, so that white residents seldom felt the need to use force, or even threats of force, to keep blacks in their place. Blacks did not accept their status without complaint, but they sensed that little could be done to change it. The tourist industry at once made the segregation system more civil and yet more suppressive. Tourism and the large number of service-related jobs connected with it placed black workers in a subservient status as waiters, waitresses, cleaning women, and doormen. The clientele they served was confined to the white race, and these occupations reemphasized in graphic terms the secondary status of black residents. At the same time tourism encouraged a civil, even pleasant relationship between the races since the industry depended for its success on satisfying the tourists and at least an appearance of harmony was necessary to encourage tourists to visit St. Augustine. A militantly racist community or a hostile group of black workers would have had a devastating impact on this business. For their part, blacks were generally inclined to conduct themselves in a cordial manner since tourism offered some a more lucrative occupation than serving as maids in homes or hired hands on farms and fishing boats. The treatment blacks received from whites in the tourist industry also tended to be better than in other occupations.

The relative freedom enjoyed by black residents in this Jim Crow society made life more tolerable, but blacks were never able to escape the pressures of racism. If violence against local blacks did not regularly occur in St. Augustine, it did in neighboring north and northwest Florida, reminding them of the tenuousness of their position. Furthermore, despite the relatively relaxed segregation customs practiced in St. Augustine, whites were no less committed to Jim Crow than those in more conservative areas of the Deep South. Any black who strayed too far outside the system was quickly cautioned about his proper place. For many whites in St. Augustine, segregation was as integral and necessary an institution as the family or the church. It was not one they would abandon lightly. In normal times white residents could be expected to treat blacks quite cordially and permit a modest degree of flexibility within the Jim Crow system, but there was never a sense that they were prepared to abandon segregation. Even racial moderates evinced little interest in changing the status quo.[3]

This commitment to segregation pervaded the white community throughout the twentieth century even as St. Augustine exhibited a marked civility in relations between the races compared to Deep South communities in particular during the pre-1945 period. When segregation stood in jeopardy, it was this fixation with a system based on race that caused St. Augustinians to abandon civil customs and behavior. Heavily influenced by the traditions of the past, many residents in this historic community were sufficiently committed to maintaining the status quo that they were fully prepared to block any racial changes. Thus, during the racial crisis in 1963 and 1964 a large majority of whites readily supported Dr. Shelley's stubborn resistance to a biracial committee because they feared such a group would lead to racial change.

St. Augustine's opposition to racial progress in the early 1960s was further strengthened by the prominence of political and law enforcement officials who were steeped in the Cold War rhetoric of the post–World War II period. Though they were not members of the John Birch Society, they generally shared the organization's outlook. Most were also close friends of the leader of the Birch Society—Dr. Hardgrove Norris. When Dr. Hayling initiated demonstrations in 1963, these political and law enforcement figures were ill prepared to adjust to a new era in race relations. In addition to their racial prejudices, local police and political leaders perceived the civil rights movement as a communist plot which threatened the very fabric of southern society.

Complicating the civil rights confrontation in St. Augustine was the militancy of Dr. Robert Hayling. Though Hayling proved to be a very effective leader in mobilizing a civil rights campaign, he lacked the personal skills to conduct negotiations with white leaders. He felt personally frustrated by the white community's ability to define the place of blacks (especially his place) and anxious to be free to shape his own future. Hayling's temperament was also ill-suited to the politics of compromise and prolonged meetings, and his outbursts of anger undermined the credibility of the movement in the eyes of more moderate whites and blacks and gave credence to the charges leveled against the civil rights movement by John Birch sympathizers. Although Hayling's anger was understandable in light of the violence perpetrated against him and his family, his growing stridency, especially his threat to arm himself and his aides, seriously impeded the efforts of civil rights forces.

Nevertheless, Hayling was a most capable organizer whose intelligence and assertiveness commanded respect and a loyal following among young people. Without his style of leadership, the civil rights protest would not have taken place in St. Augustine, and it is certain that SCLC would not have entered the community in 1964.[4]

By the spring of 1964, the Hayling-led civil rights movement had been distinctly unsuccessful in its efforts to desegregate the community and desperately needed outside support. White moderates, alienated by Hayling's militancy and influenced by friends in the John Birch Society, abandoned the middle ground, allowing Mayor Shelley and then Hoss Manucy to speak for the community. Without the intervention of the Reverend Martin Luther King, Jr., and SCLC in 1964, St. Augustine's black community would have made little if any progress and the local movement would have probably collapsed.

King's involvement proved to be a mixed blessing, however. Though SCLC was able to mobilize support from outside the community through the press, the organization often appeared only mildly interested in the local community and the aims of its movement. Throughout the spring of 1964, King kept one eye on events in Washington, D.C., and relied on developments there to gauge his course of action in St. Augustine. In his study of the Selma campaign of 1965, the political scientist David Garrow observed that King and his aides used "a strategy of nonviolent coercion" to maintain the spotlight on Selma and keep pressure on Congress to insure adoption of the Voting Rights Act of 1965. While no one in SCLC would acknowledge that the organization manipulated events in St. Augustine to facilitate passage of the 1964 Civil Rights Act, the Reverend Fred Shuttlesworth and Hosea Williams both commented that one of SCLC's primary goals during the St. Augustine campaign was to bring about enactment of the 1964 legislation.[5]

King also argued that it was essential that blacks be directly involved in the effort to desegregate the South and that it not be done for them by Congress, the press, or northern whites. He believed that it was important for blacks to realize that they had acquired these rights through their own initiatives. King and his aides wanted to avoid the difficulties of the first Reconstruction when northern support for black rights collapsed and so did the newly acquired freedoms. If blacks were involved in the struggle to obtain equal rights, King was convinced they would be unwilling to allow them to be sacrificed subsequently. In addition, such a movement would warn whites that blacks would not take their newly acquired rights lightly.[6]

In his president's report to SCLC in 1964, King declared that "when we are idle, the white majority very quickly forgets the injustices which started our movement and only think of the demands for progress as unreasonable requests from irresponsible people. . . . And so it was necessary," he continued, "for us to remind the nation of the reason the Civil Rights Bill came into existence in the first place. For this task, we chose the Nation's Oldest City." Thus St. Augustine became a stage upon which black leaders sought enactment of a law which would undo many of the inequities of the past and create a place for blacks in the mainstream of American society. Garrow has noted that King's political sagacity throughout this period has largely gone unnoticed by most scholars and has seldom been referred to by civil rights aides. But King demonstrated repeatedly in Selma and St. Augustine that he had the political acumen to know how to mobilize the nation, Congress, and the media behind the civil rights movement and thereby insure adoption of the long neglected reforms.[7]

King's concern with race relations nationally necessarily circumscribed his ability to understand events in St. Augustine and respond effectively to them. Thus, when SCLC pulled out of the community in July, it did so with what seemed little regard for the interests of the black community and the future of race relations. SCLC had achieved its main objective—passage of the Civil Rights Act.

The financial and personal burden of St. Augustine was simply too great to maintain, particularly when SCLC had made promises to participate in civil rights activities elsewhere. King acknowledged SCLC's responsibility when he wrote that "some communities, like this one, had to bear the cross."[8] This was not information that SCLC advertized widely since such pragmatism would have had disastrous consequences if it reached the press and the public.

St. Augustine, especially the black community, paid a heavy price for inviting King into the city. King and his aides dominated the movement during their participation, establishing their own goals and agenda, leading demonstrations, and negotiating with city and federal officials. Yet they failed to develop or encourage a grass roots movement which would provide the black community with leadership and direction following their departure. The Reverend Vivian later commented, "[Our] only failure was the lack of capacity to back up our activities after we left." King, he added, was not particularly interested in conducting follow-up campaigns. The local movement lost most of its leadership and support with the departure of SCLC, and was confronted by a hostile white community which resented the fact that blacks had sought outsiders to assist them, and that the quadricentennial and the city's economy had been devastated by the demonstrations. In this environment there was little hope for reconciliation and racial progress. In fact, black residents were faced with repeated acts of intimidation and violence during the fall of 1964 and throughout 1965. SCLC leaders promised to return if conditions in the community deteriorated and provided a summer workshop and college scholarships to black teenagers in the community in an attempt to ward off criticism of their departure. But when events worsened in St. Augustine, SCLC decided not to return, nor, apparently, did the organization seriously consider it. Thus while King and his SCLC staff helped to provide considerable momentum and direction for racial change in the community, their failure to develop a grass roots movement, their reluctance to return, and the alienation they helped to foster between blacks and whites portended a difficult future for race relations in the community. Though eminently successful in fostering racial progress at the national level, SCLC's strategy left local blacks in a precarious position from which they would be able to extricate themselves only with great difficulty and further federal assistance.[9]

Certainly, King and SCLC could not be held solely nor even chiefly accountable for the deteriorating relations in St. Augustine; indeed, white leaders not only rejected every civil rights proposal to end the crisis, they also encouraged militants to intervene by their persistent opposition to racial change. Further, with the passage of the civil rights bill, King would have willingly departed if city officials agreed to establish a biracial committee—hardly a radical step in 1964. Nevertheless, the racial outlook and Cold War mentality of civic leaders combined to cast a heavy pall over the prospect of racial change.

Throughout the racial crisis in 1964, the state and federal governments closely monitored events in St. Augustine. Governor Bryant sent a large contingent of state officers to maintain the peace, and an aide reported daily about developments in the community. Although Bryant sought an end to the violence in St. Augustine, his public statments criticizing the civil rights demonstrations often encouraged militant resistance. He also did little to promote a negotiated settlement either during or after the crisis. The federal government by contrast generally supported the efforts of SCLC, but refused to take specific action since President Johnson had determined that nothing should interfere with passage of the civil rights bill. The FBI, however, often worked at cross purposes with the position taken by the White House, as when agents knowingly passed along information to local law enforcement officials who in turn gave it to Klan leaders. The absence of a coherent state or federal policy impeded the efforts of SCLC and materially aided civic leaders and militants in their defiance of racial reform.

Did the demonstrations in St. Augustine insure passage of the Civil Rights Act of 1964? While events in St. Augustine were not referred to during the congressional debates, the extensive media and press coverage of the demonstrations in the nation's oldest city helped to mobilize the public behind the act and to remind congressmen that conditions in the South were worsening for blacks and would continue to deteriorate without federal legislation. Certainly the assassination of President Kennedy and the political leadership of President Johnson insured passage of the act, but the campaigns in Birmingham in 1963 and St. Augustine in 1964 pricked the conscience of the nation, spurring an alliance of blacks and whites behind civil rights reform. Without these protests, the Civil Rights Act of 1964 could not have been possible.

Throughout the St. Augustine campaign, King and SCLC consistently sought to attract and maintain media coverage to assist them in the desegregation effort and to win national support for the civil rights bill. King's understanding of the significance of the press to the civil rights cause developed during the abortive Albany campaign. He realized that northern public and financial support and subsequently federal assistance would only be provided if SCLC could capture the attention of the press. As John Lewis noted about reporters, "Only a few . . . really understood what was going on." Those who did were often natural allies of the movement. "They were even an extension of the movement—they identified with it," Lewis recalled. Other newsmen had to be persuaded of the significance of the movement. To gain their interest, King and his aides developed strategies that were bold and dramatic but which also increased the chances for violence. Hosea Williams utilized the evening marches in St. Augustine because they had been so successful in obtaining media coverage in Savannah. He thought that the press had a fixation with violence and gave the movement greater coverage whenever violence occurred. While agreeing with Williams, Pat Watters emphasized that "the press's ability to comprehend violence never included appreciation for its more important counterpoint—Negro nonviolence."[10]

SCLC leaders learned from the Albany campaign that civil rights demonstrators had to be trained in the ways of nonviolence: they had to be seen as defenseless victims seeking to correct the injustices of the past. As with striking laborers in the late nineteenth century, civil rights workers had to avoid initiating or partaking in the violence if they wanted to retain the cooperation of the press and the public. Thus SCLC field operatives conducted clinics on nonviolence throughout the South after the Albany disaster. Those who demonstrated a lack of patience or an inclination to resort to force were asked to leave and not participate in the demonstration. SCLC's ability to avoid violence and to gain widespread public sympathy and financial assistance for their position attested to the triumph of their tactics.

The success SCLC achieved in planning and conducting demonstrations did not, however, facilitate their efforts to reach a compromise with civic leaders. The St. Augustine campaign demonstrated once again the prominent role white leaders continued to play in denying black citizens equal rights and equal access. While rednecks and Klan elements often appeared on the front lines to do battle with civil rights activists, civic leaders manipulated events behind the scenes to block racial progress. Carl Holman of the National Urban Coalition remarked in 1974 that "a lot of blacks had it figured wrong. They thought that poor whites acted viciously and badly, but that 'quality' whites did not. That was wrong. Racism comes much more naturally, and to a much broader spectrum of whites, then we could have imagined." William Chafe's study of Greensboro underscores Holman's observation. In that New South city the white elite pursued a policy of benevolent paternalism which was designed to keep blacks in their place.[11]

In St. Augustine the white leadership in the early 1960s was not nearly so subtle. Mayor Joseph Shelley, his fellow commissioners, Judge Charles Mathis, and County Attorney Robert Andreu refused to discuss any proposals by SCLC that might disrupt the status quo. Civic leaders were strengthened in their opposition by a militant redneck class, led by J. B. Stoner, the Reverend Connie Lynch, Hoss Manucy, and a more sophisticated, white collar group, affiliated with the John Birch society and led by Dr. Norris. City officials and Birch proponents often worked closely together to defeat the efforts of King and his followers. While there was no such cooperation between city officials and Klan leaders, the two groups clearly worked side by side, with Sheriff Davis often serving as an intermediary, to block the efforts of SCLC and the desires of many local black residents. The white leadership thus acted as the brains behind the civil rights resistance with the militants providing the brawn. Furthermore, white civic leaders controlled the instruments of oppression through the government, courts, police, and business.

Prominent business leaders evinced little concern with the civil rights developments in 1963 and early 1964 since they did not begin to feel their effects until late 1964. Only then did they encourage a series of compromises to end the economic difficulties. Even in 1965 when they led the efforts to restrict the racial violence in order to salvage the quadricentennial celebration, they did not pursue any meaningful plans which would improve the racial character of the city. After 1965 business leaders retreated from a leadership position on race relations altogether, sanctioning, in effect, the racial polarization that emerged.

St. Augustine also felt the pressure of an ethnic minority which generally opposed extending equal rights to black residents. Many Minorcan citizens participated in demonstrations with other white militants, while others supported the position of Shelley. Minorcans shared many of the community's racial prejudices, and seemed anxious for this reason and for concerns about status to keep blacks in their place. The threat of job competition certainly weighed heavily on the minds of many Minorcans who were only slightly better off than most blacks.

The failure of the religious community to exercise its moral and ethical influence during the civil rights crisis compounded the conflict for St. Augustine. The absence of a voice of moderation seriously limited any chance for peaceful compromise. The churches, especially the large and influential Catholic Church, could have played this role very effectively with the proper leadership. When one religious leader did urge a moderate course, he was discounted by his parishioners and the community as a racial heretic. With the church as timid and biased in its leadership as the other leading institutions in the community, the emergence of a moderate position among white residents was repeatedly stymied.

The absence of such moderation during the critical two-year period from 1963 to 1965 and to a lesser degree until 1970 affected the involvement of older black citizens in the civil rights movement and undermined the unity of the movement. Those over forty generally refrained from participating in the protest activities because they feared the loss of their jobs. In fact, many blacks who had jobs in the tourist industry, as domestics, and as tenant farmers were cautioned by their employers against such involvement. Because of their limited experience and the stories they heard of racial violence elsewhere in the South, they felt little resentment of their lot in St. Augustine. Their lack of participation and, in some cases, criticism of the movement jeopardized the efforts of Hayling and King. White leaders were able to argue, as Shelley did repeatedly, that most blacks thought race relations were fine and that only outsiders and young militants favored change.[12] Local blacks who participated in the movement tended to be high school and college students or recent residents of St. Augustine. Those who did not participate generally comprised the upper ranks of black society, worked for the city as teachers, secretaries, or garbage collectors, or served as maids or servants for white residents. As happened in other communities across the South, most black clergy believed the civil rights movement was trying to proceed too fast, and they proved reluctant advocates of SCLC's desegregation efforts. Hayling's failure to cultivate their support in the first year of the civil rights movement no doubt limited their participation.

In the immediate post-1964 period, race relations lost all semblance of the cordiality that had previously existed in St. Augustine. A distinct hostility between the races pervaded the community, exhibiting itself in the violence and intimidation conducted indiscriminately against black residents, not just civil rights activists. Further, white leaders resisted school desegregation as long as possible, and only agreed to a plan after the federal court threatened the county with a cutoff of federal funds.

As the crisis eased in late 1965, moderate forces in the community gradually began to assume positions of influence. Initially, they argued that the quadricentennial celebration would only be a success if white militants were prevented from engaging in further acts of violence against blacks. They became more assertive when the Birch Society attacked the PTA. With their victory over the Birch Society in 1968, moderates had established their place in St. Augustine. Not insignificantly, the participation of moderates in civic affairs did not bring about racial progress; rather it meant racial stability and an end to violence. White moderates did not favor further changes in the status of black citizens and generally opposed affirmative action. They also continued to treat blacks with a civility that was reminiscent of the days of Jim Crow.

Clearly the racial crisis had severely strained race relations and made civil rights developments unpalatable to many white residents. With continued opposition from the white community, the decline of readily identifiable issues (especially after the passage of the Voting Rights Act of 1965), the departure of several important black leaders in the period 1966–68, and the loss of northern support generally following the urban riots of the mid-1960s, the civil rights movement in St. Augustine lost much of its momentum and membership by the end of the decade.

Despite these developments, the decades of the 1960s and 1970s witnessed a number of significant changes for black residents. Such changes allowed for a more cordial environment, but they proved no panacea for black conerns. The Civil Rights Act of 1964, the Voting Rights Act of 1965, and the Supreme Court decision in *Green* v. *County School Board* (a decision involving freedom of choice plans in New Kent County, Virginia) in 1968 permitted blacks to enter restaurants, hotels, and other public facilities, to vote without restrictions, and to attend desegregated schools. The behavior of law enforcement officers was also circumscribed by legal guidelines, insuring that blacks would be treated with some degree of courtesy and respect. A dialogue gradually developed between black activists and civic leaders, leading to improvements in roads and recreation and sewer facilities. These reforms did not come without a struggle and without pressure from a revitalized civil rights movement in the mid-1970s. And while the federal government and federal courts generally retreated from their vigorous support of civil rights, both branches of government firmly resisted efforts to resegregate during the 1970s and 1980s. The Attorney General's office filed several suits against school systems which sought to circumvent integration guidelines, and the courts endorsed busing to achieve integration even though they restricted its use in Dayton and Atlanta. Altogether these developments significantly improved the quality of life for blacks in the United States and, more particularly, in St. Augustine.[13]

Even with these changes, however, there were a number of developments in St. Augustine which proved disconcerting to blacks and detrimental to further racial progress. During the 1970s and 1980s, geographic segregation in the community increased as whites moved in larger numbers to Anastasia Island, across the bay from the city. Moreover, the YMCA still maintained segregated facilities despite numerous protests from civil rights leaders. But by far the worst aspect of life for blacks was the economic situation. From all indications blacks remained in the same economic position relative to whites that they held during the 1940s and 1950s. Virtually no progress was achieved in this area, and the majority of black residents continued to live on the edge of poverty.

The city did little to relieve the distress. The police department, still under the leadership of Chief Stuart, continued to employ only one black and the fire department, with its requirement that firemen sleep together during duty hours, employed none. Though black employment increased in other government areas, it remained confined to blue collar, secretarial, and janitorial positions. Racial advancement moved sluggishly through the 1970s, reflecting the difficulties of a small civil rights movement trying to cope with white leaders who were unwilling to grant black residents full access to power and equal status with whites.[14]

In contrast to such New South cities as Atlanta, Dallas, Charlotte, and Tampa, there were many small towns which were only slightly affected by the civil rights revolution. Because racial patterns were rooted in the nineteenth century and in some cases even earlier, they were not readily changed. Moreover, these communities did not experience the social and economic vitality of the New South cities during the post–World War II period. As a consequence, their white leaders did not view change as necessarily a positive development. This was especially true in St. Augustine where residents tended to venerate the past and spend large sums of money to preserve it. In addition to the relative absence of social and economic change in these small communities, the highly personal nature of many of these societies made it very difficult for blacks to organize and, if they did, to persuade whites to accept civil rights reform. The vast majority of these towns never experienced a civil rights demonstration and, despite the changes mandated by the federal government and the courts, they managed to avoid federal scrutiny and retained many of the racial customs of the past.

St. Augustine differed from nearly all these small communities because it had such a unique heritage and because it was confronted by a major civil rights crusade. This heritage not only bred a conservative view of society, it also encouraged a certain smugness and self-satisfaction with the quality of life in St. Augustine. Civic leaders contended that their community offered a perfect blend of history, recreation, environment, and business; they also believed that blacks had been well treated. This complacency revealed itself still further when business leaders discouraged efforts to recruit new industry for fear it would detract from the town's character. The John Birch Society appealed directly to the community's committment to the past and to its smugness about the present, while the civil rights demonstrations and the condemnation of St. Augustine's racial practices by the media and the nation only further galvanized white opposition to racial reform. Though there was little that civic leaders could do to resist the political, social, and educational changes mandated by the federal courts and the federal government, they could stifle economic developments that would improve the status of blacks. The town's major economic activity, tourism, offered few opportunities to black residents, and the decision not to recruit new industry effectively impeded black chances for social and economic advancement in St. Augustine.

Without economic readjustments and an improved economic environment, blacks have not been able to exercise fully the hard-won legal and civil rights they achieved in the 1960s. Many of the political promises have been fulfilled, but the economic and social gains that seemed in the offing as a result of federal legislation and court edicts of the 1960s have not been attained. Throughout the South in many small, tradition-bound cities like St. Augustine, where a very conservative racial outlook shaped public opinion and where change in any form did not occur easily, the 1970s was a decade of frustration for blacks as southern whites gradually reasserted their control and northern whites lost interest and enthusiasm in continuing the civil rights struggle. Thus, despite many improvements since 1959, the second Reconstruction has yet to provide a quality of life for black citizens that even closely approximates that of whites in the nation's oldest community.

Notes

1. Shell-Shocked in St. Augustine: The Celebration

1. *Washington Post* and *New York Times*, June 20, 1964, p. 1.

2. *Gainesville Sun*, June 26, 1964, p. 7b; William Brink and Louis Harris, *The Negro Revolution in America* (New York: Simon and Schuster, 1963), p. 103.

3. *Gainesville Sun*, June 26, 1964, p. 7b. Also see *Miami Herald*, June 26, 1964, p. 1, and *New York Times*, June 26, 1964, p. 14.

4. *The Christian Century*, June 3, 1964, p. 725; *Time* (vol. 83, no. 1), January 3, 1964, pp. 13–27.

5. Pat Watters, *Down to Now: Reflections on the Southern Civil Rights Movement* (New York: Random House, 1971), p. 217; August Meier, "On the Role of Martin Luther King," *New Politics* (Winter 1965), 4:53–59; Also see David L. Lewis, *King: A Biography* (Urbana, Illinois: University of Illinois Press, 1970), pp. 46–111.

6. *New York Times*, June 26, 1964, p. 1.

7. Interview with Henry Twine, September 19, 1977, St. Augustine, Fla.; interview with the Reverend C. T. Vivian, May 4, 1983, Atlanta, Ga. Copies of all interviews are in the hands of the author and are being made available to the University of Florida Oral History Collection.

8. Interview with Clyde Jenkins, September 19, 1977, St. Augustine, Fla.

9. *New York Times*, June 26, 1964, p. 14; interview with the Reverend Fred Shuttlesworth, September 13, 1978.

10. Racial Situation, St. Augustine, Fla., June 26, 1964, 6 pages, pp. 2–4, Federal Bureau of Investigation Files, Washington, D.C. (copies of all FBI materials cited here are also available in the P. K. Yonge Library of Florida History, University of Florida, Gainesville).

11. *Ibid.*; Interview with Mrs. Mary Lee Gannon, May 6, 1977, St. Augustine, Fla.

12. *Pittsburgh Courier*, June 27, 1964, p. 1; *New York Times*, June 26, 1964, pp. 1, 14; (Jacksonville) *Florida Times-Union*, June 26, 1964, p. 10. The term "slave market,"

although commonly used in St. Augustine, was alleged to be a misnomer by local residents. Black and white residents commented that the building had served only as a farmer's market in the past. Statements from people who had lived in St. Augustine during the antebellum period indicate, however, that slaves had, in fact, been sold there on occasion, and Christina Sanchez remembers her father purchasing a slave at the market. Interviews with Dr. Joseph Shelley, September 6, 1977; Henry Twine, September 19, 1977; and A. H. Tebeault, Jr., June 13, 1978, St. Augustine, Fla.; and Michael V. Gannon, May 3, 1977, Gainesville, Fla.; Mary Irwin Bainum, *Oral Legends of St. Augustine, Florida* (St. Petersburg, Fla.: n.p., 1979), pp. 33–34.

13. *The Present-Day Ku Klux Klan Movement: Report by the Committee of Un-American Activities.* House of Representatives, 90th Cong. 1st Sess., December 11, 1967 (Washington, D.C.: GPO, 1967), pp. 12–13.

14. *Activities of the Ku Klux Klan Organization in the United States*, Part 5, Hearing Before the Committee on Un-American Activities. House of Representatives, 89th Cong., 2d Sess. (Washington, D.C.: GPO, 1966), p. 3821.

15. Trevor Armbrister, "Portrait of an Extremist," *Saturday Evening Post* (vol. 231), August 22, 1964, p. 82; *St. Augustine Record*, June 25, 1964, p. 7; Larry Goodwyn, "Anarchy in St. Augustine," *Harper's Magazine* (no. 230), January 1964, pp. 74–81.

16. Armbrister, "Portrait of an Extremist," p. 82.

17. *Ibid.*

18. *Ibid.*

19. *St. Augustine Record*, June 25, 1964, p. 7; Numan V. Bartley, *The Rise of Massive Resistance: Race and Politics in the South During the 1950s* (Baton Rouge: Louisiana State University Press, 1969), p. 47; Neil R. McMillen, *The Citizens' Council: Organized Resistance to the Second Reconstruction, 1954–64* (Urbana: University of Illinois Press, 1971), pp. 22, 51–52, 180, 309.

20. *Activities of the Ku Klux Klan*, Part 5, p. 3662; Folder, St. Johns County (Race Problems, 1964), Governor Farris Bryant Papers, Florida State Archives, Tallahassee, Fla.

21. Armbrister, "Portrait of an Extremist," p. 82.

22. *Ibid.*; Goodwyn, "Anarchy in St. Augustine," p. 79; William M. Kunstler, *Deep in My Heart* (New York: Morrow, 1966), p. 301.

23. Interview with Hank Drane, January 31, 1978, Jacksonville, Fla.

24. Andrew Young v. L. O. Davis et al. Transcript of Hearing, June 13, 1964, Accession no. 73A377, FRC Box 1E15887, Agency Box 13, Record Group 21, Federal Records Center, East Point, Ga.; Folder, Special Police Force, Letters, St. Augustine and Reports, 1964. Governor Farris Bryant Papers, Florida State Archives, Tallhassee, Fla. Report on St. Augustine, Fla., by the Reverend Elizabeth J. Miller, November 11, 1964, Subgroup A, Series I, Ss 1, St. Augustine, Fla., Box 27, Folder 10, p. 6. Martin Luther King Papers, Martin Luther King Center, Atlanta, Ga.; (Jacksonville) *Florida Times-Union*, June 26, 1954, p. 22.

25. Kunstler, *Deep in My Heart*, p. 301.

26. (Jacksonville) *Florida Times-Union*, June 26, 1964, p. 22; *New York Times*, June 26, 1964, p. 14.

27. (Jacksonville) *Florida Times-Union*, May 29, 1964, p. 24; *Miami Herlald*, June 11, 1964, p. 20a.

28. Interview with Hank Drane, January 31, 1978.

29. *Miami Herald*, June 11, 1964, p. 20a; Special Police Force, Governor Farris Bryant Papers; interview with Hank Drane, January 31, 1978.

30. (Jacksonville) *Florida Times-Union*, June 26, 1964, p. 1; Kunstler, *Deep in My Heart*, p. 14.

31. *New York Times*, June 16, 1964, pp. 1, 14; June 6, 1964, p. 10. Folder on Racial Disorders, Scrapbook on St. Augustine Civil Rights, St. Augustine Historical Society. *New York Times*, June 25, 1964, p. 19.

32. Interview with Dr. Joseph Shelley, September 6, 1977; *St. Augustine Record*, July 1, 1964, p. 1. Federal pressure was also exerted in several other ways. No federal funds were allocated to the community to celebrate the community's 400th anniversary as was originally promised. A federal charter to establish a savings and loan was also rejected. Local leader Hamilton Upchurch was informed several years later by the federal hearing officer that "St. Augustine could not have gotten the Red Cross if they had been wiped off the map in 1964." Interviews with W. I. Drysdale, October 5, 1978, by the author, St. Augustine, Fla.; and Hamilton Upchurch, January 27, 1978.

33. *St. Augustine Record*, July 1, 1964, p. 1.

34. *New York Times*, June 26, 1964, p. 14; interview with the Reverend Fred Shuttlesworth, September 9, 1978; interview with Hosea Williams, March 16, 1978, Atlanta, Ga.

2. Bluebirds and Redbirds Don't Feed Together

1. Michael V. Gannon, *The Cross in the Sand: The Early Catholic Church in Florida, 1513–1870* (Gainesville: University of Florida Press, 1967), pp. 1–3, 21–27.

2. Thomas Graham, *The Awakening of St. Augustine: The Anderson Family and the Oldest City: 1821–1924* (St. Augustine: St. Augustine Historical Society, 1978), pp. 25–54.

3. *Ibid.*, pp. 167–177.

4. U.S. Bureau of the Census, *Census of the Population: 1960*. Vol. 1: *Characteristics of the Population*, Part II, "Florida" (Washington, D.C.: GPO, 1963), p. 10.

5. Interview with the Reverend Stanley Bullock, January 17, 1978, Jacksonville, Fla.; interview with W. I. Drysdale, October 5, 1978, St. Augustine, Fla.

6. Interview with Michael V. Gannon, May 3, 1977; interview with Dr. Hardgrove Norris, September 15, 1978, Gainesville, Fla.; Interview with Hamilton Upchurch, January 27, 1978.

7. Interviews with Michael V. Gannon, May 3, 1977; and the Reverend Stanley Bullock, January 17, 1978.

8. David K. Bartholomew, "An Analysis of Change in the Power System and Decision-Making Process in a Selected County," Ed.D. dissertation, University of Florida, 1971, p. 63; James Fox, "Comparisons of Civic Beliefs of Influential Leaders, Status Leaders, Educational Personnel, and Citizens in Two Selected Florida Counties," Ed.D. dissertation, University of Florida, 1971; interview with Michael V. Gannon, May 3, 1977.

9. Jane Quinn, *Minorcans in Florida: Their History and Heritage* (St. Augustine, Fla.: Mission Press, 1975), p. 69; interview with Michael V. Gannon, May 3, 1977.

10. U.S. Bureau of the Census, *Census of the Population: 1960*. Vol. 1: *Characteristics of the Population*, Part II, "Florida," p. 10. Interview with Michael V. Gannon, May 3, 1977.

11. Interview with Michael V. Gannon, May 3, 1977.

12. Interviews with the Reverend Thomas Wright, October 6, 1977, Gainesville, Fla.; the Reverend Charles M. Seymour, October 16, 1978, Lake Providence, La.; the Reverend Stanley Bullock, January 17, 1978; Michael V. Gannon, May 3, 1977.

13. Graham, *The Awakening of St. Augustine*, pp. 19–20; John Francis Tenney, *Slavery, Secession, and Success* (San Antonio, 1934), pp. 10–14.

2. *Bluebirds and Redbirds Not Together*

14. "The Mose Site," *El Escribano* (April 1973), 10(2):50–62. In 1733 the Spanish crown decreed that slaves fleeing the English settlements and desiring to embrace Catholicism would be freed. The Mose site was two miles north of the Castillo de San Marcos. W. W. Dewhurst, *The History of St. Augustine, Florida* (New York: Putnam, 1885), pp. 170–171; Graham, *The Awakening of St. Augustine*, pp. 19–24.

15. Graham, *The Awakening of St. Augustine*, p. 20; Richard Wade, *Slavery in the Cities: The South, 1820–1860* (London, Oxford, New York: Oxford University Press, 1964), pp. 243–281.

16. Graham, *The Awakening of St. Augustine*, pp. 20–21.

17. *Ibid.*, pp. 121–122.

18. Joe M. Richardson, *The Negro in the Reconstruction of Florida, 1865–1877* (Tallahassee: Florida State University Press, 1965), pp. 96, 116–117, 148; Graham, *The Awakening of St. Augustine*, pp. 140–141; *St. Augustine Evening Record*, October 31, 1902, p. 1.

19. Richardson, *The Negro in the Reconstruction of Florida*, pp. 116–117, 148; Graham, *The Awakening of St. Augustine*, pp. 140–142, 197–198.

20. Graham, *The Awakening of St. Augustine*, pp. 198, 202; Charleton W. Tebeau, *A History of Florida* (Coral Gables, Fla.: University of Miami Press, 1971), pp. 289–290; Jerrell H. Shofner, "Custom, Law, and History: The Enduring Influence of Florida's 'Black Code,' " *The Florida Historical Quarterly* (January 1977), 55(3):287–289.

21. Interviews with Michael V. Gannon, May 3, 1977, and Hamilton Upchurch, January 27, 1978; Dunkle, "St. Augustine, Florida: A Study in Historical Geography," pp. 153, 210–217; Federal Writers' Project American Guide (Negro Writers' Unit), St. Augustine, Fla.; William C. Lee, *The Higher Learning in America's Oldest City: The Story of a Christian College* (n.p.), pp. 12–13.

22. Interview with Otis Mason, assistant superintendent of schools in St. Johns County, June 13, 1978, St. Augustine, Fla.; interview with Dr. R. W. Puryear, August 1, 1980, Winston-Salem, N.C.

23. *Ibid.*; interview with Henry Twine, September 19, 1977.

24. Interview with Henry Twine, September 19, 1977; interview with Otis Mason, June 13, 1978.

25. Interview with the Reverend Thomas Wright, October 6, 1977; Benjamin E. Mays and Joseph W. Nicholson, *The Negro's Church* (New York: Arno Press and the New York Times, 1969), p. 93.

26. U.S. Bureau of the Census, *Census of the Population: 1950.* Vol. 2: *Characteristics of the Population*, Part 10, "Florida" (Washington, D.C.: GPO, 1952), p. 27.

27. U.S. Bureau of the Census, *Census of the Population: 1960.* Vol 2: *Characteristics of the Population*, Part 11, "Florida" (Washington, D.C.: GPO, 1963), pp. 29, 127, 129, 204, 210.

28. *Ibid.*; interview with Otis Mason, June 13, 1978.

29. William H. Chafe, *Civilities and Civil Rights: Greensboro, North Carolina, and the Black Struggle for Freedom* (New York and Oxford: Oxford Univeristy Press, 1980), p. 8; Robert W. Hartley, "A Long, Hot Summer: The St. Augustine Racial Disorders of 1964," M.A. thesis, Stetson University, 1972, p. 8; interview with John D. Bailey, August 11, 1977, St. Augustine, Fla.; interviews with Henry Twine, September 19, 1977; and Mr. Clyde Jenkins, Septemer 19, 1977, St. Augustine, Fla.; interview with Hank Drane, January 31, 1978; interview with Otis Mason, June 13, 1978.

30. David Chalmers, *Hooded Americanism: The First Century of the Ku Klux Klan* (Chicago: Quadrangle, 1968), p. 378; interview with Otis Mason, June 13, 1978.

31. Interviews with Clyde Jenkins, September 19, 1977; and the Reverend Charles M. Seymour, Jr., August 16, 1978.

32. Interviews with Michael V. Gannon, May 3, 1977; Hamilton Upchurch, Frank Upchurch, and Douglas Hartley, January 27, 1978; and the Reverend Stanley Bullock, January 17, 1978; U.S. Bureau of the Census, *Census of the Population: 1950. Vol. 2: Characteristics of the Population*, Part 10, "Florida" (Washington, D.C.: GPO, 1952), pp. 10–28; U.S. Bureau of the Census, *Census of the Population: 1960*. Vol. 1: *Characteristics of the Population*, Part 11, "Florida" (Washington, D.C.: GPO, 1963), pp. 11–29.

33. *New York Times*, July 5, 1964, sec. 6, p. 30; interview with Michael V. Gannon, May 3, 1977; interview with the Reverend Stanley Bullock, January 17, 1978.

34. *St. Augustine Record*, May 19, 1954, p. 4; C. Vann Woodward, *The Strange Career of Jim Crow* (New York: Oxford University Press, 1974), p. 153.

35. Numan V. Bartley, *The Rise of Massive Resistance: Race and Politics in the South During the 1950s* (Baston Rouge; Louisiana State University Press, 1969), pp. 67–68. Bartley characterizes the southern response during the year following the *Brown* decision as one "of drift and decision, of progress and reaction." (Jacksonville) *Florida Times-Union*, May 18, 1954, p. 1; *Congressional Quarterly*, May 21, 1954, p. 637; *Tampa Tribune*, May 19, 1954, p. 10.

36. *St. Augustine Record*, May 19, 1954, pp. 1, 4.

37. Bartley, *The Rise of Massive Resistance*, pp. 68, 85.

38. *New York Times*, July 6, 1957, p. 7; May 5, 1957, p. 46. *Southern School News* (May 1957), 3(11):1. *Tampa Tribune*, December 17, 1958, p. 1; February 19, 1959, p. 1. J. Harvie Wilkinson III, *From Brown to Baake: The Supreme Court and School Integration, 1954–1978* (New York: Oxford University Press, 1979), pp. 115–117.

39. *Miami Herald*, February 28, 1961; *Tampa Tribune*, February 28 1961.

40. Interview with the Reverend Thomas Wright, October 6, 1977; Henry Twine, September 19, 1977; Otis Mason, June 13, 1978. Minutes of the St. Augustine City Commission, May 28, 1958, City Hall, St. Augustine; Fla. Allen Morris, *The Florida Handbook, 1947–48* (Tallahassee: The Peninsular Publishing Company, 1948), p. 222; Morris, *The Florida Handbook, 1951–52* (Tallahassee: The Peninsular Publishing Company, 1952), p. 204.

41. Interview with the Reverend Thomas Wright, October 6, 1977.

42. Interviews with the Reverend Thomas Wright, October 6, 1977; and Hamilton Upchurch, January 27, 1978.

43. Interview with Dr. Robert Hayling, September 28, 1978; interview with Dr. Robert B. Hayling by John H. Britton, Atlanta, Ga., The Civil Rights Documentation Project, Howard University, Washington, D.C., p. 1; interview with Otis Mason, June 13, 1978.

44. Interview with Dr. Robert Hayling, September 28, 1978; interview with Dr. Robert Hayling, Civil Rights Documentation Project, p. 1.

45. *Ibid.*

46. *Ibid.*; interview with Mrs. Rosalie Gordon-Mills, August 11, 1977.

47. Interviews with Henry Twine and Clyde Jenkins, September 19, 1977; Otis Mason, June 13, 1978; and Michael V. Gannon, May 3, 1977.

48. Doug McAdam, *Political Process and the Development of Black Insurgency, 1930–1970* (Chicago: University of Chicago Press, 1982), p. 51.

49. Interviews with Mrs. Rosalie Gordon-Mills, August 11, 1979; Henry Twine, Clyde Jenkins, September 19, 1977; Dr. Hardgrove Norris, September 15, 1978; Mr. Fred Brinkhoff, June 13, 1978; Mr. Douglas Hartley, January 27, 1978; and Hosea Williams, March 16, 1978.

50. Group II, Youth File, Series D, 5, National Association for the Advancement of Colored People Papers, Library of Congress Manuscripts, Washington, D.C.

51. Interview with Dr. Robert Hayling, September 28, 1978; interview with Mrs. Rosalie Gordon-Mills, August 11, 1977, interview with Hosea Williams, March 16, 1978.

52. Referred to in Letter to President John F. Kennedy from Mrs. Fannie Fuller-wood and Mrs. Elizabeth Hawthorne, May 4, 1963, p. 1. In Box 24, Lee White Files, President John F. Kennedy Papers, John F. Kennedy Library, Waltham, Mass. Vice-President Johnson's visit was to be the first public act by the St. Augustine Quadricentennial Commission, established by Congress on August 14, 1962, in preparation for St. Augustine's 400th anniversary in September 1965. *Pittsburgh Courier*, March 9, 1963, p. 2; Memorandum to Walter Pozen, assistant to the secretary of the Department of Interior, from Jackson E. Price, assistant director, Conservation, Interpretation and Use, May 8, 1963, Box 24, Lee White Files, JFK Papers.

53. *Pittsburgh Courier*, March 9, 1963, p. 2; also letter to President John Kennedy from Mrs. Fannie Fullerwood and Mrs. Elizabeth Hawthorne, May 4, 1963, p. 1, JFK Papers; Lyndon B. Johnson to the Reverend Martin Luther King, Jr., July 9, 1963, SCLC Papers, Subgroup A, Series I, Ss1, Box 20, folder 9, Martin Luther King, Jr., Papers, Atlanta; letter from Lyndon B. Johnson to Mrs. Fannie Fullerwood, March 7, 1963, Community Relations Service Files, Department of Justice, Washington, D.C.

54. *St. Augustine Record*, March 26, 1963, p. 8. *Florida Star News*, May 25, 1963, p. 1.

55. Letter to President John F. Kennedy from Mrs. Fannie Fullerwood and Mrs. Elizabeth Hawthorne, May 4, 1963, 2 pages, JFK Papers; St. Augustine Quadricentennial Commission, Box 24, Lee White Files, JFK Papers; Racial Situation, St. Johns County, June 5, 1963-December 30, 1963, FBI Files.

56. Demands of the St. Augustine Branch of the NAACP, MLK Papers, Box 20, St. Augustine, Fla., n.d., folder 13; Charles P. Barrier to Mayor James S. Lindsley, May 8, 1963, MLK Papers, Box 20, Folder 9.

57. *Ibid.*; *St. Augustine Record*, October 22, 1963, p. 8. Interview with Dr. Joseph Shelley, September 6, 1977; *St. Augustine Record*, June 18, 1963, p. 1.

58. *Ibid.*, June 18, 1963; Mrs. F. Fullerwood and Mrs. E. Hawthorne to Charles P. Barrier et al., May 18, 1963, MLK Papers, Box 20, Folder 9; letter to President John F. Kennedy from Congressman Bob Sikes, June 27, 1963, p. 2, JFK Papers; *St. Augustine Record*, June 19, 1963; Racial Situation, St. Augustine, Florida, June 20, 1963, p. 1, FBI Files.

59. *St. Augustine Record*, June 20, 1963, p. 1.

60. Racial Situation, St. Augustine, Florida, June 21, 1963, p. 2, FBI Files.

61. Interview with Dr. Joseph Shelley, September 6, 1977, interview with Dr. Hardgrove Norris, September 15, 1978, interview with Dr. Ron Jackson, June 6, 1978, by telephone with the author.

62. Interview with Dr. Hardgrove Norris, September 15, 1978; Tape recording in possession of the author, restricted by request of donor. (Jacksonville) *Florida Times-Union*, July 31, 1964, p. 23; interview with Dr. Joseph Shelley, September 6, 1977; *St. Augustine Record*, April 2, 1964, p. 1.

63. Interview with Dr. Joseph Shelley, September 6, 1977; *St. Augustine Record*, May 8, 1963, p. 1; (Jacksonville) *Florida Times-Union*, April 2, 1964, p. 24.

64. Interview with Dr. Joseph Shelley, September 6, 1977; interview with Dr. Hardgrove Norris, September 15, 1978; tape recording in possession of the author.

65. *Racial and Civil Disorders in St. Augustine: Report of the Legislative Investigation Commission* (Tallahassee), February 1965, pp. 63–64; Minutes of the St. Augustine City Commission, September 24, 1962–December 12, 1966; June 28, 1963, pp. 4410–4412.

66. *Ibid.*

67. *Florida Star News,* July 6, 1963, p. 1; SAC, Jacksonville to Director, FBI, Racial Situation, St. Johns County, July 2, 1963, 5 pages, pp. 1–5, FBI Files.

68. Racial Situation, St. Johns County, Fla., July 19, 1963, pp. 1–2, FBI Files; July 23, 1963, pp. 1–2.

69. Tape recording in possession of the author; Racial Situation, St. Johns County, Florida, July 25, 1963, p. 1, FBI Files; July 23, 1963, pp. 1–2.

70. *St. Augustine Record,* July 25, 1963, p. 12; *New York Times,* July 26, 1963, p. 1; Folder, St. Johns County (Race Problem, 1964), Governor Farris Bryant Papers, Florida State Archives, Tallahassee, p. 9.

71. (Jacksonville) *Florida Times-Union,* July 30, 1963, p. 20; *Florida Star News,* August 10, 1963, p. 2; Memorandum to Burke Marshall, assistant attorney general, Civil Rights Division, from John L. Murphy, chief, General Litigation Section, November 5, 1963, 3 pages. United States Department of Justice Papers, Washington, D.C., p. 2; interview with Judge Charles Mathis, Jr., October 5, 1978; Tape recording in possession of the author; County Commission Records, S., St. Johns County, Florida, September 17, 1963, p. 119; *St. Augustine Record,* November 18, 1963, p. 8.

72. *St. Augustine Record,* November 18, 1963, p. 8.

73. *Florida Star News,* August 10, 1963, p. 2; *St. Augustine Record,* December 4, 1963, p. 14; *Pittsburgh Courier,* January 25, 1964, p. 1.

74. *St. Augustine Record,* October 2, 1963, p. 10a; *Florida Star News,* October 12, 1963, p. 1; also in *The Crisis,* (November 1963), 70(9):553.

75. Letter to Organization of American States from SCLC, undated, Farris Bryant Papers, pp. 8, 9; *Florida Star News,* July 13, 1963, p. 1; *Andrew Young v. L. O. Davis et al.,* #64–133–Civ–J. Pamphlet entitled "St. Augustine, Florida: 400 Years of Bigotry and Hate," p. 4, Box 1, Judge Bryan J. Simpson Papers; interview with Dr. Robert Hayling, Civil Rights Documentation Project, p. 26. Interview with Henry Twine, September 19, 1977.

76. (Jacksonville) *Florida Times-Union,* July 30, 1963, p. 1.

77. *New York Times,* June 14, 1964, p. 59. Interviews with Dr. Hardgrove Norris, September 15, 1978; and the Reverend Charles M. Seymour, Jr., August 16, 1978.

78. Tape recording in possession of the author; Interviews with Hamilton Upchurch, January 27, 1978; Dr. Joseph Shelley, September 6, 1977; and the Reverend Charles M. Seymour, Jr., August 16, 1978.

79. Interviews with Hamilton Upchurch, January 27, 1978; and Dr. Ron Jackson, June 6, 1978.

80. Minutes of the St. Augustine City Commission, June 28, 1963, pp. 4410–4411. *St. Augustine Record,* May 10, 1963, p. 1; September 3, 1963, p. 1. St. Augustine was not in the forefront of school desegregation in Florida. Nearly 2,000 black students attended white schools in 1962. Joseph Aaron Tomberlin, "The Negro and Florida's System of Education: The Aftermath of the *Brown* Case." Ph.D. dissertation, Florida State University, 1967, p. 199.

81. *New York Times,* July 29, 1963, p. 9; interview with Hamilton Upchurch, January 27, 1978.

82. Interview with Fred Brinkhoff, June 13, 1978; *New York Times,* July 29, 1963, p. 9.

83. *Report on the Open Meeting in St. Augustine, Florida,* August 16, 1963, Florida Advisory Committee to the United States Civil Rights Commission, 3 pages, Judge Bryan J. Simpson Papers, P. K. Yonge Library of Florida History, University of Florida, Gainesville, p. 2.

84. *Ibid.*; *St. Augustine Record*, August 18, 1963, p. 16; Racial Situation, St. Johns County, August 19, 1963, p. 1, FBI Files.

85. *Report on the Open Meeting in St. Augustine, Florida*, August 16, 1963, p. 2.

86. *Ibid.*, p. 1.

87. Shelley's letter argued that the city permitted blacks to register, vote, picket, and apply for city jobs. He contended that the city had attempted to hire a second black policeman, but the man had resigned after being threatened "with dire reprisals if he took the job." He concluded by stating "that racial tension has been falsely propagandized out of proportion to its true significance."

88. (Jacksonville) *Florida Times-Union*, August 18, 1963, p. 20.

89. Morris, *The Florida Handbook*, 1951–52, p. 204; *Tabulation of the Registered Voters*, November 6, 1962, Secretary of State's Office, p. 15 (copy in the P.K. Yonge Library of Florida History, University of Florida, Gainesville).

90. *St. Augustine Record*, August 19, 1963, p. 1; August 24, 1963, p. 10; August 27, 1963, p. 1; September 1, 1963, p. 1. interview with Sheriff L. O. Davis by Edward W. Kallal, Jr., SJ IAB, Tape A, Oral History Collection, University of Florida, Gainesville; Tape A, Side 1; Progress Report, Voter Registration, St. Augustine, Fla., August 3, 1964, by Harry Boyte, Accession No. 1, Subgroup E, Ss 3, Box 139, Folder 10, SCLC Papers.

91. *St. Augustine Record*, September 3, 1963, p. 8; September 4, 1963, p. 1. *Florida Star News*, September 7, 1963, p. 1. *The Crisis* (November 1963), 70(9):553.

92. *St. Augustine Record*, September 3, 1963, p. 8; (Jacksonville) *Florida Times-Union*, November 7, 1963, p. 24; *St. Augustine Record*, October 10, 1963, p. 1; SAC, Jacksonville to Director, FBI, Racial Situation St. Johns County, September 3, 1963, p. 1, FBI Files.

93. *Pittsburgh Courier*, July 13, 1963, p. 4; *Racial and Civil Disorders in St. Augustine: Report of the Legislative Investigation Commission*, p. 143; interviews with Hamilton Upchurch, January 27, 1978; and A. H. Tebeault, Jr., June 13, 1978.

94. Interview with Sheriff L. O. Davis by Edward W. Kallal, Jr., SJ 1AB, Tape A, Side 1; interviews with A. H. Tebeault, Jr., June 13, 1978; the Reverend Thomas Wright, October 6, 1977; and Henry Twine, September 19, 1977.

95. *St. Augustine Record*, September 12, 1963, p. 10.

96. *Ibid.*, April 5, 1963, p. 1; April 22, 1963, p. 1. (Jacksonville) *Florida Times-Union*, April 4, 1963, p. 1; August 14, 1964, p. 26.

97. Benjamin Muse, *Ten Years of Prelude: The Story of Integration Since the Supreme Court's 1954 Decision* (New York: Viking Press, 1964), p. 198; Chalmers, *Hooded Americanism*, pp. 353–54.

98. Memorandum to Burke Marshall from John L. Murphy, November 5, 1963, p. 2. U.S. Department of Justice Records; Letter to Organization of American States from Southern Christian Leadership Conference, undated, p. 7. *St. Augustine Record*, October 30, 1963, p. 1; February 9, 1964, p. 2a; February 11, 1964, p. 1. Interview with Henry Twine, September 19, 1977. *Florida Star News*, Ocrober 5, 1963, p. 1.

99. Letter to Mrs. C. D. Johnson from Dr. Joseph A. Shelley, mayor-commissioner, September 17, 1963. Private Papers of Dr. Joseph A. Shelley, St. Augustine, Florida, copy in hands of author. Tape recording in possession of the author.

100. Fairchild had a $2 million federal contract pending for construction of an Air Force aerial tanker. It subsequently received the contract after promoting the black workers, *St. Augustine Record*, January 13, 1964, p. 1; *Florida Star News*, October 10, 1963, p. 1; *The Crisis* (November 1963), 70(9):553.

101. Folder, St. Johns County (Race Problem, 1964), Eyewitness Report of St. Augustine Ku Klux Klan Meeting by Reverend Irwin Cheney of Daytona Beach, 11 pages, Farris Bryant Papers, pp. 1, 2; *Miami Herald,* September 21, 1963, p. 10.

102. Folder, St. Johns County (Race Problem, 1964), Eyewitness Account of KKK Meeting, pp. 3, 4, Farris Bryant Papers.

103. *Ibid.,* pp. 5, 6.

104. Interview with Clyde Jenkins, September 19, 1977; Racial Situation, St. Johns County, Florida, September 19, 1963, p. 2, FBI Files.

105. *St. Augustine Record,* September 19, 1963, p. 1; *Miami Herald,* September 21, 1963, p. 1d; Memorandum to Burke Marshall from John L. Murphy, November 5, 1963. U.S. Department of Justice Records, p. 2; *Pittsburgh Courier,* October 19, 1963, pp. 1, 4.

106. Folder, St. Johns County (Race Problem, 1964), Eyewitness Account of KKK Meeting, pp. 7–9, Farris Bryant Papers; William M. Kunstler, *Deep in My Heart* (New York: Morrow, 1966), p. 293.

107. Folder, St. Johns County (Race Problem, 1964), Eyewitness Account of KKK Meeting, pp. 9–10, Farris Bryant Papers; Memorandum to Burke Marshall from John L. Murphy, November 5, 1963. U.S. Department of Justice Records, pp. 2, 3; *Miami Herald,* September 20, 1963, p. 24a; interview with Clyde Jenkins, September 19, 1977; *St. Augustine Record,* September 19, 1963, p. 1.

108. *St. Augustine Record,* October 17, 1963, p. 12; *Florida Star News,* October 19, 1963, p. 1; *Miami Herald,* October 17, 1963, p. 1; *St. Augustine Record,* November 6, 1963, p. 14; *New York Times,* November 6, 1963, p. 27.

109. Interview with Henry Twine, September 19, 1977.

110. Memorandum to Burke Marshall from John L. Murphy, November 5, 1963, p. 2. U.S. Department of Justice Files; *St. Augustine Record,* October 25, 1963, p. 1; (Jacksonville) *Florida Times-Union,* October 26, 1963, p. 26; *St. Augustine Record,* November 6, 7, 1963, p. 1.

111. *St. Augustine Record,* October 29, 1963, p. 1; *New York Times,* October 20, 1963, p. 24. Hayling was subsequently fined $50. *St. Augustine Record,* January 8, 1964, p. 10; Racial Situation, St. Johns County, October 29, 1963, p. 1, FBI Files.

112. *St. Augustine Record,* October 3, 1963, p. 14; October 24, 1963, p. 1. *New York Times,* October 30, 1963, p. 24. *St. Augustine Record,* February 17, 1964, p. 1.

113. *St. Augustine Record,* October 27, 1963, pp. 1, 6a.

114. *Ibid.,* November 1, 1963, p. 10; October 30, 1963, p. 1.

115. *Miami Herald,* October 18, 1963, p. 22a; *St. Augustine Record,* November 15, 1964, p. 1; Racial Situation, St. Johns County, July 23, 1963, 7 pages, pp. 3–4, FBI Files.

116. Interview with Mr. Dan Warren, by telephone with the author; Folder, Governor's Statements, Legal Matters—St. Augustine, 3 pages, p. 1, Farris Bryant Papers.

117. My emphasis. Folder, Governor's Statements, Legal Matters—St. Augustine, Governor Bryant Papers, p. 2.

118. *Ibid.,* pp. 2, 3.

119. Hartley, "A Long, Hot Summer," p. 41; *St. Augustine Record,* December 20, 1963, p. 10; interview with Dr. Robert Hayling, September 28, 1978; (Jacksonville) *Florida Times-Union,* December 20, 1963, p. 27.

120. Interviews with Henry Twine, September 19, 1977; Otis Mason, June 13, 1978; Clyde Jenkins, September 19, 1977; and Earl Johnson, May 24, 1977. All these men commented on Hayling's influence with the youth and college students at Florida Memorial College. John Dillin, *Christian Science Monitor,* July 13, 1964, p. 9.

121. Minutes of the St. Augustine City Commission, September 24, 1962–December 12, 1966, January 27, 1964, pp. 4518, 4522; *St. Augustine Record*, January 28, 1964, p. 8.

122. Memorandum for the Attorney General from Burke Marshall, November 5, 1963, Department of Justice Files; *ibid.*, Intra-Agency Memorandum to Director, Federal Bureau of Investigation from Joseph F. Dolan, assistant attorney general, June 22, 1964. Memorandum to Governor Bryant from Mal Ogden, February 10, 1964, pp. 1, 2, Farris Bryant Papers. Interview with Dan Warren, December 19, 1978. Letter to Governor Farris Bryant from Randolph C. Tucker, Jr., February 20, 1964, Folder, St. Johns County, 1964, Farris Bryant Papers. *St. Augustine Record*, February 9, 1964, p. 2a; February 11, 1964, p. 1. Interview with Clyde Jenkins, September 19, 1977. Racial Situation, St. Johns County, Florida, November 1, 1963, p. 1, FBI Files. Memorandum to Governor Bryant from Mal Ogden, February 10, 1964, pp. 1, 2, Farris Bryant Papers. *St. Augustine Record*, February 9, 1964, p. 1. Pat Watters, *Down to Now: Reflections on the Southern Civil Rights Movement* (New York: Pantheon, 1971), p. 280.

123. Memorandum to Governor Bryant from Mal Ogden, February 10, 1964, p. 2, Farris Bryant Papers. Also in *St. Augustine Record*, February 9, 1964, p. 1.

124. Memorandum to Governor Bryant from Mal Ogden, February 10, 1964, pp. 2, 3, Farris Bryant Papers.

125. Interviews with Dr. Joseph Shelley, September 6, 1977; Hamilton Upchurch, January 27, 1978; W. I. Drysdale, October 5, 1978; Judge Charles Mathis, Jr., October 5, 1978; Michael V. Gannon, May 5, 1977; and Dan Warren, December 19, 1978.

126. Interviews with Dr. Robert Hayling, September 28, 1978; Clyde Jenkins and Henry Twine, September 19, 1977; and Earl Johnson, May 24, 1977.

3. The Invasion

1. Interviews with Henry Twine, September 19, 1977; Dr. Robert B. Hayling, September 28, 1978; Dr. Joseph Shelley, September 6, 1977; and Sheriff L. O. Davis, SJ 1AB, Tape A, Side 2, Oral History Collection.

2. Interviews with Henry Twine, September 19, 1977; Catherine Twine, September 6, 1977; and the Reverend C. T. Vivian, Atlanta, Ga., May 4, 1983.

3. Lyndon B. Johnson to the Reverend Martin Luther King, Jr., July 9, 1963, MLK Papers, Box 20, Folder 9; Hobart Taylor, Jr. to the Reverend Wyatt Tee Walker, August 8, 1963, MLK Papers, Box 20, Folder 9; interview with the Reverend C. T. Vivian, May 4, 1983.

4. Interview with the Reverend Fred Shuttlesworth, September 13, 1978; John Herbers, *The Lost Priority: What Happened to the Civil Rights Movement in America?* (New York: Funk and Wagnalls, 1970), p. 68; transcript of a tape-recorded interview with the Reverend C. T. Vivian (February 20, 1968), The Civil Rights Documentation Project, Howard University, Washington, D.C., p. 45; Wyatt Tee Walker to Dr. King, n.d., MLK Papers, Box 20, Folder 13.

5. Martin Luther King, Jr., "Of the Civil Rights Bill," *Southern Christian Leadership Conference Newsletter* (March, 1964), 11(6):7; interview with the Reverend Fred Shuttlesworth, September 13, 1978; interview with the Reverend C. T. Vivian, Howard University, p. 52.

6. *Christian Science Monitor*, April 1, 1964, p. 1.

7. Interviews with the Reverend Fred Shuttlesworth, September 13, 1978; and Hosea

Williams, March 16, 1978. *Racial and Civil Disorders in St. Augustine. Report of the Legislative Investigation Commission* (Tallahassee: n.p., 1965), pp. 72, 76, 77. *St. Augustine Record,* March 22, 1964, p. 1. *Racial and Civil Disorders in St. Augustine,* pp. 1, 76, 77. *Miami Herald,* March 31, 1964, p. 4a.

    8. Interview with Dr. Joseph Shelley, September 6, 1977; *Racial and Civil Disorders in St. Augustine,* p. 78.

    9. Interview with Dr. Joseph Shelley, September 6, 1977; *Boston Globe,* March 30, 1964, p. 1.

    10. Racial Situation, St. Johns County, Florida, March 20, 1964, p. 1, FBI Files; March 27, 1964, p. 2. Interview with Hosea Williams, March 16, 1978. *St. Augustine Record,* March 22, 1964, p. 1. Interview with Clyde Jenkins, September 19, 1977.

    11. Racial Situation, St. Johns County, Florida, March 27, 1964, p. 1, FBI Files; SAC, Jacksonville to Director, FBI, March 29, 1964, p. 1, FBI Files; *St. Augustine Record,* March 29, 1964, p. 1, and March 30, 1964, p. 1; Racial Situation, St. Johns County, Florida, March 31, 1964, p. 1, FBI Files; *St. Augustine Record,* March 30, 1964, p. 1.

    12. Racial Situation, St. Johns County, Florida, April 1, 1964, p. 1, FBI Files; Scrapbook on St. Augustine Civil Disorders, April 1, 1964, Folder on Racial Disorders, St. Augustine Historical Society.

    13. Robert K. Massie, "Don't Tread on Grandmother Peabody," *Saturday Evening Post* (vol. 237), May 16, 1964, p. 76; *David Robinson et al. v. State of Florida et al.,* #64–108–CR–J. Transcript of Findings by Judge Bryan Simpson, April 2, 1964, p. 4, Box 1, Judge Bryan Simpson Papers, P. K. Yonge Library of Florida History, University of Florida, Gainesville, Fla., *Washington Post,* March 30, 1964, p. 1.

    14. Interview with Hank Drane, January 31, 1978; Dr. Martin Luther King, Jr., to Mrs. Malcolm Peabody, April 1, 1964, MLK Papers, Box 20, Folder 9.

    15. *New York Times,* April 2, 1964, p. 18, and April 1, 1964, p. 1.

    16. Massie, "Don't Tread on Grandmother Peabody," p. 76; *New York Times,* April 1, 1964, p. 1.

    17. Racial Situation, St. Johns County, Florida, April 2, 1964, and April 3, 1964, p. 1, FBI Files.

    18. (Jacksonville) *Florida Times-Union,* April 2, 1964, p. 24; interview with Hosea Williams, March 16, 1978; Hartley, "A Long, Hot Summer; The St. Augustine Racial Disorders of 1964," Masters thesis, Stetson University, 1972, p. 52; Dr. Martin Luther King, Jr., to Dr. Robert Hayling, April 1, 1964, MLK Papers, Box 20, Folder 9.

    19. Interviews with Dr. Hardgrove Norris, September 15, 1978; Frank Upchurch, January 27, 1978; and W. I. Drysdale, October 5, 1978.

    20. (Jacksonville) *Florida Times-Union,* April 3, 1964, p. 27.

    21. Dr. William Sanders, Organization of American States from the Southern Christian Leadership Conference, undated, Farris Bryant Papers, p. 8; interview with Dr. Robert B. Hayling, The Civil Rights Documentation Project, Howard University, p. 27.

    22. *New York Times,* April 3, 1964, p. 1; *Pittsburgh Courier,* April 11, 1964, p. 4.

    23. *St. Augustine Record,* April 3, 1964, p. 1.

    24. *New York Times,* April 9, 1964, p. 30.

    25. *St. Augustine Record,* April 13, 1964, p. 1, and April 23, 1964, p. 1.

    26. County Commission Record, April 14, 1964, p. 271; Minutes of the City Commission, April 17, 1964, p. 4579.

    27. *St. Augustine Record,* May 20, 1964, p. 1. In a letter to NBC, Hayling criticized Shelley's comments, especially those about himself and requested equal time to rebutt Shelley's statement. NBC did not respond to Hayling's proposal, believing, perhaps, that both

sides had had a chance to air their views. Dr. Robert Hayling to Mr. Jerry Madden, National Broadcasting Company, Inc., June 6, 1964, MLK Papers, Box 20, Folder 10.

28. (Jacksonville) *Florida Times-Union*, May 6, 1964, p. 30; Hartley, "A Long, Hot Summer," p. 4.

29. Interview with Sheriff L. O. Davis, SJ 1AB, Oral History Collection, University of Florida; interview with Clyde Jenkins, September 19, 1977; Tape recording in possession of the author.

30. Tape recording in possession of the author.

31. Activities of Ku Klux Klan in the United States, Part 5. Hearings Before the Committee on UnAmerican Activities, House of Representatives, 89th Cong., 2d Sess. (Washington: GPO, 1966), p. 3668.

32. Tape recording in possession of the author; David Chalmers, *Hooded Americanism: The First Century of the Ku Klux Klan* (Chicago: Quadrangle, 1968), p. 378.

33. Tape recording in possession of the author.

34. Interview with Hank Drane, January 31, 1978; *St. Augustine Record*, June 10, 1964, p. 12; Yvonne Johnson, Petitioners v. L. O. Davis, Virgil Stuart, and Charles C. Mathis, Respondents, June 9, 1964, p. 3. Judge Bryan Simpson Papers; William M. Kunstler, *Deep in My Heart* (New York: Morrow, 1966), p. 275.

35. Earl Black, *Southern Governors and Civil Rights: Racial Segregation as a Campaign Issue in the Second Reconstruction* (Cambridge: Harvard University Press, 1976), p. 226. *St. Petersburg Times*, May 18, 1964, p. 384.

36. Racial Situation, St. Johns County, Florida, April 27, 1964, p. 1, FBI Files; Memorandum from John L. Gibson to SCLC, May 2, 1964, 4 pages, MLK Papers, Box 20, Folder 10, p. 2.

37. Memorandum from John L. Gibson to SCLC, May 2, 1964, 4 pages, MLK Papers, Box 20, Folder 10, pp. 1–3.

38. *Ibid.*

39. *Ibid.*

40. Southern Christian Leadership Conference Executive Staff Meeting, May 4, 1964, 4 pages, MLK Papers, Box 20, Folder 13, p. 1.

41. Wyatt Tee Walker to Dr. King, "Suggested Approach and Chronology for St. Augustine," 3 pages, n.d., MLK Papers, Box 20, Folder 13, p. 1; interview with the Reverend C. T. Vivian, May 4, 1983.

42. *Ibid.*

43. *Ibid.*

4. You're Going To Have To Integrate

1. Wyatt Tee Walker to Dr. King, "Suggested Approach and Chronology for St. Augustine," 3 pages, n.d., MLK Papers, Box 20, Folder 13, p. 1.

2. (Jacksonville) *Florida Times-Union*, May 19, 1964, p. 21; *Florida Star News*, May 23, 1964, p. 1; Dr. Martin Luther King, Jr., to Attorney General Robert Kennedy, n.d., SCLC Papers, Box 27, Folder 37, May, 1964—Statement on St. Augustine, Florida. King also urged Kennedy to withdraw federal support "morally or financially" from the quadricentennial celebration in St. Augustine; SCLC Code of Discipline, Private Papers of Barbara Gallant, Gainesville, Florida.

3. (Jacksonville) *Florida Times-Union*, May 27, 1964, p. 29; interview with Dan Warren, December 19, 1978; David L. Lewis, *King* (Champaign: University of Illinois Press, 1978), pp. 243, 246–248; (Jacksonville) *Florida Times-Union*, May 27, 1964, p. 29.

4. Interview with Hosea Williams, March 16, 1978; Rosalie Gordon-Mills, August 11, 1977; Henry Twine, September 19, 1977.

5. Paul Good, *The Trouble I've Seen: White Journalist—Black Movement* (Washington, D.C.: Howard University Press, 1975). p. 76.

6. Interview with Hosea Williams, March 16, 1978; Howell Raines, *My Soul Is Rested: Movement Days in the Deep South Remembered* (New York: Bantam, 1978), pp. 486–489.

7. Interview with Hosea Williams, March 16, 1978.

8. Martin Luther King, Jr., *Why We Can't Wait* (New York: Harper and Row, 1963), p. 59.

9. *St. Augustine Record*, May 27, 1964, p. 1; interview with Henry Twine, September 19, 1977.

10. Good, *The Trouble I've Seen*, pp. 80–81; *Andrew Young v. L. O. Davis*, #64–133–Civ–J, Box 1, Judge Bryan Simpson Papers, pp. 6–7.

11. *Jacksonville Journal*, May 29, 1964, p. 22; *St. Augustine Record*, May 29, 1964, p. 1.

12. *St. Augustine Record*, June 2, 1964, p. 1.

13. Report on St. Augustine, Fla., by the Reverend Elizabeth J. Miller, November 11, 1964, 8 pages, MLK Papers, Box 20, Folder 12, pp. 2–3.

14. *New York Times*, June 9, 1964, p. 17.

15. *St. Augustine Record*, May 31, 1964, p. 1; interview with Hank Drane, January 31, 1978.

16. Telegram from Martin Luther King, Jr., to President Lyndon B. Johnson, May 29, 1964, 3 pages, Martin King, Jr., Name File, Lyndon Baines Johnson Papers, the Lyndon Baines Johnson Library, Austin, Tex.

17. Memorandum for the Files, Subject: St. Augustine, Fla., June 1, 1964; Letter from Lee C. White to Dr. King and Dr. Hayling, June 11, 1964, LBJ Papers.

18. Memorandum for the Files, Subject: St. Augustine, Fla., June 1, 1964, LBJ Papers.

19. *Ibid.*

20. SAC, Jacksonville to Director, FBI, Racial Situation, St. Johns County, Fla., July 23, 1963, pp. 1–6, FBI Files; July 27, 1963, pp. 1–2. Interview with the Reverend C. T. Vivian, May 4, 1983.

21. *Jacksonville Journal*, June 5, 1964, p. 1; interview with Dr. Joseph Shelley, September 6, 1977.

22. Minutes of the City Commission, 9/24/62–12/12/66, June 1, 1964, p. 4615; *St. Augustine Record*, June 10, 1964, p. 1; (Jacksonville) *Florida Times-Union*, June 10, 1964, p. 14.

23. Transcript of editorial by Frankie Walker, June 12, 1964, WFOY News, St. Augustine, Fla., copy in P. K. Yonge Library of Florida History, University of Florida; *Pittsburgh Courier*, June 6, 1964, p. 4.

24. *Miami Herald*, June 14, 1964, pp. 14a–15a; SAC, Jacksonville to Director, FBI, Racial Situation, St. Johns County, Fla., May 28, 1964, p. 1, FBI Files; June 15, 1964, p. 3.

25. Interviews with W. I. Drysdale, October 5, 1978; and Mrs. Mary Lee Gannon, May 6, 1977, St. Augustine, Fla., interview with Holstead "Hoss" Manucy by Edward W. Kallal, Jr., SI2A, Oral History Collection, University of Florida, Gainesville, Fla., *Miami Herald*, June 14, 1964, p. 14a.

26. Interviews with Michael V. Gannon, May 2, 1977; and the Reverend Stanley Bullock, January 17, 1978.

27. Racial Situation, St. Johns County, Fla., June 1, 1964, pp. 5–6, FBI Files; SAC, Jacksonville to Director, FBI, Racial Situation, St. Johns County, Fla., May 31, 1964, p. 1, FBI Files.

28. *Miami Herald,* June 14, 1964, p. 14a.

29. Interview with Holstead "Hoss" Manucy by Edward W. Kallal, Jr., SJ2A; SAC, Jacksonville to Director, FBI, Racial Situation, St. Johns County, Fla., May 28, 1964, p. 1, FBI Files.

30. SAC, Jacksonville to Director, FBI, Racial Situation, St. Johns County, Fla., June 9, 1964, p. 1; June 8, 1964, pp. 1–2.

31. Memorandum for the Files, Subject: St. Augustine, June 10, 1964, LBJ Papers.

32. Report to Governor Bryant from E. F. Emrich, June 5, 1964, Folder on Executive Orders, Master File, Farris Bryant Papers.

33. *New York Times,* June 6, 1964, p. 10; *Washington Post,* June 28, 1964, p. 19a; *Miami Herald,* June 10, 1964, p. 1.

34. Good, *The Trouble I've Seen,* p. 77.

35. Judge's Notes and Authorities, June 9, 1964, Judge Bryan J. Simpson Papers; *Jacksonville Journal,* June 10, 1964, p. 10.

36. Executive Order No. 1, June 16, 1964, Executive Orders—St. Augustine, Master File, Farris Bryant Papers.

37. Racial Situation, St. Johns County, Florida, June 11, 1964, p. 1, FBI Files.

38. *Miami Herald,* June 12, 1964, pp. 1, 2a; Folder on Special Police Force, Letters—St. Augustine and Reports, 1964, June 11, 1964, Farris Bryant Papers.

39. *Ibid.; New York Times,* June 12, 1964, p. 17.

40. *Ibid.*

41. *Ibid.*

42. Memorandum, M. Carl Holman, information officer, to William L. Taylor, general counsel, June 11, 1964, Lee White File, Box 5, LBJ Papers; Memorandum to the President from Douglass Cater, June 11, 1964, Lee White File, Box 5, LBJ Papers.

43. Memorandum for the Files, Subject: Conversation with Wyatt Tee Walker, June 13, 1964, Lee White File, Box 5; Lee C. White to Mr. Wyatt Tee Walker, June 10, 1964, Martin Luther King, Jr., Name File, LBJ Papers.

44. Interview with Dan Warren, December 19, 1978; *St. Augustine Record,* June 12, 1964, p. 1; Washington Capital News Service, June 13, 1964, p. 1, Racial Situation, St. Augustine, Fla., Racial Matters, FBI Files.

45. Interview with Dr. Joseph Shelley and Dr. Hardgrove Norris by A. G. Heinsohn, private papers of Dr. Hardgrove Norris, copy in hands of author; George A. Smathers to the Reverend Martin Luther King, Jr., June 13, 1964, MLK Papers, Box 20, Folder 10.

46. Pat Watters, *Down to Now. Reflections on the Southern Civil Rights Movement* (New York: Random House, 1971), p. 110; interview with Dr. Joseph Shelley, September 6, 1977; County Commissioners Record, S, June 6, 1964, p. 322, St. Johns County, Fla.; Donald Buck to Farris Bryant, June 15, 1964, Folder, St. Johns County, 1964, Farris Bryant Papers.

47. *Pittsburgh Courier,* June 13, 1964, p. 10; *Miami Herald,* June 13, 1964, p. 2a; *New York Times,* June 13, 1964, p. 21.

48. Folder on Special Police Force, Letters—St. Augustine, and Reports, 1964, June 12, 1964, pp. 3–5, Farris Bryant Papers; Report on Racial Situation in St. Augustine, Fla., June 15, 1964, pp. 3–5, FBI Files; *New York Times,* June 13, 1964, p. 21; Good, *The Trouble I've Seen,* pp. 96–98.

49. *Ibid.*

50. Good, The Trouble I've Seen, pp. 96–98; Watters, *Down to Now,* p. 290.

51. Carl Holman, information officer, to William L. Taylor, general counsel, June 11, 1964, LBJ Papers.

52. Executive Order No. 1, June 16, 1964, Executive Orders—St. Augustine, Master File, Farris Bryant Papers.

53. *New York Times,* June 12, 1964, p. 17.

54. *Ibid.,* June 16, 1964, p. 34; (St. Augustine) *Ancient City Liberator,* June 30, 1964, p. 4.

55. Interview with Hosea Williams, March 16, 1978; interview with Clyde Jenkins, September 19, 1977; Report on St. Augustine, Fla., by the Reverend Elizabeth J. Miller, November 11, 1964, 8 pages, MLK Papers, Box 20, Folder 12, p. 2.

56. SAC, Jacksonville to Director, FBI, June 16, 1964, p. 1, FBI Files.

57. Folder on Special Police Force, Letters—St. Augustine, and Reports, 1964, June 17, 1964, pp. 2–4, Farris Bryant Papers; Racial Situation in St. Augustine, Fla., June 18, 1964, pp. 1–2, FBI Files.

58. *St. Augustine Record,* June 18, 1964, p. 10.

59. Folder on Special Police Force, Letters—St. Augustine, and Reports, 1964, June 16, 1964, pp. 1–2, Farris Bryant Papers; Folder on Master File, Executive Orders—St. Augustine Executive Order No. 2, June 20, 1964, Farris Bryant Papers.

60. Racial Situation, St. Johns County, Fla., June 19, 1964, pp. 1–2, FBI Files; Folder on Special Police Force, Letters—St. Augustine, and Reports, 1964, June 18, 1964, Monson Motel Swimming Pool, 3 pages, Farris Bryant Papers; interview with Frank Upchurch, January 27, 1978.

61. *Miami Herald,* June 19, 1964, p. 20a; *St. Augustine Record,* June 18, 1964, p. 1; *New York Times,* June 19, 1964, p. 1; Report on Racial Situation, St. Johns County, Fla., June 19, 1964, pp. 1–2, FBI Files.

62. *Ibid.;* Folder on Special Police Force, Letters—St. Augustine, and Reports, 1964, June 18, 1964, Monson Motel Swimming Pool, 3 pages, Farris Bryant Papers.

63. Folder on Special Police Force, Letters—St. Augustine, and Reports, 1964, June 18, 1964, Monson Motel Swimming Pool, 3 pages, Farris Bryant Papers; *Washington Post,* June 19, 1964, p. 2a.

64. *Ibid.*

65. *Washington Post,* June 19, 1964, p. 2a.

66. Racial Situation, St. Augustine, Fla., June 17, 1964, p. 3, FBI Files.

67. *Ibid.*

68. *Ibid.,* June 19, 1964, pp. 1–4.

69. *Racial and Civil Disorders in St. Augustine, Report of the Legislative Investigation Committee* (Tallahassee: n.p., 1965), pp. 102–103; *St. Augustine Record,* June 19, 1964, p. 1; Presentment of Grand Jury to the Honorable Howell W. Melton, Presiding Circuit Court Judge, June 18, 1964, MLK Papers, Box 20, Folder 10; (Jacksonville) *Florida Times-Union,* June 20, 1964, p. 22.

70. Answer to Presentment of Grand Jury, June 18, 1964. Folder on Special Police Force, Letters—St. Augustine, and Reports, 1964, 2 pages, Farris Bryant Papers; (Jacksonville) *Florida Times-Union,* June 20, 1964, p. 22; *Racial and Civil Disorders in St. Augustine,* p. 106; Response to the Grand Jury Presentment, n.d., MLK Papers, Box 20, Folder 10.

71. (Jacksonville) *Florida Times-Union,* June 20, 1964, p. 22; *Washington Post,* June 20, 1964, p. 2a; *Miami Herald,* June 28, 1964, p. 14; SAC, Jacksonville to Director, FBI, June 24, 1964, p. 1, FBI Files; *Christian Science Monitor,* June 22, 1964, p. 10.

72. Report on St. Augustine, Fla., by the Reverend Elizabeth J. Miller, November 11, 1964, 6 pages, MLK Papers, Box 20, Folder 12, p. 1.

73. Folder on Special Police Force, Letters—St. Augustine, and Reports, 1964,

June 18, 1964, pp. 3–4, Farris Bryant Papers; Racial Situation, St. Augustine, Florida, June 19, 1964, p. 3, FBI Files; *New York Times*, June 19, 1965, p. 16.

74. Folder on Special Police Force, Letters—St. Augustine, and Reports, 1964, June 19, 1964, pp. 4–5, Farris Bryant Papers; Racial Situation, St. Augustine, Fla., June 22, 1964, pp. 2–3, FBI Files.

75. Folder on Special Police Force, Letters—St. Augustine, and Reports, 1964, June 20, 1964, pp. 6–8, Farris Bryant Papers; Racial Situation, St. Augustine, Fla., June 22, 1964, pp. 3–4, FBI Files.

76. *Ibid.*

77. *Ibid.*; *St. Augustine Record*, June 20, 1964, p. 1; *New York Times*, June 27, 1964, p. 1.

78. Racial Situation, St. Augustine, Fla., June 22, 1964, p. 3, FBI Files; Folder on Governor's Statements, Legal Matters—St. Augustine, June 20, 1964, Farris Bryant Papers; *St. Augustine Record*, June 21, 1964, p. 1.

79. David R. Colburn and Richard K. Scher, *Florida's Gubernatorial Politics in the Twentieth Century* (Gainesville: University Presses of Florida, 1980), pp. 78–80, 227–228.

80. *Ibid.*, pp. 232–233.

81. *Miami Herald*, June 20, 1964, p. 1a.

82. Filmed Statements by Governor Farris Bryant, June 22, 1964, *Andrew Young v. L. O. Davis et al.*, #64–133–Civ–J, Judge Bryan J. Simpson Papers.

83. Folder on Special Police Force, Letters—St. Augustine, and Reports, 1964, June 20, 1964, pp. 7–8, Farris Bryant Papers; Racial Situation, St. Augustine, Fla., June 22, 1964, p. 4, FBI Files.

84. *Andrew Young v. L. O. Davis*, Accession #73A377, Record Group 21, FRC Box 1E15887, Agency Box 13, 64–141, 7, Federal Records Center; *St. Augustine Record*, June 21, 1964, p. 1.

85. Racial Situation, St. Augustine, Fla., June 25, 1964, pp. 1–2, FBI Files.

86. *St. Augustine Record*, June 21, 1964, p. 1.

87. Report on St. Augustine, Fla., by the Reverend Elizabeth J. Miller, November 11, 1964, 6 pages, MLK Papers, Box 20, Folder 12, pp. 3–4.

88. *New York Times*, June 21, 1964, p. 69; *Pittsburgh Courier*, July 11, 1964, p. 2.

89. Folder on Special Police Force, Letters—St. Augustine, and Reports, 1964, June 17, 1964, Farris Bryant Papers.

90. Folder on Special Police Force, Letters—St. Augustine, and Reports, 1964, Incident at Monson Motel Swimming Pool, June 19, 1964, 2 pages, Farris Bryant Papers; *ibid.*, St. Augustine Beach—Violence, June 22, 1964. *New York Times*, June 26, 1964, p. 14.

91. Interview with the Reverend Fred Shuttlesworth, September 13, 1978; *New York Times*, June 26, 1964, p. 14.

92. Memorandum from John L. Murphy, chief, General Litigation Section, to John Doar, first assistant, Civil Rights Division, June 23, 1964. United States Department of Justice Files, Washington, D.C.

93. Racial Situation, St. Augustine, Fla., June 26, 1964, pp. 3–4, FBI Files; (Jacksonville) *Florida Times-Union*, June 26, 1964, p. 22; *New York Times*, June 26, 1964, p. 14.

94. *New York Times*, June 26, 1964, p. 1; *Miami Herald*, June 27, 1964, p. 1a.

95. SAC, Jacksonville to Director, FBI, Racial Situation, St. Augustine, Fla., June 27, 1964, p. 2, FBI Files.

96. Racial Situation, St. Augustine, Fla., Racial Matters, June 29, 1964, pp. 1–2, FBI Files.

97. Interview with Dr. Joseph Shelley, September 6, 1977; interview with Dr. Joseph Shelley and Dr. Hardgrove Norris by A. G. Heinsohn, n.d.; *St. Augustine Record*, July 1, 1964, p. 1; John Dillin, *Christian Science Monitor*, July 2, 1964, p. 1.

98. Interview with Dan Warren, December 19, 1978.

99. Interview with Dr. Robert Hayling, August 16, 1967, The Civil Rights Documentation Project, Howard University.

100. (Jacksonville) *Florida Times-Union*, July 2, 1964, p. 18.

101. (St. Augustine) *Ancient City Liberator*, June 30, 1964, p. 2, copy in hands of author; Dr. R. B. Hayling and Henry Twine to Fellow Citizens and Interested Friends, September 22, 1964, 3 pages, SCLC Papers, Box 139, Folder 10; Winston W. Davidson to unnamed, May 13, 1965, MLK Papers, Box 20, Folder 12.

102. Racial Situation, St. Augustine, Fla., July 6, 1964, p. 1, FBI Files; *Lucille Plummer et al. v. James E. Brock et al.*, #64–187–Civ–J, Judge Bryan J. Simpson Papers.

103. James Brock, Owner, Monson Motor Lodge, St. Augustine, Fla., July 16, 1964, pp. 8–9, FBI Files; *New York Times*, August 6, 1964, p. 16.

104. James Brock, Owner, Monson Motor Lodge, St. Augustine, Fla., July 16, 1964, pp. 1–3, FBI Files; *St. Augustine Record*, July 16, 1964, p. 1.

105. (Jacksonville) *Florida Times-Union*, July 15, 1964, p. 25; *St. Augustine Record*, July 6, 1964, p. 1.

106. Martin Luther King, Jr., and C. T. Vivian to Dr. Robert B. Hayling, n.d., MLK Papers, Box 20, Folder 12. *St. Augustine Record*, July 31, 1964, p. 6; *New York Times*, July 1, 1964, p. 1.

107. *St. Augustine Record*, July 17, 1964, p. 1; Racial Situation, St. Augustine, Fla., July 20, 1964, p. 1, FBI Files; *New York Times*, July 18, 1964, p. 6.

108. Pat Watters, *Down to Now*, p. 110; John Herbers, *The Lost Priority; What Happened to the Civil Rights Movement in America?* (New York: Funk and Wagnalls, 1970), p. 70; Martin Luther King, Jr., and C. T. Vivian to Dr. Robert B. Hayling, n.d., MLK Papers, Box 20, Folder 12.

109. Carl Brauer, *John F. Kennedy and the Second Reconstruction* (New York: Columbia University Press, 1977), pp. 316–317; Doris Kearns, *Lyndon Johnson and the American Dream* (New York: Harper and Row, 1976), pp. 148–150; Steven F. Lawson, *Black Ballots: Voting Rights in the South, 1944–1969* (New York: Columbia University Press, 1976), p. 286.

110. Kearns, *Lyndon Johnson*, pp. 148–150.

111. Newspaper Scrapbook on the St. Augustine Civil Rights Movement, August 7, 1964, St. Augustine Historical Society. Also *St. Augustine Record*, August 14, 1964, p. 1.

5. A Judge for the Times

1. Transcript of Proceedings before Honorable Bryan J. Simpson, June 8, 1964, p. 204. *Yvonne Johnson et al. v. L. O. Davis et al.*, #64–141–Civ–J, Accession #73A377, FRC Box 1E15887, Agency Box 13, Record Group 21, Federal Records Center, East Point, Ga.; *St. Augustine Record*, October 27, 1963, pp. 1, 6a.

2. *David Robinson et al. v. State of Florida et al.*, #64–108–Civ–J. Transcript of Findings by Judge Bryant Simpson, April 2, 1964, pp. 3–4, Box 1, Judge Bryan Simpson Papers, P. K. Yonge Library of Florida History, University of Florida, Gainesville, Fla.; *ibid.*, p. 10.

3. Leon Friedman, "The Federal Courts of the South: Judge Bryan Simpson and

His Reluctant Brethren," in Leon Friedman, ed., *Southern Justice* (New York: Random House, 1965), p. 187.

4. *Ibid.*, pp. 193–194.

5. *Andrew Young v. L. O. Davis et al*, #64–133–Civ–J, Findings of Fact and Conclusions of Law by Judge Bryan Simpson, June 9, 1964, pp. 12–13, Box 1, Judge Bryan Simpson Papers.

6. *Ibid.*, p. 9, and Additional Findings of Fact in Connection with Civil Contempt Proceedings of August 17, 18, and 19, p. 4.

7. Executive Order Number 2, issued by Governor Farris Bryant, June 20, 1964, pp. 1–5, copy in case file *Young v. Davis*, #64–133–Civ–J, Box 1, Judge Bryan Simpson Papers.

8. *Florida Star News*, May 18, 1963, p. 1.

9. *St. Augustine Record*, May 12, 1964, p. 1; *Jacksonville Journal*, June 11, 1964.

10. (Jacksonville) *Florida Times-Union*, May 28, 1978, p. 1.

11. *Ibid.*; interview with Judge Bryan Simpson, Jacksonville, Fla., January 27, 1978.

12. (Jacksonville) *Florida Times-Union*, May 28, 1978, p. 1; interview with Judge Bryan Simpson, Jacksonville, Fla., January 17, 1978.

13. (Jacksonville) *Florida Times-Union*, June 11, 1964; interview with Judge Bryan Simpson, Jacksonville, Fla., January 17, 1978.

14. Interviews with Judge Bryan Simpson, Jacksonville, Fla., January 17, 1978; and Earl Johnson, Jacksonville, Fla., January 17, 1977.

15. Interviews with Dr. Joseph Shelley, St. Augustine, Fla., September 6, 1977; and Dr. Hardgrove Norris, St. Augustine, Fla., September 15, 1978.

16. *Young v. Davis*, Findings of Fact and Conclusion of Law, June 9, 1964, p. 1–19, Box 1, Judge Bryan Simpson Papers.

17. *Ibid.*; Memorandum, n.d., 2:20 P.M. FBI agent, Mr. Kittle, telephoned Simpson and informed his secretary that FBI agent Brown, who was in St. Augustine, had information suggesting that "numerous Klansmen had been deputized by Sheriff Davis in the event there are racial demonstrations in St. Augustine; they bear no arms but do have the power of arrest. The Sheriff said he did this because he heard that the negroes were bringing in an army of a thousand or more, and he needed help." Kittle viewed the use of Klansmen as law enforcement officials with grave concern. *Young v. Davis et al*, Excerpts from Testimony of L. O. Davis, June 2, 1964. Accession #63A377, FRC Box 1E15887, Agency Box 13, Record Group 21, Federal Record Center, East Point, Ga.

18. *Young v. Davis*, Excerpts from Testimony of L. O. Davis, June 3, 1964, Federal Records Center.

19. *Young v. Davis*, Findings of Facts and Conclusion of Law, June 9, 1964, pp. 1–2, 13–14, Box 1, Judge Bryan Simpson Papers.

20. *Ibid.*, p. 16.

21. *Ibid.*, p. 17.

22. Executive Order Number 1, issued by Governor Farris Bryant, June 15, 1964, pp. 1–7, copy in *Young v. Davis*, #64–133–Civ–J, Box 1, Judge Bryan Simpson Papers.

23. *Andrew Young v. L. O. Davis*, #64–133–Civ–J, Partial Transcript of Hearing Testimony of Verle Pope, p. 129, Accession #73A377, FRC Bos 1E15887, Agency Box 13, Record Group 21, Federal Records Center; *ibid.*, Testimony of Dan Warren, pp. 3–18.

24. Executive Order Number 2, issued by Governor Farris Bryant, June 20, 1964, pp. 1–5, copy in case file *Young v. Davis*, #64–133–Civ–J, Box 1, Judge Bryan Simpson Papers.

25. *Young v. Davis*, #64–133–Civ–J, *Order To Show Cause*, June 22, 1964, pp.

1–3, Box 1, Judge Bryan Simpson Papers; *ibid.*, *Response to Order To Show Cause*, 5 pages, pp. 2–4.

26. Friedman, "The Federal Courts of the South," p. 204.

27. *Young v. Davis*, #64–133–Civ–J, Accession #73A377, FRC Box 1E15887, Agency Box 13, Record Group 21, pp. 64–141, 7, Federal Records Center.

28. Statement by Governor Farris Bryant, Folder—Governor's Statements, Legal Matters—St. Augustine. Farris Bryant Papers, Florida State Archives, Tallahassee, Fla.

29. Folder—Governor's Statements, Legal Matters—St. Augustine, Farris Bryant Papers.

30. *Ibid.*

31. Friedman, "The Federal Courts of the South," p. 206.

32. Interviews with Governor Farris Bryant, Jacksonville, Fla., and with Judge Bryan Simpson, Jacksonville, Fla., January 17, 1978; *Young v. Davis*, #64–133–Civ–J, Notes of Judge Simpson, Box 1, Judge Bryan Simpson Papers.

33. *Yvonne Johnson v. L. O. Davis*, #64–141–Civ–J, Accession #73A377, FRC Box 1E15891, Agency Box 13, Record Group 21, Transcript of Proceedings before Judge Bryan Simpson, June 18, 1964, pp. 120–122, Federal Records Center.

34. *Ibid.*; Friedman, "The Federal Courts of the South," p. 200.

35. *Johnson v. Davis*, #64–141–Civ–J, Transcript of Proceedings before Judge Simpson, June 18, 1964, p. 122, Federal Records Center, East Point, Ga.

36. *Ibid.*

37. *New York Times*, June 12, 1964, p. 1; *Johnson v. Davis*, #64–141–Civ–J, June 19, 1964, p. 2, Box 1, Judge Bryan Simpson Papers.

38. Memorandum from Alvin J. Bronstein to Henry Schwarzchild, August 13, 1964, p. 2, Lawyers Constitutional Defense Committee, Inc. Files, ACLU Papers, Princeton University, Princeton, N.J.

39. *Plummer v. Brock*, #64–187–Civ–J, Transcript of Hearing pp. 93–95, Accession #73A377, FRC #1–15873, Agency Box 13, Record Group 21, Federal Records Center, East Point, Ga. *Plummer v. Brock*, #64–187–Civ–J, Transcript of Oral Findings, Judge Bryan Simpson Papers.

40. *Lucille Plummer, v. James Brock*, #64–187–Civ–J. Judge Simpson's Notes, Box 1, Judge Bryan Simpson Papers.

41. *Plummer v. Brock*, #64–187–Civ–J. Transcript of Hearing, pp. 210–211. Accession #73A377, FRC #1D015872, Agency Box 13, Record Group 21, Federal Records Center.

42. *Plummer v. Brock*, #64–187–Civ–J. Judge Simpson's Notes, Box 1, Judge Bryan Simpson Papers.

43. *Ibid.*; (Jacksonville) *Florida Times-Union*, August 19, 1964, p. 27.

44. *Plummer v. Brock*, #64–187–Civ–J. Judge Simpson's Notes, Box 1, Judge Bryan Simpson Papers; *ibid.*, Transcript of Oral Findings.

45. *Plummer v. Brock*, #64–187–Civ–J. Transcript of Oral Findings, Box 1, Judge Bryan Simpson Papers; *St. Augustine Record*, August 5, 1964, p. 1.

46. *Ibid.*

47. *New York Times*, August 6, 1964, p. 16.

48. *St. Augustine Record*, August 19, 1964, p. 1; August 20, 1964, p. 1.

49. *Ibid.*, September 4, 1964, p. 2; September 16, 1964, p. 2.

50. *Charles Lance, Jr., Appellant v. Lucille Plummer, et al.*, Appelles (two cases), No. 21904, 22035. United States Court of Appeals, Fifth Circuit, December 9, 1965. Federal Reporter, 2d Series, Vol. 353, F.2d (St. Paul: West Publishing Company, 1966).

51. *St. Augustine Record*, September 17, 1964, p. 10.

52. Correspondences Unfavorable to Simpson's Decisions, File 1, Box 3, Judge Bryan Simpson Papers.

53. Interviews with Dr. Joseph Shelley, September 6, 1977; Dr. Hardgrove Norris, September 15, 1978; and Judge Charles Mathis, Jr., October 5, 1978; tape recording in possession of the author.

54. Interview with Dr. Hardgrove Norris, September 15, 1978; tape recording in possession of the author.

55. Interview with Dr. Joseph Shelley, September 6, 1977; tape recording in possession of the author.

56. Interviews with Dr. Joseph Shelley, September 6, 1977; and with Dr. Hardgrove Norris, September 15, 1978; tape recording in possession of the author.

57. *Ibid.*

58. Interviews with Dr. Joseph Shelley, September 6, 1977; and Judge Charles Mathis, Jr., October 5, 1978; tape recording in possession of the author.

59. Alvin J. Bronstein to Henry Schwarzchild, August 13, 1964, LCDC Files, pp. 4, 5; *Robert B. Hayling, et al. v. Flagler Hospital, Inc., et al.*, p. 1, Box 1, Judge Bryan Simpson Papers; *St. Augustine Record*, August 14, 1964, p. 8.

60. *New York Times*, December 2, 1965, p. 37.

61. Friedman, "The Federal Courts of the South," p. 193; interview with Earl M. Johnson, May 24, 1977, Jacksonville, Fla.

6. Every Job Had a Name and a Face

1. David K. Bartholomew, "An Analysis of Change in the Power System and Decision-Making Process in a Selected County," Ed.D. dissertation, University of Florida, 1971, pp. 63, 103–104; James Fox, "Comparisons of Civic Beliefs of Influential Leaders, Status Leaders, Educational Personnel, and Citizens in Two Selected Florida Counties," Ed.D. dissertation, University of Florida, 1971, p. 102; interviews with Michael V. Gannon, May 3, 1977; W. I. Drysdale, October 5, 1978; Hamilton Upchurch, January 27, 1978; John D. Bailey, August 11, 1977; and the Reverend Stanley Bullock, January 17, 1978.

2. Harry S. Ashmore, *An Epitaph for Dixie* (New York: Norton, 1957), pp. 125–126.

3. Quoted in Kenneth K. Bailey, *Southern White Protestantism in the Twentieth Century* (New York: Harper and Row, 1964), p. 148; Reed Sarratt, *The Ordeal of Segregation: The First Decade* (New York: Harper and Row, 1966), pp. 285, 286. Writing in 1977, Calvin Trillin declared that Georgia's "most powerful businessmen wanted as little integration as possible, but they also wanted as little trouble as possible accompanying the integration that had to come." Calvin Trillin, "Remembrance of Moderates Past," *The New Yorker*, March 21, 1977, p. 88. William Brophy, "Active Acceptance—Active Containment: The Dallas Story," pp. 138–150; Paul Lofton, "Calm and Exemplary: Desegregation in Columbia, South Carolina," pp. 70–81; John Quincy Adams and Charles Sallis, "Desegregation in Jackson, Mississippi," pp. 236–256; Elizabeth Jacoway, "Taken by Surprise: Little Rock Businessmen and Desegregation," pp. 15–41; and Carl Abbott, "The Norfolk Business Community: The Crisis of Massive Resistance," pp. 98–119 in *Southern Businessmen and Desegregation*, Elizabeth Jacoway and David Colburn, eds. (Baton Rouge: Louisiana State University Press, 1982).

4. Numan V. Bartley, *The Rise of Massive Resistance: Race and Politics in the South During the 1950s* (Louisiana State University Press, 1969), pp. 313–315. Bartley also con-

tended that the church, schools, unions, and corporations reacted to racial crisis only "when stability of southern society and, consequently, their own vested interests were more threatened by massive resistance than by token social change did these great institutions make a meaningful contribution to the course of southern politics" (p. 294).

Even in such New South cities as Greensboro and Tampa, historians have argued that businessmen did not willingly accept the new social changes. Steven Lawson notes that in Tampa, businessmen "lacked the dedication necessary to sustain an intensive drive to remove the last vestiges of employment discrimination." William Chafe goes a step further and suggests that white leaders simply modified the older forms of control. "Through black political appointments and capitulation on issues like school desegregation," he writes, "white leaders had successfully 'co-opted' members of the black middle class, giving them an investment in the prevailing system of political and economic authority." Steven Lawson, "From Sit-In to Race Riot: Businessmen and Blacks in Tampa and the Pursuit of Moderation, 1960–67," p. 279, and William Chafe, "Greensboro, North Carolina: Perspectives on Progressivism," p. 69, in Jacoway and Colburn, eds. *Southern Businessmen and Desegregation.*

5. Interview with Michael V. Gannon, May 3, 1977; Hamilton Upchurch, January 27, 1978; Douglas Hartley, January 27, 1978; and the Reverend Stanley Bullock, January 27, 1978.

6. Bartholomew, "An Analysis of Change in the Power System and Decision-Making Process in a Selected County," pp. 99, 104.

7. One business leader noted that Wolfe's opposition to new business should not be surprising since "his pet project is the history of St. Augustine." Bartholomew, "An Analysis of Change," p. 104.

8. *New York Times*, July 5, 1964, sec. 6, p. 30; interview with the Reverend Stanley Bullock, January 17, 1978; *Wall Street Journal*, June 19, 1964, p. 1; interview with Michael V. Gannon, May 3, 1977.

9. Local Chapter of the Southern Christian Leadership Conference to Dr. William Sanders, Organization of American States, n.d., Farris Bryant Papers, p. 7; *Florida Star News*, July 13, 1963, p. 1.

10. Interview with Michael V. Gannon, May 3, 1977.

11. *Ibid.*; interview with Hamilton Upchurch, January 27, 1978.

12. Interviews with Dr. Joseph Shelley, September 6, 1977; Judge Richard O. Watson, January 9, 1977; Michael V. Gannon, May 3, 1977; Hamilton Upchurch, January 27, 1978; the Reverend Stanley Bullock, January 17, 1978; and Hank Drane, January 31, 1978.

13. Robert W. Hartley, "A Long, Hot Summer: The St. Augustine Racial Disorders of 1964," unpublished M. A. thesis, Stetson University, 1972, p. 93. The Birch Society declared that the civil rights movement had "been deliberately and almost wholly created by the Communists . . . ," *St. Augustine Record*, August 22, 1965, p. 7a; *New York Times*, June 14, 1964, p. 59.

14. Interviews with Hamilton Upchurch, January 27, 1978. Similar views were expressed by Dr. Ron Jackson and Judge Richard O. Watson. Interviews with Dr. Ron Jackson, June 6, 1978; and Judge Richard O. Watson, January 9, 1977.

15. (Jacksonville) *Florida Times-Union*, April 3, 1964, p. 27; *Report on the Open Meeting in St. Augustine, Florida*, August 16, 1963, Florida Advisory Committee on the United States Civil Rights Commission, 3 pages, Judge Bryan J. Simpson Papers, p. 2; *New York Times*, July 29, 1963, p. 9. The committee alleged that "a void" existed in leadership at the higher levels of business and industry on racial matters. *Report on the Open Meeting in St. Augustine, Florida*, p. 5.

16. *New York Times*, July 30, 1963, p. 1; interviews with Hamilton Upchurch,

January 27, 1978, and Dr. Joseph Shelley, September 6, 1977; *Miami Herald*, September 15, 1963, p. 42. City Manager Charles Barrier felt strongly that a businessman should have the right to refuse service to any customer. "Well, let's say you were back in Atlanta," he told a reporter, "and you walked into a nice restaurant, like the Dinkler Plaza, without a tie and coat on, and the manager asked you to leave. Wouldn't he be within his rights? It's the same exact thing," Paul Good, *The Trouble I've Seen: White Journalist-Black Movement* (Washington, D.C.: Howard University Press, 1975), p. 86.

17. *St. Augustine Record*, June 17, 1963, p. 1; interview with Dr. Robert Hayling, September 28, 1978.

18. *Wall Street Journal*, June 19, 1964, p. 1. *Florida Star News* carried an article shortly after the Easter demonstrations noting how vulnerable the state's economy was to racial protest. The author wrote that "continued racial disturbances will eventually seriously affect even the richest of these members of the politico-economic power structure and then and only then will they bring the politicians into line." Norman E. Janes, "Let's Talk Politics," *Florida Star News*, April 18, 1964, p. 2.

19. (Jacksonville) *Florida Times-Union*, April 3, 1964, p. 27.

20. *New York Times*, April 9, 1964, p. 30. *St. Augustine Record*, April 13, 1964, p. 1; May 20, 1964, p. 1; April 23, 1964, p. 1. The Reverend Martin Luther King, Jr., to Mr. Robert McNamara, Secretary of Defense, June 3, 1964, SCLC Papers, Box 134, Folder 13.

21. *New York Times*, June 7, 1964, p. 48.

22. Interviews with Dr. Joseph Shelley, September 6, 1977; and W. I. Drysdale, October 5, 1978. (Jacksonville) *Florida Times-Union*, April 3, 1964, p. 27; *New York Times*, July 3, 1964, p. 8.

23. *Wall Street Journal*, June 19, 1964. Most business leaders, including Wolfe, opposed SCLC's demands for immediate integration and equality between the races. Wolfe told a newsman that he believed "Negroes are being accepted and employed to do any job they are qualified to do." However, he added, "I don't think it helps any to talk about the matter of equality. Take John D. Rockefeller, for example. If you were to say I wasn't equal with him, well, I would know that I'm not. But saying it wouldn't help our relationship any. Patience. If there's one word in life I love, it's patience." Good, *The Trouble I've Seen*, p. 87.

24. Interview with John D. Bailey, August 11, 1977. Also, interviews with Hamilton Upchurch and Frank Upchurch, January 27, 1978; W. I. Drysdale, October 5, 1978; and A. H. Tebeault, Jr., June 13, 1978.

25. *Wall Street Journal*, June 19, 1964; one motel owner reported twenty cancelled reservations in one day. *Atlanta Journal and Constitution*, July 5, 1964, p. 80.

26. Mrs. M. A. Willie to Governor Farris Bryant, July 20, 1964. Folder, St. Johns County, 1964, Farris Bryant Papers. *Wall Street Journal*, June 19, 1964.

27. Interview with Dr. Hardgrove Norris, September 15, 1978.

28. *Miami Herald*, September 15, 1963, p. 4a; *New York Times*, May 31, 1964.

29. *St. Augustine Record*, June 6, 1964, pp. 6a, 6b; June 7, 1964, pp. 6a, 7a.

30. Interviews with Hamilton Upchurch, January 27, 1978; Holstead Manucy, SJ2a, Oral History Collection, University of Florida; and J. B. Stoner, SJ3a, Oral History Collection, UF.

31. *New York Times*, June 6, 1964, p. 10; June 18, 1964, p. 8a.

32. *Ibid.*; *Atlanta Journal and Constitution*, July 5, 1964, p. 80.

33. *New York Times*, June 18, 1964, p. 25; interview with the Reverend Fred Shuttlesworth, September 13, 1978.

34. *Miami Herald*, June 18, 1964, p. 1a; *New York Times*, June 25, 1964, p. 19.

35. Report on Racial Situation, St. Johns County, Fla., June 19, 1964, pp. 1–2,

FBI Files; Folder on Special Police Force, Letters—St. Augustine, and Reports, 1964, June 18, 1964, Monson Motel Swimming Pool, 3 pages, Farris Bryant Papers; (Jacksonville) *Florida Times-Union*, June 20, 1964, p. 22; *Miami Herald*, June 19, 1964, p. 1.

36. *New York Times*, June 14, 1964, p. 59; *Atlanta Journal and Constitution*, July 5, 1964, p. 80.

37. Interview with Dr. Joseph Shelley, September 6, 1977; interview with Dr. Joseph Shelley and Dr. Hardgrove Norris by A. G. Heinsohn, n.d.; *St. Augustine Record*, July 1, 1964, p. 1.

38. Folder, St. Johns County, 1964, July 1, 1964, Farris Bryant Papers; (Jacksonville) *Florida Times-Union*, July 2, 1964, p. 18.

39. Special Report from St. Augustine, Fla., by Willie M. Bolden, MLK Papers, Atlanta, Box 20, Folder 13; Results of Public Accommodation Tests, July 20, 1964, MLK Papers, Atlanta, Box 20, Folder 11.

40. *Lucille Plummer, et al. v. James E. Brock, et al.*, #64–187–Civ–J. Judge Bryan Simpson's Notes, Judge Bryan Simpson Papers; (Jacksonville) *Florida Times-Union*, July 16, 1964, p. 25.

41. (Jacksonville) *Florida Times-Union*, July 16, 1964, p. 25. *Lucille Plummer, v. James Brock*, Transcript of testimony of James E. Brock, July 28, 1964, pp. 18–19. Accession #73A377 FRC #1E–15823, Agency Box 13, Record Group 21, Federal Records Center; John Dillin, *Christian Science Monitor*, July 3, 1969, p. 6.

42. *St. Augustine Record*, July 24, 1964, p. 1. Brock asserted that "beyond any question of doubt . . . the Molotov-Cocktail was a result of the meeting we had that evening." Testimony of James E. Brock, *Plummer v. Brock*, p. 56, Federal Records Center.

43. *St. Petersburg Times*, July 26, 1964, p. 1b. Also *St. Augustine Record*, July 26, 1964, p. 16. Stoner alleged that businessmen "insisted on me eating free" until the Chamber of Commerce switched sides. Interview with J. B. Stoner, April 6, 1976, SJ3A.

44. *St. Augustine Record*, July 20, 1964, p. 1; August 5, 1964, p. 1; *New York Times*, August 6, 1964, p. 16. *Plummer v. Brock*, Transcript of Oral Findings, August 19, 1964, p. 10, Judge Bryan J. Simpson Papers; interview with Judge Bryan Simpson, January 17, 1978.

45. Interviews with Hamilton Upchurch and Frank Upchurch, January 27, 1978, and A. H. Tebeault, Jr., June 13, 1978. *St. Augustine Record*, August 11, 1964, p. 1.

46. *Pittsburgh Courier*, September 26, 1964, p. 4.

47. *Wall Street Journal*, August 6, 1965, p. 1.

48. *St. Augustine Record*, January 22, 1965, p. 5.

49. Memorandum from Hal Hunton, August 3, 1965, St. Augustine, Fla., 4 pages. Community Relations Services Files, Department of Commerce, Washington, D.C., pp. 3–4.

50. *Ibid.*, August 3, 1965, CRS Files, pp. 3–4; Progress Report from Harold Hunton, September 23, 1965, 2 pages, CRS Files, p. 1.

51. Bartley, *The Rise of Massive Resistance*, p. 313; interview with the Reverend Stanley Bullock, January 17, 1978.

7. The Most Segregated Hour in America

1. Weldon James, "The South's Own Civil War," in Don Shoemmaker, ed., *With All Deliberate Speed* (New York: Harper, 1957), p. 23. Also see Ernest Q. Campbell and Thomas F. Pettigrew, *Christians in Racial Crisis: A Study of Little Rock's Ministry* (Washington, D.C.; Public Affairs Press, 1959), pp. 1–2. St. Augustine did not have a synagogue.

2. Kenneth K. Bailey, *Southern White Protestantism in the Twentieth Century* (New York: Harper and Row, 1964), p. 142.

3. "Protestantism Speaks on Justice and Integration," *The Christian Century*, February 5, 1958, 75:164–166; Bailey, *Southern White Protestantism*, pp. 142–144.

4. Frank Loescher, *The Protestant Church and the Negro* (New York: Association Press, 1948), pp. 78–79, the Reverend Nelson Smith of Birmingham went further than Loescher, contending that Christianity hasn't failed in helping black Southerners, "It hasn't even . . . tried." *Washington Post*, March 17, 1965, p. A13.

5. Samuel Hill, "Southern Protestantism and Racial Integration," *Religion in Life* (Summer 1964), 33:421–429. Also see Numan V. Bartley, *The Rise of Massive Resistance: Race and Politics in the South During the 1950s* (Baton Rouge: Louisiana State University Press, 1969), p. 296.

6. Ernest Q. Campbell, "Moral Discomfort and Racial Segregation—An Examination of the Myrdal Hypothesis," *Social Forces* (March 1961), p. 229. Campbell contended that ministers who failed to act during a crisis "held a set of values and beliefs centered around their occupational role obligation, the effect of which was to quiet any self-aggression that otherwise might develop."

7. Hill, "Southern Protestantism and Racial Integration," *Religion in Life*, p. 424; Robert Penn Warren, *Segregation* (New York: Random House, 1956), p. 100. Campbell and Pettigrew noted "that the farther away the ministers are from their home churches, the more liberal they are on all issues." Campbell and Pettigrew, *Christians in Racial Crisis*, p. 172.

8. Campbell and Pettigrew, *Christians in Racial Crisis*, p. 132; Bartley, *The Rise of Massive Resistance*, pp. 296–304.

9. Interview with Michael V. Gannon, May 3, 1977.

10. Hill, "Southern Protestantism and Racial Integration," *Religion in Life*, p. 426. Hill writes that the development of warm friendships created little concern for "bringing those of the social 'outgroup' into the local congregation."

11. Interviews with the Reverend Stanley Bullock, January 17, 1978, Jacksonville, Fla. the Reverend Charles Seymour, Jr., August 16, 1978; and Michael V. Gannon, May 3, 1977.

12. *Ibid.*

13. Interview with the Reverend Charles Seymour, Jr., August 16, 1978.

14. Folder VI, 33, National Press Club Address, Washington, D.C., July 19, 1962, Martin Luther King, Jr., Papers, Boston University, Boston.

15. Interview with the Reverend Charles M. Seymour, Jr., August 16, 1978.

16. *Ibid.*

17. *Ibid.*; also, interview with Michael V. Gannon, May 3, 1977.

18. *Miami Herald*, September 21, 1963, p. 1D.

19. *St. Augustine Record*, August 24, 1964, p. 1.

20. 147 D 16, Reel 33, Papers of Joseph P. Hurley, Archbishop of Florida, P. K. Yonge Library of Florida History, University of Florida, Gainesville; interview with Michael V. Gannon, May 3, 1977.

21. Interview with Michael V. Gannon, May 3, 1977.

22. 145 E 1 and 146 A, Reel 33, Papers of Joseph P. Hurley.

23. 147 D 16, Reel 33, Papers of Joseph P. Hurley; interview with Michael V. Gannon, May 3, 1977.

24. Box No. 28, Papers of Joseph P. Hurley; interview with Michael V. Gannon, May 3, 1977.

25. Interview with Michael V. Gannon, May 3, 1977.

26. *Ibid.*

27. Folder on Racial Disorders, Scrapbook on St. Augustine Civil Rights, June 21, 1964. St. Augustine Historical Society, St. Augustine, Fla., Irvine Nugent to the Very Reverend Monsignor John P. Burns, June 18, 1964, MLK Papers, Box 20, Folder 10.

28. *New York Times,* April 6, 1964, p. 21; *Miami Herald,* June 15, 1964, p. 1; interview with the Reverend Stanley Bullock, January 17, 1978; *Christianity Today,* July 17, 1964, "Spotlight on St. Augustine," by Adam C. Taft, Tallahassee, Florida, 3 pages, SCLC papers, Box 134, Folder 13, pp. 1–2.

29. J. LeRoy Conel to the Mayor and Clergy of St Augustine, Florida, July 25, 1965, MLK Papers, Box 10, Folder 12.

30. *Ibid.*; interview with the Reverend Charles M. Seymour, Jr., August 16, 1978.

31. Interview with the Reverend Charles M. Seymour, Jr., August 16, 1978.

32. *Ibid.*; interview with the Reverend Stanley Bullock, January 17, 1978; interview with A. H. Tebeault, Jr., June 13, 1978.

33. Interview with the Reverend Charles M. Seymour, Jr., August 16, 1978.

34. *Ibid.*; interview with the Reverend Stanley Bullock, January 17, 1978.

35. Robert K. Massie, "Don't Tread on Grandmother Peabody," *The Saturday Evening Post* (vol. 237), May 16, 1964, p. 76.

36. Interview with the Reverend Stanley Bullock, January 17, 1978.

37. *Ibid.*; *The Florida Alligator,* June 12, 1964, 56(147):1.

38. Interviews with the Reverend Stanley Bullock, January 17, 1978; and with the Reverend Charles M. Seymour, Jr., August 16, 1978.

39. Interview with the Reverend Charles M. Seymour, Jr., August 16, 1978; "To the Vestrymen of the Diocese of Florida," from Vestrymen at Trinity Episcopal Church, 3 pages, n.d., Private Papers of the Reverend Stanley Bullock, Jacksonville, Fla.

40. *St. Augustine Record,* April 13, 1964, p. 1.

41. *Ibid.*

42. *The Jacksonville Journal,* January 27, 1956.

43. "Resolution by the Vestry of Trinity Episcopal Church," 1 page, April 30, 1964, Private Papers of the Reverend Stanley Bullock.

44. Interview with the Reverend Stanley Bullock, January 17, 1978.

45. Interview with the Reverend Charles M. Seymour, Jr., August 16, 1978.

46. Interview with the Reverend Stanley Bullock, January 17, 1978; interview with Dr. Hardgrove Norris, September 15, 1978; and interview with A. H. Tebeault, Jr., June 13, 1978.

47. "Church Breaks With Diocese," 1 page, Private Papers of the Reverend Stanley Bullock; "To the Vestrymen of the Diocese of Florida," pp. 1–2, Private Papers of the Reverend Stanley Bullock.

48. "Church Breaks With Diocese," 1 page, Private Papers of the Reverend Stanley Bullock.

49. Interview with the Reverend Charles M. Seymour, Jr., August 16, 1978; interview with the Reverend Stanley Bullock, January 17, 1978.

50. *St. Augustine Record,* June 22, 1964, p. 8; interview with the Reverend Charles M. Seymour, Jr., August 16, 1978; and interview with the Reverend Stanley Bullock, January 17, 1978.

51. *Ibid.* A white youth called Stines a "Nigger lover" as he departed from the church after the service and warned about remaining once "the cops leave here."

52. Interview with the Reverend Charles M. Seymour, Jr., August 16, 1978.

53. *Ibid.* Interview with the Reverend Stanley Bullock, January 17, 1978; Bishop

Hamilton West to the Reverend Charles M. Seymour, 2 pages, n.d., Private Papers of the Reverend Stanley Bullock.

54. West to Seymour, 2 pages, n.d., Bullock Papers.

55. Transcript of Vestry Meeting of July 1, 1964, with Bishop Hamilton West, 4 pages, Private Papers of the Reverend Stanley Bullock, p. 1.

56. *Ibid.*, pp. 2–4. Because Trinity parish had been established before the Diocese of Florida, it was in the unique position of owning its property and building (all other church property belonged to the Diocese). Through an oversight, the lands of Trinity had never devolved to the Diocese after it had been created. Tebeault's proposal sought to take advantage of this loophole, but the majority of the vestry members felt such a step was much too radical.

57. Interview with the Reverend Charles M. Seymour, Jr., August 16, 1978.

58. Interview with Mr. and Mrs. Henry Twine, St. Augustine, Florida, September 18, 1977; interview with the Reverend Stanley Bullock, January 17, 1978.

59. Interview with the Reverend Stanley Bullock, January 17, 1978; Private Papers of the Reverend Stanley Bullock.

60. *St. Augustine Record*, August 24, 1964, p. 1; interview with Michael V. Gannon, May 3, 1977.

61. *Ibid.*

62. John A. Griffin to Harold Hunton, February 25, 1965. Community Relations Service Files, Washington, D.C.

8. No Real Controversies

1. *St. Augustine Record*, July 3, 1964, p. 1.

2. Newspaper Scrapbook on the St. Augustine Civil Rights Movement, August 7, 1964. St. Augustine Historical Society, St. Augustine, Fla., also *St. Augustine Record*, August 14, 1964, pp. 1, 8; Further Presentment of Grand Jury to the Honorable Horace D. Riegle, Presiding Circuit Judge, n.d., MLK Papers, Box 20, Folder 11.

3. *Ibid.*; interview with the Reverend Stanley Bullock, Jacksonville, Fla., January 17, 1978.

4. Newspaper Scrapbook on the St. Augustine Civil Rights Movement, August 17, 1964. St. Augustine Historical Society.

5. *Miami Herald*, July 11, 1964, p. 1.

6. Speeches, Director, Community Relations Service, July, 1964–July, 1965, Undersecretary of Commerce, August 1964, Collection No. 2, Box No. 64, Address to Southern Regional Council, Atlanta, Ga., November 20, 1964, Governor LeRoy Collins Papers, 1955–1961, University of South Florida, Tampa; *ibid.*, LeRoy Collins Clippings, 1961–65, July 28, 1964.

7. David R. Colburn and Richard K. Scher, *Florida's Gubernatorial Politics in the Twentieth Century* (Gainesville: University Presses of Florida, 1980), p. 78.

8. *Miami Herald*, July 11, 1964, p. 1.

9. *Florida Star News*, September 18, 1964, p. 1; *St. Augustine Record*, July 22, 1964, p. 1.

10. *St. Augustine Record*, July 22, 1964, p. 1; September 21, 1964, p. 8. Progress Report, Voter Registration by Harry Boyte, August 3, 1964, SCLC Papers, Box 139, Folder 10; (Jacksonville) *Florida Times-Union*, September 22, 1964.

11. (Jacksonville) *Florida Times-Union*, June 18, 1964, p. 22; *Florida Star News*, August 29, 1964, p. 1; *St. Augustine Record*, September 2, 1964, p. 1.

12. SCLC Weekly Project Report from Fred Martin, September 14–19, 1964, SCLC Papers, Box 139, Folder 10, p. 2.

13. Progress Report—St. Augustine, Fla., Harold T. Hunton, September 23, 1965, 3 pages, p. 1, Community Relations Service Files.

14. *Ibid.*, p. 1; Hal Hunton to File Case No. 5, August 3, 1965, St. Augustine, Fla., 6 pages, pp. 2–3, CRS.

15. Hal Hunton to File Case No. 5, August 2, 1965, pp. 4–5, CRS; *ibid.*, September 23, 1965, p. 2.

16. Hal Hunton to File Case No. 5, August 3, 1965, pp. 3–5, CRS.

17. *Daytona Beach Sunday News Journal*, February 21, 1965.

18. *Ibid.*, March 23, 1965, p. 9.

19. Racial and Civil Disorders in St. Augustine, Report of the Legislative Investigation Committee (n.p., February 1965), pp. 54–57, 58–61.

20. *Miami Herald*, January 10, 1965; *St. Augustine Record*, September 4, 1964, p. 1.

21. *New York Times*, July 5, 1964, Sec. 6, p. 30.

22. *St. Augustine Record*, November 16, 1964, p. 8; *Response to Order To Show Cause, Young v. L. O. Davis*, #64–133–Civ–J, Folder St. Augustine, 1965, Box 3, Judge Bryan Simpson Papers, P. K. Yonge Library of Florida History. SCLC asserted that it would be a mockery to hold the quadricentennial without having all people of St. Augustine share in full citizenship. *St. Augustine Record*, March 21, 1965, p. 9a.

23. *Wall Street Journal*, August 6, 1965, p. 1; *Miami Herald*, January 10, 1965. Reflecting upon the postcrisis period, Otis Mason commented that "many blacks were hoping as a result of national exposure things would get better. But it didn't happen immediately."

24. *Florida Star*, March 27, 1965, pp. 1, 10.

25. *Ibid.*

26. *Ibid.*

27. *St. Augustine Record*, July 31, 1964, p. 1.

28. Hal Hunton to File Case No. 5, St. Augustine, Fla., August 3, 1965, p. 2, CRS.

29. Interview with Mrs. Rosalie Gordon-Mills, St. Augustine, Fla., August 11, 1977; interviews with Mr. and Mrs. Henry Twine, St. Augustine, Fla., September 18, 1977.

30. *St. Augustine Record*, April 15, 1964, p. 1; April 19, 1965, p. 1; April 23, 1964, p. 1; May 2, 1965, p. 1b.

31. *Ibid.*, May 2, 1965, p. 1b; May 3, 1965, p. 1.

32. Hal Hunton to File Case No. 5, St. Augustine—Emerging Racial Crisis, July 23, 1965, p. 1, CRS; Southern Christian Leadership Conference to Mr. LeRoy Collins, July 8, 1965, and SCLC to President Lyndon Johnson, July 9, 1965, CRS.

33. *St. Augustine Record*, June 6, 1965, p. 10.

34. *New York Times*, July 18, 1965, p. 39; *Florida Star*, July 3, 1965, p. 1.

35. Newspaper Scrapbook on the St. Augustine Civil Rights Movement, Folder on Racial Disorders, July 22, 1965.

36. *St. Augustine Record*, July 23, 1965, p. 1.

37. *Ibid.*, June 6, 1965, p. 10.

38. (Jacksonville) *Florida Times-Union*, July 24, 1965, p. 22; *New York Times*, July 24, 1965, p. 8.

39. Colburn and Scher, *Florida's Gubernatorial Politics*, p. 80.

40. (Jacksonville) *Florida Times-Union*, July 24, 1965, p. 22; *New York Times*, July 24, 1965, p. 8.

41. *Miami Herald*, September 5, 1965; *Daytona Journal*, September 3, 1965.

42. *Daytona Journal*, September 3, 1965, and September 4, 1965; Recommendations from the Negro Community for the City of St. Augustine, Fla., St. Augustine Files, CRS; transcript of interview with Dr. Robert B. Hayling by Mr. John H. Britton, August 16, 1967, The Civil Rights Documentation Project, Howard University, p. 25.

43. *Daytona Journal*, September 4, 1965.

44. Interview with W. I. Drysdale by the author, St. Augustine, Fla., October 5, 1978; interview with Hamilton Upchurch, St. Augustine, Fla., January 27, 1978.

45. *Daytona Journal*, September 4, 1965; Lucille Plummer to Dr. King, May 20, 1965, MLK Papers, Box 20, Folder 12.

46. *Wall Street Journal*, August 5, 1965, p. 1.

47. Spotlight on St. Augustine by Adam C. Taft, Tallahassee, Fla., *Christianity Today*, July 17, 1964, 3 pages, SCLC Papers, Box 134, Folder 13, p. 1.

48. *Daytona Journal*, September 4, 1965; interview with Otis Mason, St. Augustine, Fla., June 13, 1978.

49. Progress Report—St. Augustine, Fla., Harold T. Hunton, September 23, 1965, p. 1, CRS; *Daytona Journal*, September 4, 1965.

50. (Jacksonville) *Florida Star*, September 12, 1965, p. 1; *St. Augustine Record*, September 29, 1965, p. 12.

51. *Florida Star*, December 5, 1965, p. 1.

52. *St. Augustine Record*, December 2, 1965, p. 10.

53. Courtney Siceloff to the Florida Advisory Committee, December 7, 1965, p. 2, Judge Bryan Simpson Papers; *ibid.*, p. 3; interview with the Reverend Stanley Bullock, Jacksonville, Fla., January 17, 1978.

54. Irving N. Tranen to Conciliation Files, St. Augustine, Fla., February 19, 1966, pp. 1–2, CRS; Hal Hunton, St. Augustine, St. Johns County, Fla., December 21, 1965, pp. 1–2, CRS; Hal Hunton to File Case No. 5, St. Augustine, Fla., August 3, 1965, pp. 3–6, CRS.

55. *St. Augustine Record*, January 19, 1965, p. 8; January 13, 1965, p. 9.

56. *St. Augustine Record*, January 11, 1965, p. 8; February 25, 1965, p. 10.

57. Courtney Siceloff to the Florida Advisory Committee, December 7, 1965, pp. 2–4, Box 3, Judge Bryan Simpson Papers.

58. *Ibid.*

59. *Ibid.*, p. 4.

60. Interview with Otis Mason, St. Augustine, Fla., June 13, 1978; interview with Mrs. Rosalie Gordon-Mills, St. Augustine, Fla., August 11, 1977; interview with Henry Twine, St. Augustine, Fla., September 19, 1977; interview with Dr. R. W. Puryear, August 1, 1980, Winston-Salem, North Carolina.

61. *St. Augustine Record*, September 2, 1969, p. 1.

62. *New York Times*, July 4, 1969, p. 1.

63. *St. Augustine Record*, July 9, 1969, p. 1.

64. *Ibid.*

65. *Ibid.*, July 10, 1969, p. 1.

66. *Ibid.*, September 3, 1969, p. 8; July 3, 1970, p. 1; July 11–12, 1970, p. 1.

67. Colburn and Scher, *Florida's Gubernatorial Politics*, pp. 234–235.

68. *St. Augustine Record*, June 4, 1970, p. 1. Interview with W. Douglas Hartley, St. Augustine, Fla.

69. *St. Augustine Record*, August 14, 1970, p. 1.

70. *Ibid.*, August 12, 1970, p. 1.

71. David K. Bartholomew, "An Analysis of Change in the Power System and Decision-Making Process in a Selected County," Ed.D. dissertation, University of Florida, 1971, p. 80; James N. Fox, "Comparison of Civic Beliefs of Influential Leaders, Status Leaders, Educational Personnel, and Citizens in Two Selected Florida Counties," Ed.D. dissertation, University of Florida, 1971, p. 76.

72. *St. Augustine Record*, May 28, 1973, p. 5.

73. *Ibid.*, May 30, 1973, pp. 1, 16.

74. Interview with Arnett Chase, St. Augustine, Fla., July 20, 1975, by Professor James Button, University of Florida, Gainesville.

75. U.S. Bureau of the Census, *Census of the Population, 1970.* Vol. 1. *General Social and Economic Characteristics*, Part II, "Florida" (Washington, D.C.: GPO 1972), pp. 11–410, 420, 425; *Key West Citizen*, June 15, 1977, p. 46.

76. *Ibid.*, Interviews with Henry Twine, September 19, 1977; Hamilton Upchurch, October 5, 1978; and Otis Mason, June 13, 1978.

77. *Ibid.*

78. Newspaper Scrapbook, July 14, 1974, St. Augustine Historical Society.

79. *Ibid.*

Conclusion

1. Interviews with Clyde Jenkins, September 19, 1977; and Rosalie Gordon-Mills, August 11, 1977.

2. William H. Chafe. *Civilities and Civil Rights: Greensboro, North Carolina and the Black Struggle for Freedom* (New York: Oxford University Press, 1980), pp. 337–355; interview with the Reverend Charles Seymour, August 16, 1978.

3. Interviews with the Reverend Charles Seymour, August 16, 1978; and Otis Mason, June 13, 1978.

4. Interviews with Robert Hayling, September 28, 1978; Hosea Williams, March 16, 1978; the Reverend Stanley Bullock, January 17, 1978; and Rosalie Gordon-Mills, August 11, 1977.

5. David J. Garrow, *Protest at Selma: Martin Luther King, Jr. and the Voting Rights Act of 1965* (New Haven: Yale University Press, 1978), pp. 221–222; interviews with the Reverend Fred Shuttlesworth, September 9, 1978; and Hosea Williams March 16, 1978.

6. *SCLC Newsletter* (October 1963), 11(1):5, 7; Martin Luther King, Jr., *Where Do We Go From Here? Chaos or Community* (New York: Harper and Row, 1967), p. 90.

7. President's Report, 1964, SCLC Papers, Box 130, Folder 6; Garrow, *Protest at Selma*, pp. 230–231.

8. *St. Augustine Record*, July 31, 1964, p. 1; Pat Watters, *Down to Now; Reflections on the Southern Civil Rights Movement* (New York: Random House, 1971), p. 110.

9. Interview with the Reverend C. T. Vivian, May 4, 1983.

10. Interview with Hosea Williams, March 16, 1978; Watters, *Down to Now*, pp. 18, 70.

11. J. Harvie Wilkinson III, *From Brown to Bakke: The Supreme Court and School Integration, 1954–1978* (New York: Oxford University Press, 1979), p. 212. For a more detailed expression of this viewpoint, one should consult V. O. Key, Jr., *Southern Politics in State and Nation* (New York: Vintage, 1949), p. 9. Key contended that southern white elites were largely responsible for the suppression of blacks.

12. Interviews with Rosalie Gordon-Mills, August 11, 1977; Henry Twine, Sep-

tember 19, 1977; Catherine Twine, September 19, 1977; Hank Drane, January 31, 1978; the Reverend Charles Seymour, August 16, 1978; and Hosea Williams, March 16, 1978.

13. Interviews with Henry Twine, September 19, 1977; Catherine Twine, September 19, 1977; J. A. Webster, August 15, 1980; and Otis Mason, June 13, 1978. Harvard Sitkoff, *The Struggle for Black Equality, 1954–1980* (New York: Hill and Wang, 1981), pp. 227–228.

14. Interviews with Henry Twine, September 19, 1977; and Hamilton Upchurch, October 5, 1978. *1980 Florida Statistical Abstract* (Gainesville: The University Presses of Florida, 1980), pp. 79, 81, 105, 160.

Index